TONIGHT AT NOON

TONIGHT AT NOON

A Love Story

Sue Graham Mingus

PANTHEON BOOKS

NEW YORK

Copyright © 2002 by Sue Graham Mingus

All rights reserved under International and Pan-American
Copyright Conventions. Published in the United States by
Pantheon Books, a division of Random House, Inc., New York,
and simultaneously in Canada by Random House of
Canada Limited, Toronto.

Pantheon Books and colophon are registered trademarks of
Random House, Inc.

Library of Congress Cataloging-in-Publication Data
Mingus, Sue
Tonight at noon : a love story / Sue Graham Mingus.
        p.   cm.
Includes index.
ISBN 0-375-42115-7
1. Mingus, Charles, 1922–   2. Jazz musicians—United States—
Biography.   3. Mingus, Sue.   4. Musician's spouses—United
States—Biography.   I. Title.
ML418.M45 M46 2002
781.65'092—dc21   [B]   2001056042

www.pantheonbooks.com

Book design by Mia Risberg

Printed in the United States of America
First Edition
9   8   7   6   5   4   3   2   1

For
Susanna and Roberto

TONIGHT AT NOON

Prologue

On a cold January morning before dawn, in the holy village of Rishikesh in northern India, I scattered Charles Mingus's ashes in the Ganges as he had asked me to do, immersing myself with them in the freezing river according to Hindu custom, certain that the raw air beneath the dark range of the Himalayas was made for the life of the spirit and for reincarnation, as he believed. I walked to my one-room house on the Ganges, shivering and dripping water along the sand, and imagined that one day I would nail a small sign above the entrance with his name and dates and the title of one of his tunes, "Tonight at Noon." That was musician talk for time displacements on the gig, the topsy-turvy hours of work, an acknowledgment of a reversal in the order of things. Perhaps, I thought, it was the new life he had already imagined.

As I continued along the beach I remembered something he'd said about Charlie Parker: "You know, I was thinking about Bird's death . . ." We were sitting together in the patio outside our last home in Mexico, warming ourselves in the sun. "When Bird died there was that clap of thunder. It was a happy death. I felt good about it. As if everything was all right, as if Bird had died in order to look out for a whole lotta guys . . ." He laughed. "Probably the beboppers!

"You know, Bird's music was very intuitive," he continued. "There was something sacred about it. I don't know if it was from the devil or from the angels, but the music itself was almost superhuman. I remember I was talking to him once about Buddhism—he knew all about it—and he was telling me about yoga and Buddha and then all of a sudden we saw the club owner raise his hand, and Bird said: 'Well, it's time to go. Let's finish the discussion on the bandstand.' "

Charles was silent, remembering.

"So that's what he said," he repeated. "He said: 'Let's finish the discussion on the bandstand.' . . . You see, I always knew he was as superstitious about the music as I was."

Two weeks earlier, on a cloudy January afternoon, fifty-six sperm whales swam through the shallow coastal waters of Baja in northwest Mexico, landed like a monstrous tidal wave, and perished on the beach. Several hundred kilometers to the east in a small village called Cuernavaca, my husband, Charles Mingus, died the same afternoon. He was fifty-six years old. The following day, Mingus and the whales were consumed by fire: Mingus inside a crematorium on the outskirts of Mexico City and the whales in funeral pyres along the coast.

Mingus would have appreciated the coincidence. After all, he was a man of omens and doubtless would have recalled the mysterious thunderclap in a cloudless sky the day Charlie Parker passed on. He'd told the story often enough: how he was carrying his bass up Fifth Avenue to a recording session that afternoon, March 12, 1955, when Bird died; how he'd looked up at the sparkling sun and heard the heavens rumble. And though, later on, he once said he might have heard the thunder in his head, it hardly mattered. He knew Bird had flown off with a clap of thunder, just as I knew Mingus left town with the whales.

The day after Charles died, his second son, Eugene, and I sat on a curbstone beneath the crematorium chimney in an old Mexican graveyard and watched the dark brown smoke curl off to the east. "He's going in the right direction," Eugene said, nodding at the sky. He knew that in less than a week I would follow the smoke, traveling east to a holy village in the foothills of the Himalayas to scatter his father's ashes in the Ganges River.

I imagined that part of the reason Charles had asked me to carry his ashes to the far side of the world was to avoid the club owners and booking agents, the gangsters and promoters who had hassled him throughout his career. After all, a quiet passage for his spirit from this world to the next required distance—halfway around the earth, if necessary—from their mojo and interference. At important events he'd always kept to himself. Backstage before a concert, for example, he meditated alone. I was telling Eugene how one night at the Village Vanguard, a jazz club in New York where the dressing room was a kitchen and the usual gang was partying inside, he had shouted that only Bird understood the spiritual side of the music.

Eugene and I were sitting side by side, sharing scraps of memory, trying to feel close. I'd met him only once before he arrived in Mexico to care for his father and to help offset the changing guard of undependable male nurses who regularly flew down to Mexico from an agency in San Francisco and rarely stayed for more than a few weeks. Months before in New York, Charles had been diagnosed with a terminal nerve illness called amyotrophic lateral sclerosis (ALS), popularly known as Lou Gehrig's disease, and had been given three to six months to live. By the time we arrived in Mexico, seeking a miraculous cure under the guidance of a prominent witch and *curandera* named Pachita, he was already on borrowed time. And so he had sent for his son. Eugene was strong, he was family, and we needed all the help we could get—Charles being one of the difficult cases, as the nursing agencies invariably called him.

Earlier, inside the crematorium, I'd insisted they open the coffin to make certain Charles was inside. This was a foreign country: we were used to mishaps. The attendants undid the blue sheet in which he was wrapped and exposed his head. His right eyelid was open. The soft brown eye stared ahead. Eugene closed it and pushed his father's lips together, after first checking the gold inside his teeth. He'd assisted in hospitals, he reminded me, and knew the score—the insider mischief I might not imagine.

After the attendants lowered the coffin through a trap door to the final platform below, Eugene rose abruptly to his feet and set off down a long hallway as if he had something in mind. I followed him to the end of the corridor where he pushed his way through a closed door to a room above the furnaces that appeared to be a small chapel. As I watched with curiosity, he began to poke about in the dim light. In all the months we'd worked together, I was never certain what was brewing in his head. Now I wondered if he had come inside to pray. Or whether he planned to slip some artifact inside his sleeve. Or whether, after all, he just wanted to waste time before the cremation began.

Before long he discovered an old piano in a corner of the room, opened its lid, and began to improvise some spare, halting chords to his father below. Soon, however, the tenuous chords sprang loose and now Eugene was rocking on his heels, standing before the open keyboard in his clean starched jeans, humming along hoarsely like Major Holly talking to his bass, thrashing out note after note as he accompanied himself on the keys.

I stood in the shadows near the piano, wondering at his boldness, wondering if it was a protest, some impromptu cocky response to the confusion that the complex man who was his father had brought to

Eugene's world. Or whether it was just a spontaneous farewell, a last one-sided exchange that swelled and echoed off the chapel walls. And then, as I was listening, a door flew open behind the altar and a priest ran in. The priest halted just inside the doorway for a moment while his astonished eyes adjusted to the light. When at last he saw us in the corner—saw Eugene, who was lost inside the rising choruses of his song—the priest raised a pallid arm from the folds of his great black cloak and, shaking with indignation, waved us from the room.

"*Fuera!*" the priest shouted. And then again: "*Afuera!*"

Eugene closed the piano lid carefully. "Just making my tribute," he said quietly over his shoulder as we made our way out. Then he added with a modest shrug, "of nothing!"

Expelled from the sanctuary, Eugene and I sat silent and reflective beneath the crematorium chimney. The intimacy of illness with its urgency and passion, and the new rapport we had been forced to establish over half a year, still vied with family conflicts from the past. There had been thirty intervening years since Charles had split up with Eugene's mother, Jeanne. Eugene had barely known his father, a man driven by art and by his appetites, whose life was mostly on the road. Now, in Mexico, we had lived and journeyed together, a sort of pickup family, coursing through mountains and flatlands and volcanic wastes, consorting with witches, preparing iguana blood elixirs, harvesting a thousand snails on the elegant bathroom walls of our villa, storing manure compresses in the fridge, overseeing voodoo operations with flashing knives in the dark. At night we sped along roads lit only by the moon in a special van so that Charles, paralyzed in his wheelchair, could rock to sleep. In the daytime, Eugene stood tall above his father's chair: strong, complicated, laconic, amused, his feelings impossible to gauge. At times the weed he smoked relaxed his mood; other times he brooded. Father and son. Nurse and patient. Homeboys together.

"We had a repertoire," Eugene said one afternoon to his father while massaging him and telling stories, discussing his former partner in the "grease business" in Los Angeles, describing the days of popping oil barrels in Chinatown, risking shady ventures at night and working cheap.

I laughed. "Rapport, you mean."

"Niggers say repertoire," Charles said immediately. "That's what they mean. He knows what he's saying."

Homeboys together, arguing about money, sharing jokes, engaged in a silent tug-of-war, their exchanges cryptic or raunchy, rarely relaxing their guard. Years before, Eugene had been left behind. Now, at least physically, he was back and in charge. There were times when one sensed the dark, unresolved issues between them. Other times, despite so much baggage from the past, there were moments of shining transcendence that erased all the rest, sweet brief lapses that pushed their personal agendas aside.

One afternoon Charles was complaining, in his fashion. "I could have gotten well," he reproached me. "I have the wrong nurses. I need a team. People who believe."

"We believe," I said.

"Eugene says I believe in witches. He says Pachita has crazy people around who like knives, who want to be cut, who could get well without being cut . . ."

"It doesn't matter about Eugene. It matters what you believe."

"He went to Mexico City. He left me the night of the operation. He doesn't think I can get well."

"Yes, he does. He wants you to walk, he believes," I insisted.

That evening Eugene miraculously pulled Charles up out of bed without the Hoyer lift, pivoted him around on his feet, and made him take two or three faltering steps. Then, instead of putting him directly into the chair, Eugene held him up in a standing position. Charles began to arch his back while I placed his hands on Eugene's shoulders for support and helped him lift his head, until finally he was able to hold it up himself. He raised his head higher and higher and then, throwing it back, he raised it higher still, his eyes rolling upward, his neck stretching until, as we watched him—

moved by his soaring emotion and by ours—we saw him stand up once again as a man. I thought of the music he had written long ago—"Pithecanthropus Erectus"—out of his feelings for the first human on earth who had drawn himself up triumphantly on two feet. Now, as we stared at him, Charles called out, looking heavenward: "Where have I been?"

I saw Eugene's eyes shining as he held his father, and I knew this time he believed.

In the cemetery Eugene lingered beside me. "We still have the coffin," he said. "I mean, it's paid for. It seems a shame to waste. I was thinking I might ship it home to my aunt."

"It's not much of a gift," I said quickly. I was used to his whims; most of his inspired inventions on Charles's behalf had sprung from them. I supposed he wanted the coffin as a stash to transport home the marijuana plants he had nursed throughout the summer. His taste for "smoke" had become an obsession as the days worsened and Charles's disease grew and matured like the weed. I used to imagine his harvesting activities helped sustain him through our nights of illness—that he anticipated the balmy sun-filled hours the next day when he would carry some new sap or syrup to his plants, whistling and tramping across the fields. I imagined they shimmered in his mind during our sickbed marathons, though I didn't know for sure.

"It's a hell of a gift," I said again.

He was staring at the crematorium chimney, idly counting off the bricks. "Yeah," he reflected. "And there might be trouble at customs."

"Or a lot of overweight . . ."

He settled back, dismissing the idea as easily as he'd conceived it. Together we watched the dark brown smoke blow eastward for two hours and a half, smoke growing lighter as time went on, fire consuming bone, smoke turning white and then whiter and finally pure white at the end. Charles would have had something to say about that, I thought.

I remembered a conversation not long before Charles and I left New York. We were sitting together on our small balcony above Tenth Avenue at dusk, watching the sun collapse behind New Jersey. He already knew he was dying. "I may come back to earth as someone else," he was saying as he stared across the river. "I'll be somewhere with no name, practicing on my cello." He laughed. "And studying Bach, Beethoven, and Mingus . . .

"You know, I've had the physical thing already. Next time I want to be a star. I want to be flashing all night long. A star stays up there till it burns out and becomes something else. If I come out of this, I'll have a lot to say. But just in case . . . I want to be buried in the Ganges. I don't really want to come back no more." He was silent. He circled his good arm around me, the one he could still use to bang against the side of his wheelchair when he wanted to keep time.

"I've had a whole lot of karmas, baby," he said. "I'm really a dumb cat. I don't know that much music. It's from God. All of it. God is eternal life."

He had just spoken on the phone with his friend Booker-the-tailor about the writings of Swami Vivekananda and the Hindu parables. Booker was dying, too.

"Those cats had more to say," he'd told Booker as they sat in their separate homes, trying to make sense of things, Mingus in his wheelchair in our Manhattan apartment, Booker propped up in bed in Queens. "They're the only ones who got through to me. Their religion is open and democratic, they worship *all* the prophets. There's no prejudice at all!"

Booker had laughed. He and Charles had been friends since the sixties, long before Booker had gone off to jail for defending his small clothing store on Avenue B with a knife, stabbing one of the neighborhood extortionists who'd regularly held him up for cash as adroitly and deservedly (certain parties agreed) as he once swatted a rat off his ironing board with a scissors in the back of his shop. In those days, Booker had designed African dashikis for leaders of the new black consciousness, many of whom lived or worked nearby. Down the block, activist Rap Brown held political meetings in the back room of Bunch's Restaurant. Civil rights leader Stokely Carmichael came by for lunch. Booker called his line of clothing "The New Breed," and Charles was one of his loyal customers. Now Booker had been released from prison in Ossining with tuberculosis in order to die at home.

Booker laughed again. He reminded Charles of the old days, late nights on the bandstand when Mingus would call out the names of all the prophets in a jackhammer roll: *"Buddha! Moses! Krishna! Confucius! Mohammed! a-a-a-nd Jeee-sus Christ!"* Then he'd look into the audience and shout one more time: *"All the prophets!!"*

"Oh yeah," Mingus replied. He laughed, too. "As soon as I read Vivekananda I was enlightened even though I was raised in a Western church. You know, my friend Farwell Taylor used to take me to the Vedanta Society when I was young. I found more truth in what they were saying than anything in the Holiness or Methodist scene. I mean, most people are so bugged by the political system, the church, and the gangsters that they don't know what life is, man. They don't have time to find out."

They were both under sedation and they spoke to each other in thick voices.

"I'll come by in my wheelchair and I'll bring you some pie," Charles promised Booker. After a long pause, he said: "They ain't got no cure for what I got, but I'm going to get out of this bed. I'm going to get out of this *bed.* I'm going to get *out* of this bed. I'm going to die on my *feet.* All right, baby, I love you. I'm gonna let you go."

At the cemetery Eugene and I were joined by Arturo and Jesus, two Mexican nurses who had come to pay their respects. They sat on large white stones a few feet away, speaking quietly in Spanish while the smoke from their cigarettes curled in the air, joining the smoke from the crematorium above. Arturo, who had been our strength for so many months, who had stood so huge in the sickrooms of our villa, looked pale and small in his shirtsleeves under the open sky. Eventually, a man wearing baggy trousers and a soiled white cap arrived from the crematorium carrying the box of ashes. Eugene and I transferred the ashes to a small urn, fingering the warm contents, inspecting them for pieces of cranium and bone as Hindu custom required, while each of us—with the single-minded, lunatic possessiveness of the bereaved—was thinking of keeping something, a souvenir.

"I hope you didn't take anything," I said sharply to Eugene, later on.

"I thought about it," he admitted. "But I didn't want him to reincarnate incomplete. I didn't want him missing a finger or some toes."

Eugene and I drove back silently through the mountains at dusk, a high wind bending the trees and shaking the van. Instead of Charles strapped behind us in his wheelchair, there was only a metal urn, the metamorphosis too enormous for discussion.

One

I met Charles Mingus shortly before midnight in July 1964. I'd gone down to the Five Spot, a jazz club in lower Manhattan, because the producer of a film I was acting in had commissioned a jazz soundtrack from saxophonist Ornette Coleman—at least he thought he had commissioned a soundtrack—and my friend Sam Edwards, who was working on the film, suggested I check out the scene. I didn't know the first thing about jazz. Sam warned me I was not with it, especially for someone in New York, but added in his usual upbeat fashion that anyone could learn. Members of the cast had given me an Ornette Coleman album called *Something Else,* and I had listened over and over to a Miles Davis record called *Miles Ahead,* because the director of the film had played it over and over in the apartment where we were shooting during the long intervals between takes. That was the extent of my baptism into the music.

Sam picked me up at my apartment on the Upper West Side and we headed down to the Village Gate, where the trumpet player

Dizzy Gillespie was performing. Around midnight when Dizzy's set ended, we drove across town to the Five Spot to hear Mingus. In those days the Five Spot was one of the liveliest jazz hangouts in New York City. Jazz was peaking and both Charles Mingus and Thelonious Monk, who had recently appeared on the cover of *Time* magazine, could play at the same place for six months straight and keep people coming. It was a time, Sam explained, when Charles Mingus was referred to in the press as jazz's angry man.

I'd barely heard of Mingus, though echoes of his reputation had filtered down: the ornery, sometimes violent, often unjust, blustery figure who fired his musicians onstage, hired them back, denounced the audience for inattention, picked fights, mastered his instrument, dominated his music, vented his political beliefs on stage, presented a larger-than-life personality, and created on-the-spot performances for all to see. He was the essence of a sixties "happening," people said—those spontaneous events of the era that were everywhere around town.

Intermission had just begun when we arrived, and musicians were still lingering near the stage. We found a couple of seats at the bar and Sam ordered me a gin and tonic. I was unwinding from a visit home to my dad's—not really home, which had been Milwaukee, but my father's retirement place in Florida where I'd gone to discuss family problems: mine, marital and economic; his, an end-of-life hobbling illness.

He'd discovered that my phone wasn't working when he tried to call, and when I told him my marriage was close to being off the hook as well, he'd suggested I come down to talk it over. I'd soaked up the sun during our long discussions and now, back in New York, was hoping to blur the details of life for a few more hours, relaxing in a club. I was tanned and dressed in off-white clothes from head to toe. "Like a bottle of milk," Sam said, laughing, when he saw my cream-colored ensemble—skirt, blouse, matching summer heels. "You could be a blurb for your home state. America's Dairyland in linen."

I informed him it was silk, not linen, and that even my father had complimented me at the airport—an event I was still savoring, considering that our family had always avoided praise. For once, I said, Mom's convent ghosts were not kicking in. Sam knew about the Convent of the Sacred Heart where my mom had spent her childhood. I'd told him about the prestigious finishing school for Catholic young ladies whose rituals and distaste for excess and display were as alive and disapproving six decades later as they had been at the turn of the century.

I was touched by the unlikely attention my father had lavished on me earlier in the day and couldn't help bragging to Sam as we sat together on our stools, waiting for the music to begin.

"He gazed at my silk dress, my high heels and jewelry—I'm not usually so dressed up—and he saw my pinned-up hair, a whiff of hairspray holding it in place, and he told me I was a beautiful woman. Perhaps it was the first time he saw me. I think he was proud." The waiter had set down my drink and then run off to get Sam's, which he'd forgotten. "Of course he was shy about it, it was such an intimate thing to say. We never talked about looks in our family, you know. I don't remember compliments at all—not even about our accomplishments. They were dangerously linked to vanity in Mom's mind. And then, of course, my parents had expectations; you were expected to do well without flattery or approval. That's how they were." I looked at Sam. "I mean, my brothers and I didn't feel deprived."

I was aware that I was justifying what might seem like a spartan fear of excess or of personal expression.

"Well, here's to fatherly praise." Sam raised his glass. After surveying the room, he pointed to someone at a distant table and said it was Mingus. I'd already noticed the individual who was eating alone at a table for four, a man so aloof and removed from the late-night mob around him that he seemed like a remote island plunked down by accident in a sea of people. His sleeves were rolled up, a steak bone was in his fist, and his eyes were focused on the round plate of food before him, as intense and private as a holy man meditating on his chakra. He looked as if he might lavish the same brooding intensity on everything he touched. For the moment it happened to be his dinner.

I liked him immediately. I liked his aloneness in the tumultuous room, his concentration on the outsized beef bone at hand. He was consumed in the act of eating, lost in the pleasure of it despite the Saturday night frenzy and noisy tourist crowd around him, an unselfconscious, perspiring, focused man, exposed and unimpressed, a man too concentrated within himself for fear. My own life had been one of order and balance, founded on grammar and taste and impeccable manners, and yet something about the man across the room seemed oddly familiar, like someone I already knew, a relation in the family, some critical presence or weight like my father, looming beyond scale or size—although Mingus was not physically heavy then, nor was my father ever. I suppose now that it was just some soothsayer wraith blowing down my neck, some fanciful wind from the future revealing for an instant, like a photo developed too soon and out of sequence, the far-off snapshot ahead.

There is a tiny snapshot on my wall at home, centered inside an oversized frame. It is myself, aged five, a postage stamp of childhood. In the tattered photo I am flanked by two stalwart nannies who grasp my hands. They are tall and erect and stand at attention. Even now I can feel my hands locked in theirs. They were in charge of running the kitchen, in charge of me. Although orders came from above— from my mother who watched scrupulously over the preparation of food, the table settings, the lighting of candelabra, the preparation of my hair with a hot curling iron each morning before school—they ran interference for her and upheld the law.

Our meals were formal occasions at which my brothers wore ties and freshly ironed shirts, a bell summoned the maids, and my father carved at the head of the table. Although formalities were altered when the war broke out and young women could earn a better, more independent living working in defense factories instead of serving in homes, dinners remained a crucial ritual that continued long afterward. They were a branding iron of form that burned through our lives and those of our children, whatever our circumstances. Even years later, in the days when I ran a newspaper and held frequent boisterous editorial meetings/banquets at home, Charles sprawled large and brooding over his favorite dishes at the head of the table, we consumed our meals under flickering candles, sat straight before our place settings, and covered our laps with linen. The corruption of table manners remained unthinkable. It was linked forever with the echoes of Mom's vivid descriptions of her early convent discipline—the gothic punishments for a small elbow leaning on the dining table or a mistaken choice among the silver forks.

The expressions of the women in the snapshot are stern and protective beneath hats that slant rakishly low over their foreheads. Their long coats are slightly open; perhaps it is the first mild day at the end of winter, though the trees in the distance are bare, suggesting several weeks before spring. The women's lives are not about to blossom either, one imagines, although they are young enough and perhaps—but no, I cannot imagine them as anything but jailkeepers. Outfitted in a double-breasted coat with matching hat, I squint irritably at my father with his box camera, my hands locked in theirs. One day I will escape to Europe, marry a freethinking Italian sculptor, and, when he dies, marry Charles. It is already written in the snapshot.

But wait, there is another picture beside it—my mother, still young, taken by a professional photographer. She is beautiful and wears a beige linen dress, seated on a white wooden bench in the garden. She is carefree and gracious and without disappointment, years before her suicide. She holds a protective hand behind me as I balance on top of the bench and squint into the sun, seemingly unfettered. I am allowed my acrobatics, allowed to climb tall trees and back fences and explore the carefully designed world that is offered. I am given an illusion of independence, an abiding sense of freedom and the right to claim that freedom, that will last a lifetime.

As I watched, Mingus rose from the table and shouldered his way through the crowd. When he reached the bar, a bearded young man who was standing near us complained to him about Dizzy Gillespie's antics onstage at the very club Sam and I had just left. "Did you listen to him play?" Mingus responded immediately. Before the young man could reply, he continued: "Next time just listen to him blow his horn." Mingus stood at the bar near the ice buckets, looking glum. He'd been telling audiences to listen for more years than anyone could remember. Now, as the house cook moved past him, Mingus recalled another failure—an overcooked steak from the night before— and launched into a passionate complaint. The Chinese cook, who was called Samelschitt after his favorite expression, waited for the storm to run its course.

"Same old shit," he said under his breath and disappeared into the kitchen.

Mingus called for a bottle of Bordeaux—his own, which he'd evidently brought from home—and was standing so close to our stools that, as he drifted into wine talk with the bartender, I stole a glance at his eyes. They were large innocent eyes, I thought, vulnerable and questioning, deep brown amused eyes that darted about the room while he remained fixed on his conversation with the man at the bar. I decided to ask Mingus whether he'd seen Ornette Coleman, the musician Sam and I were looking for, whose free style of playing was still causing disputes among jazz fans.

"You mean the calypso player?" Mingus replied scornfully. He looked at me with curiosity. "You his old lady?" he asked.

"His mother?" I said. I hadn't the faintest notion what he meant. Mingus laughed. "No, baby, I mean his woman, his lady."

"He's writing some music for a movie I'm in."

"You in a movie?" He seemed surprised. "With those teeth?"

Now I laughed. "It's an underground movie," I said. "They're not fussy." A missing tooth in the back of my mouth was hardly visible—certainly it had never been singled out by a curious stranger.

"Isn't your daddy rich?" Mingus persisted. I looked sideways at Sam. He was sitting straight-backed and noncommittal, staring at himself in the mirror across the bar. I imagined he was waiting to see exactly how far down this communication failure was headed.

"I lived in Italy," I said. "The dentists aren't so great. I suppose it's not important." I turned back to Sam.

Sam Edwards edited an arts magazine called *The Second Coming* and had spent the afternoon examining stills from Robert Frank's new film. Robert had been the cameraman on *Pull My Daisy,* a documentary about beat poets narrated by Jack Kerouac, and was now completing his first feature film. My costar in Robert Frank's film was a French actor named Martin LaSalle. Martino, as we called him, had played the lead in Robert Bresson's *Pickpocket,* a movie famous among film cognoscenti. I'd fallen asleep at a special screening of *Pickpocket,* sandwiched between my future movie director and future leading man, and had earned an unfair reputation for being blasé, although the movie was achingly slow and the notion of being on-screen myself with Martino still seemed unreal.

I was living with my husband and my children, Susanna and Roberto, trying to make ends meet, modeling for an occasional photographer and landing the lead in Frank's film. My family of four had come to the States five years earlier from Rome. Half a dozen years before that, I'd graduated from Smith College, gone in search of a Europe my mother had imagined—different, to be sure, from the one I found—spent two years in Paris, and then moved on to Italy.

The reason—if one could say the following events had anything to do with reason—for the utterly spontaneous transfer of our family to New York, went more or less like this:

Because my brother Bob had won third prize in the Irish Sweepstakes together with a friend, and because the horse's name involved my deceased mom's maiden name as well as part of her former address, and because he now considered himself an agent of destiny summoned to bring his younger sister and her Italian family (whom he had already fallen in love with during a visit to Rome) back home, he helped organize our trip, found a gallery for Alberto's work, and had a house waiting for us in the country when we arrived. At the bidding of friends, who encouraged us to think in terms of success, Alberto and I left our mattress, our most costly possession, behind in Rome.

We departed from Venice, the only passengers on a cargo ship bound for the States, guests of the ship's owner, who was a friend of a Venetian countess named Adele who had long supported Alberto's art. (The countess's second husband, Giulio Machi, was a filmmaker who had been a prisoner of war and comrade of Alberto's in a British concentration camp in India for nearly seven years. The Italian government was too poor to bring its soldiers home after the war and they stayed where they were for an extra year. During that last year Alberto was allowed to travel through India making art for the British—transformed from a prisoner to a personage with his own majordomo or butler—in a last surreal touch. Giulio himself had returned to India several years later to make a film called *India Favolosa* with the cameraman Claude Renoir, a nephew of the film director Jean Renoir.) As we headed out to sea, our ship passed directly beneath the countess's palace windows on the Grand Canal. From the ornate balconies above our heads her servants gaily waved colorful carpets and silk wall hangings or whatever banners they could find. Twenty-two days later, in Norfolk, Virginia, Alberto and I and our children arrived at a long black dock lined with coal barges where, from our high perch, we could see my brother far below, a lone speck of white waiting by himself at the end of the pier. As we drove north, through the still-segregated South of 1958, we entered a strange world of hula hoops, Elvis Presley, and people who were

separated by the color of their skin. It seemed a long way from
Rome.

That was how, in the late 1950s, we went from our small but elegant apartment in the Villa Brasini to a cottage in the backwoods of
New Jersey, and finally to Manhattan, the nature of our life changing
as radically as the landscape.

"I hear you." Mingus smiled unexpectedly as he prepared to leave
for the bandstand. It was time for the next set. The stage lights were
on and he looked at me again. Then he said: "Still, if I was your
daddy, I'd fix your teeth!"

Sam drew him into a last-minute conversation about Dizzy's
music, and I couldn't help adding my own view—similar to the
bearded fan's at the bar—that Dizzy was playing to the tourists, juggling his maracas and clowning for the crowd. The showbiz aspect
of it, a sense of dismissal and condescension to the audience that
included me, was annoying. Mingus gave a last resigned sigh and
murmured again about the rewards of listening. I was beginning to
get the point.

He continued to linger beside my stool. "I'll play something for
you," he said finally, as he turned to leave. He headed over to the
piano, where he intercepted the piano player and sat down on the
bench himself. Quietly he began to pick out a melody on the keys,
tentative and reflective, as if he were playing at home.

Off to the right, his musicians were gathering on the bandstand.
He glanced at them, slowly got up, and walked over to the center of
the stage. Then, in one swift movement and without a word to his
sidemen, he picked up his double bass and launched into an up-
tempo version of "Fables of Faubus," his personal indictment of
Orville Faubus, the governor of Arkansas, the man who had pre-
vented a teenage black girl in Little Rock from entering and integrat-
ing her high school class.

"Tell me someone . . . who is ridiculous . . . !" he shouted to his drummer, Dannie Richmond.

"Gov . . . ner . . . Fau . . . bus!" his drummer shouted back.

"Why is he so sick . . . and ridiculous . . . Dannie?"

"Two-four-six-eight . . . brainwash and teach you hate . . . !"

Two hours later he finished the set with an intricate bass solo and retired to the kitchen that doubled as a dressing room—one of the many irritations in the world of the jazz artist, as Sam explained, which Mingus addressed nightly before his audiences. Earlier in the evening he'd admonished the bartender for ringing the cash register during one of his bass solos and, later on, had scolded some noisy patrons seated in front of the stage for clinking ice in their glasses.

"Isaac Stern doesn't have to put up with that shit," he said, staring straight at the offending table.

It was late. We called for the tab and Sam escorted me home in a cab.

On the way home, I told Sam his earlier swipes about America's Dairyland weren't entirely out of line, that the Midwest still clung to me like summer pollen: I remembered Sunday afternoons driving across the state, my father at the wheel of our royal-blue Buick, unintentionally rakish beneath his gray fedora, as we crisscrossed the countryside and observed the cows. They were everywhere you looked, dappling the landscape, stark and dignified and familiar, standing quietly across a thousand remembered childhood afternoons, slow comfortable cows with soft brown eyes, blank and tranquil like my life.

"They were still as statues," I said.

"Wisconsin sculpture," Sam agreed from his side of the cab.

"Well, there wasn't much going on at the museums," I said, laughing, "if that's what you mean. Anyone looking for formal culture headed south, ninety miles to Chicago, for season tickets to the symphony or visits to the Art Institute. But Sundays we went for drives and . . ."

"You miss the cows." Sam nodded. "It's perfectly natural."

I said it was more likely that I missed being on my own and free. I said even my husband had told me recently I didn't make a man secure, that I always had a "ticket in my pocket to Florida," as he put it, his way of explaining some failure in me, some inability to belong with total conviction to married life. Although we were friends, still sharing the details of our dreams and sorrows, our marriage was nearly over. I jumped out in front of my apartment as Sam vanished in the night. I stood on the curb for a while watching the patch of stars visible above the trees on Riverside Drive and wondered whether I would return to the club.

The week after I met Mingus, I drove down to the Five Spot by myself on a Thursday, or "listeners' night," as the musicians called it, when the room was less crowded. I sat at a table directly in front of the bandstand where a waiter had placed me, wondering whether I should have asked for a seat less visible, a seat farther back. I rarely went out by myself and had never been to a jazz club alone. I was glad when the waiter seated someone named Ivan Black at my table, a soft-spoken, pale, middle-aged man who introduced himself as a publicity agent for another club. He was also a black history scholar, he added modestly, moonlighting in the trenches of New York nightlife. He seemed to possess a brainy reserve of uncommon facts that he delivered to outsiders like me, as well as to friends and musicians who sat around and bought him drinks, listening to his accounts of centuries and civilizations that never made it to the classroom—not yet, at least, but things were changing. It was 1964, the year the Civil Rights Act was passed, and a new politics was emerging.

Despite all the talk of change, Ivan went on, Mingus was unimpressed. (Soon there would be a new slogan—"Black is beautiful"—and a new hairdo—the Afro—and still, Mingus would tell reporters, it was the same "schitt" as before.) Mingus had invented his own spelling of "schitt," Ivan explained, that was acceptable on the printed page in publications to which Mingus wrote frequently about music or racism or the hypocrisy of the record industry—open letters to critics in which the word "schitt" figured prominently. "Mingus can tell you a lot about life," Ivan said, laughing as the house lights dimmed, "if you catch him in the right mood." We settled back, waiting for the music to begin.

In the middle of the set, as he had done throughout the evening, Ivan leaned over to explain something to me. This time, however, his words ran on too long. Mingus glowered from the stage. Simultaneously, within the density of the music, a growling bass solo emerged that featured such irate bowing, such dissonant slurs and scratches of protest, that we all snapped to attention. The scratches continued, becoming almost deafening until, satisfied by their effect, Mingus modulated to a tender chorus of "She's Funny That Way."

At the end of the set, an argument broke out at the table next to ours: a customer protesting the undivided attention Mingus required of the audience. "Yeah, well, it's demanding music. You have to listen," another at the table replied. "Mingus isn't background. He's not for mealtimes. I mean . . ." He laughed suddenly. "How could you eat dinner, man? That's what Dexter Gordon said. 'You'd choke on your spaghetti!' " Mingus walked past our tables at that moment and headed for the kitchen. Together with Ivan Black, for the first time in my life, I went backstage.

Inside the kitchen two of Mingus's sidemen were unhooking their horns and calling out food orders to the cook. Behind them Mingus sat on a stool drinking from a large flask of red wine. He lowered the bottle from his lips and looked at me without smiling. He didn't extend a greeting and I didn't wait for one.

"Why were you so insulting the other evening?" I heard myself ask. He looked perplexed. He was wearing a long chain around his neck from which dangled wristwatches, rings, and various talismans.

"*You* were insulting," he said instinctively. He hadn't the foggiest notion what I was talking about.

I laughed. "Why do you wear all that around your neck?"

He was silent for a moment. He set the bottle of wine down on the floor. He looked at me, perhaps to gauge whether he would allow the question. He decided once again to let it ride.

"They're presents," he said slowly. "From women. You know, from fans." Then, as if he had just decided it, he added, "They're good luck . . ." He looked up at me. "How come you're here? You listen to the music?" he asked. "Are you an heiress? Or a call girl? Or a spy? . . ." There was a slight edge to his voice. "Or did somebody send you?"

Ivan Black began a discussion about Hannibal. I decided it was time to leave and fished in my purse for the keys.

"I'll walk you to your car," Mingus said unexpectedly. "You shouldn't be alone on the streets at this hour."

He accompanied me down the block, holding my arm protectively and making certain that I locked the front door of my old station wagon behind me before he headed back up the street. A few moments later, as I drove past the club, he was lingering in the doorway waving, his bowlegs silhouetted against the light.

"Take care of yourself," he called out to me. "Ain't nobody safe out there no more." His voice trailed off.

I ran into Mingus a few weeks later on a hot summer evening in Central Park where we both had gone to see James Earl Jones in a production of *Othello*. It was part of the Shakespeare in the Park series and I had walked across the park with friends from my children's school who, like me, flocked to any inexpensive cultural event the city offered. When we arrived at the ticket line, Mingus was standing in the middle of an animated crowd that seemed to be agreeing with his unfavorable opinion of the seating arrangements at the theater. It was his habit, I later learned, to involve those within earshot in personal matters. It was a form of protection, he once explained, against the enemy, the unknown adversary. He needed witnesses at the ready, and to this end he engaged stoop sitters in conversation en route to work, chatted amicably with cops, and had an army of supporters poised to vouch for him in countless bars throughout the city. There was danger everywhere, and he, for one, would not be found among the friendless or unprepared.

He saw me with my friends and invited us to join him. As we sat together in the bleachers of the Delacorte Theater watching the play, he consulted a leather briefcase frequently, snapping it open and shut. This briefcase—his Pandora's box, as someone later called it—was full of medicine bottles, knives, black pepper, music scores, earplugs, telephone numbers, a bottle of Courvoisier, several meerschaum pipes, and lots of money. Mingus removed the tiny yellow-lensed Swiss watchmaker glasses he was wearing and replaced them with dark goggles. He filled a pipe with great care, lit several matches, and blew smoke toward the darkening sky. He swallowed a pill from a bottle and screwed the cap on noisily. He wiped the lenses of a tiny pair of opera glasses with a large handkerchief and handed them to me. He counted some bills. He put his arm about me in a distracted moment and quickly withdrew it. And all the while, despite his activities, he remained absorbed by the action onstage.

At intermission, when I asked about the layers of bills in his briefcase, he explained that carrying lots of money, usually in thick stacks of small bills, was a habit he had cultivated years before. His explanation was simple: he was black. When "creative anger" didn't work—a system he described for getting front tables at restaurants, personal attention, or simply admittance through the door—money did. He said he had special custom-made shirts designed with secret pockets on the shoulders and under the armpits in which he regularly carried wads of bills.

When *Othello* was over, he asked if I'd have dinner with him at a steak house nearby. I made arrangements to meet my friends later on, and then Mingus and I headed across the park. As we walked along, a jazz writer he knew who was carrying a John Coltrane record under his arm approached and began to question him about the great saxophone player. "Don't ask me, man. I'm just a poor bass player," Mingus replied. He linked arms with me protectively for a brief moment, as he had on the street outside the Five Spot, and was silent while the three of us walked on. It was an uneasy silence. Mingus seemed torn between dismissing this fellow who was in the way and unburdening himself of matters pressing on his soul.

"He went back to India, man," Mingus said finally. "Back to Indian-type pedal point music. He hit a streak." The writer began to share some opinions of his own but Mingus wasn't listening. "Why doesn't he do other things too?" Mingus asked out loud. "Why do guys stylize themselves? Don't they know in the summertime you wear thin clothes and straw hats and then in the wintertime you got a right to play a different tune? You don't have to be stylized. A preacher preaches a different sermon every Sunday. He doesn't preach the same one. You turn to a different page." He stopped on the path and pulled some matches out of his pocket. "It's very sad." The matches were followed by a large flat lighter from which he raised an enormous flame and slowly began to light his pipe. The writer tried to talk again, but Mingus wasn't listening. "It's very sad," he continued. "That's why I haven't made it. Because I'm turning pages all the time. Because I have a special page I want to get to. If I throw that page open . . ." He stopped. We had reached Fifth Avenue, where he decided to turn right and let the writer walk on ahead.

"Well, see you, man," he said abruptly and took my arm again. Then he walked over to the curb to hail a cab. Two or three taxis slowed down and then continued on without stopping. Mingus's mood shifted. He shouted at the next cab, ran after it, and managed to kick the rear fender with his foot, letting out a holler at the same time as if he had been struck by the car.

"I've got your number!" he yelled after it. "I'm gonna sue your ass!" (In later, calmer years, he would carry a fold-up leather seat on a steel tripod for "sitting out" in style any redneck, honky driver who might pass him by, like the night he left a standing ovation at Carnegie Hall in 1974 after one of his concerts and—unable to flag down a taxi—sat down on his collapsible chair in the middle of Fifty-seventh Street and read a newspaper.)

We walked for a few blocks and caught a cab in front of the Plaza Hotel. It was easier to find a driver there who overlooked the color of your skin in favor of the green inside your wallet, he said. In the middle of our ride, Mingus changed his mind about dinner and said there was something important he needed to show me first. He ordered the driver instead to Grand Central Terminal. When we arrived, he jumped out of the cab and swiftly led me downstairs, hurrying through the halls and corridors until we reached a corner that echoed our voices along a wall. I waited at one end of the long wall while he spoke in a low whisper from the other side, unexpected words of tenderness that roared from across the room, shy words of love that slid along the grimy walls of Grand Central as distant and unreal as the graffiti they swept past.

"I love you," he was saying. "I want you to be my woman." I laughed off his words. They were sounds in a station from a man I hardly knew. Still, I went on listening. I listened to his flood of words and to his long stories for most of the night. Ivan Black would have said I'd caught him in the mood.

We taxied a few blocks to Gallagher's Steak House, where Mingus seemed to be a regular. After a lavish meal we walked along the dark West Side streets of Manhattan and then back through the park, past the zoo, walking nowhere through the night, nowhere, at least, where outsiders might intrude. Perhaps he felt the world's heavy hand was far away. And so we walked, side by side, our shoulders touching now and then, a couple minding our own business in the dark, while he explained how he'd wanted to be a pimp, how gangsters were running his world, how the clubs were full of women called "chippies," and how in the middle of his pain and his sins he was trying to find God.

"I broke with the life," he said. "I couldn't stand it. It was driving me crazy. I only had two girls but I knew it was wrong. Maybe I just didn't want to become a snake or a rat or a roach when I died. Maybe it was that simple . . . It had mainly to do with religion, with my karma." I listened as his streams of biography, brave and unprotected, flowed through the night, history crammed into private codes, language bright and distant as the moon above, all of it delivered in a nonstop mumble at the speed of light. I barely understood a word. I knew only that he was exposing his truth, raw and without apology. When he finally slowed down, he began to talk about his cowardice and his fears. And then he remembered Fats Navarro, the trumpet player whom he said he had written about in a book.

"You know, Fats wasn't afraid of anything," he said. "Especially death. Fats always talked about 'Everybody afraid to die, I ain't afraid to die.' " We were marching south on Eighth Avenue now, somewhere in the Forties, past bowling alleys and late-night delis, and still he had not stopped talking. I had forgotten long ago about my friends. "Well, one night the bus broke down," he continued. "We were on one of those tours with Lionel Hampton and we had to wait a couple of hours on the road. It was outside a town where they had this dam and some rafters, you know? Those wide concrete rafters that run across a bridge?" He stopped and looked at me for a while as if I might understand something in silence he could not put into words.

"I liked Fats," he began again more slowly. His voice was tender, as it had been at the train station. "He was my sitting partner on the bus and my sleeping partner in the hotel. So I said: 'I'll play follow-the-leader with you, Fats.' And Fats said: 'All right.' So I started walking on the rafters until they got so high I said: 'I'm going back now, Fats.' And then Fats protested. He said: 'You said we playin' follow-the-leader, Mingus. Now I'm gonna lead!'

"Well, man! He went to the top of this kind of bridge and he walked across the narrow plank and he turned around and said: 'Mingus, don't be afraid! You 'fraid to die!' And then he walked all the way across that thing and turned around and came back . . . Well, I couldn't do that. Not then, anyway. I'd be gone!"

Mingus stood in the shadows on the street, lost in recollection. Then, as if to include me, he leaned over and gently touched my face. The sky was growing light on the horizon between the chunks of sky-scrapers. It was almost dawn.

"Now, maybe it's different," he said finally. "I'm older now. A man has to know how to die."

During the rest of the summer we met for coffees or meals on the run in the middle of our separate lives. He'd arrive with a shrieking of brakes at some small coffee shop, cool in his brown leather pants and leather vest, his open sandals and tiny shades, skinny and sharp, no hint he'd once weighed three hundred pounds. ("Mingus?" people would say. "Nah, he's fat. Must be someone else.") He'd enter the shop, stake out the terrain, address the smattering of customers— quietly focused on their meals or newspapers—about some issue on his mind with all the noise and color and abandon necessary to de-flect whatever hostile scenarios he imagined were in their heads. He'd pitch us dead center into the lives of everyone in the shop.

Since childhood I'd been trained to look away from disruptive scenes, ignore private feuds or public brawls, remain respectfully un-involved. All that was over now. Charles's need to drag into broad daylight the dangers he imagined crouching out of sight wasn't "something else," in the jargon of the times, nor was it "a horse of another color," as my British father might have said. For Charles, it was just the norm—disarming the enemy, flushing the bush.

As for my father, he'd been in the cavalry and horses figured in his speech. You were on your high horse, or someone ought to be horse-whipped, or he might quote: "It ain't the 'eavy armor that 'urts the

'orses' 'ooves, it's the 'ammer, 'ammer, 'ammer on the 'ard 'ighway"—
a Cockney observation he'd once heard in a pub and quoted with delight whenever he'd had a few drinks. "A horse of another color"
was an expression I soon learned to avoid around Charles, along
with "blackmail" ("call it whitemail"), "iron out the kinks," and any
number of other unsuspected kegs of dynamite. Words were important and Charles was on his own mission to clear the air.

There was a lot of new vocabulary I had to learn. In a restaurant,
if he said there was a "soul in the kitchen," it meant the cook was a
brother. A brother meant someone with the same color skin as his. If
a person was "booked," it meant his days on earth were numbered,
he'd soon travel on. When Charles said, "I crossed my legs on him,"
it meant he was healthy and in shape: he'd lost enough weight so he
could cross his legs. (He might do it—cross his legs—and then look
significantly at an opponent sitting opposite him who possibly had
no idea of the ominous message he was being sent.) In moments of
emergency, I often hadn't a clue myself what directive he was giving.
I'd learned Italian, but this was a language of invention with no fixed
text. You had to get the hang of it by feel.

Sometimes he would end his late-night set with a few bars from a
popular 1930s tune called "The Object of My Affection."

"It'll never happen," an actor who was sitting at my table one
night mused aloud. He was one of the stars of the Negro Ensemble
Theater Company, situated around the block from the Five Spot.

"What won't?" I asked.

"What the tune says," he said, laughing. " 'Change my complex-
ion from white to rosy red.' " There were subtexts as well: it was a
corny society tune, an object of derision, a tune that symbolized an
entire social stratum—my own stratum, for that matter. I thought of
the debutante balls at home, the steamer trunk full of long formal
dresses I'd taken to Europe after college and never worn—my life
changing midstream in Paris.

I'd been presented to society when I was eighteen, standing at the top of a spindly staircase under a spotlight in my long white gloves and formal, modest dress—not the slinky one I'd begged Mom to buy—while my name was announced to a crowded ballroom and I maneuvered the descent to where my oldest brother was waiting below. He escorted me to a cotillion in the center of the floor where thirty-five or forty young women were living out a tradition that, even then, like the royal families of the world, was rapidly losing ground. (Those formal gowns I took abroad rotted inside my trunk in the basement of the American House at the Cité Universitaire along with several hundred other unreclaimed trunks belonging to young ladies who, like me, moved into the ateliers of Paris and left their former lives and dresses behind with their luggage.)

Mingus continued to charge through the moments I saw him as if his life were at stake, summoning the same intensity at a hot-dog stand, where he ordered every topping on the cart, that he unleashed on honky cabdrivers who ignored him on the street. At breakfast he might order racks of lamb—he was on a protein diet then—at dinner, a dozen scrambled eggs. His daily menu was as personal, passionate, and noisy as his political assaults on the status quo. I was mesmerized by his excesses, his boldness, his monumental refusal to compromise what he believed.

When we first met I'd asked him about some ugly marks I noticed on his wrist. Attaching little importance to the story, he described a wager he'd made a few days before with a French film director, whose documentary on tribal life, *The Sky Above, the Mud Below,* was playing in art theaters around town. He and the director had been drinking at the Five Spot, following an afternoon rehearsal there. Over several fiascoes of red wine, the director had told him that as the result of a war injury, he had no feeling in his left hand.

"A black man in this country has no feeling either," Charles replied immediately. "He's used to pain." He then challenged the director to a contest in which they took turns burning cigarette holes into their wrists, one after another, until finally the director with compassion conceded. Five holes into the wager, it was obvious Mingus never would. "You just kept on?" I asked with disbelief. He merely shrugged.

One of his closest friends from his childhood days in Watts, trombone player Britt Woodman, who had performed in Duke Ellington's band for a dozen years, told me that when Mingus was a young man he carried a lasso with him as he charged on his motorcycle past the manicured front lawns of Los Angeles homes. When he spotted a black jockey figurine, he would lasso off its head. Sometimes, Britt said, Mingus would strike out in specific retaliation after a confrontation with a honky homeowner in a redneck bar. Britt, who everyone agreed was one of the kindest, least confrontational men to ever walk the earth, smiled with pride at his recollection.

Charles's values arrived in such unorthodox forms that, in spite of myself, I rejected most of them out of hand. His irony was at odds with my faith in the obvious, with a childhood's worth of not being tricked. I'd grown up in the safest city in the United States. Milwaukee had the toughest police force, the lowest crime rate, the cleanest streets, the fewest traffic accidents per capita in the country. Even my entry into the world was free of struggle, a Caesarean lifted from my mother's womb without a wrinkle. Flanking the expensive part of town, Lake Michigan loomed, endless as the ocean, tame as the spaniels on our front lawn, familiar and gray as the fedora my father wore to the office or tipped politely to the ladies who gathered with my mother to roll bandages for the Red Cross twice a week. After the bandages, bridge tables were assembled and immaculate playing cards were stacked perpendicular to the corners as carefully as my life.

The summer afternoons were measured and predictable like the mathematical equations inside my father's head, his wild inventor's brain concealed and ticking beneath his proper hat. I sat on flat rocks at the end of a flowering ravine and dreamed my way across the water. They were motionless afternoons when the leaves on the big elm trees were still and watchdogs dozed in the shade, when the only sound was the whirring of sprinklers on a dozen lawns a short slice away from the nine-hole golf course at the end of the block. On such afternoons I watched the gray water slap against the rocks and waited, defined by summers as free from turbulence as the lilac bush outside my window, summers that would provide the placid underpinnings and, eventually, the suit of mail that absorbed life's surprises and still allowed, as one friend noted, my "exasperating optimism."

Was it necessary to apologize for well-being, I wondered. I woke up happy. I attributed it to a fortunate metabolism or to bland summers or to an easy birth. Sheer energy dispelled the gloom. Even when I was surrounded by early-morning sufferers, I rose from bed with hope despite the irritation it provoked and my inability to account for it.

In mid-September, Mingus announced that he was heading out to the Monterey Jazz Festival in California. Along with other compositions he'd written, he planned to present an extended work about integration that he called "Meditations for a Pair of Wirecutters." We were sitting at a Madison Avenue deli uptown and he was bringing me up to date. "It's fully orchestrated," he said from across the table, as people around us were ordering from their breakfast menu and he was ordering a high-protein array of meat and cheeses from the dinner page. "Sometimes I call it 'Meditations on Integration' and sometimes 'Meditations on Inner Peace.' " The waitress had left to discuss his burgeoning order with some higher authority. "I mean, we'll be performing it with an expanded band. We'll rehearse it for three days out there. You know, in Europe we were only playing with a quintet."

I wasn't sure why the expanded band was special, but he was exuberant and his high spirits were growing higher. He explained that the piece he'd written had become a hymn to injustice, that he'd dedicated it to black Americans imprisoned behind electric barbed wire in the South.

"Where are they imprisoned?" I asked immediately. He took for granted that his assertions were self-evident. I was constantly catching up. Sometimes I only half believed him. They were facts out of my range. It was hard to separate his excesses from his truths, although frequently they were the same. He said he'd heard about the internments from his saxophonist Eric Dolphy before their final tour together. He said he couldn't get them out of his mind.

"They don't have ovens and gas faucets in this country yet," he said grimly, as the waitress reappeared with a hunk of Gorgonzola and a giant steak. "But they have electric fences. So I wrote a prayer about some wire cutters. I wrote a prayer we'd find some scissors and get out!"

A week later, moments after the concert was over in Monterey, he called me in New York from a phone backstage. He said the crowd had roared its approval for five solid, unbelievable minutes while he paced back and forth across the raised platform of the bandshell, his leather sandals flapping against his bare feet while the crowd stood up and screamed. He said he never even looked up, he was too scared. At rehearsal he'd told his trumpet player, Lonnie Hillyer, that the music was a prayer and he, Lonnie, was the preacher. "I told him it's like when disorganization comes in and you've got to straighten it out," he said. "I told him it's like a minister in church or like a Jewish rabbi. Everybody's shouting at you. You've got to chant and put them back into condition." He was on a roll. I barely had a chance to speak. He said he'd been playing to God and that he felt close to death. Next day I read about it in the press. "I felt pains in my chest," he'd told a reporter. "I felt them once before and it scared me. This time it didn't matter. I said, 'To hell with it, I'll go on playing what I'm playing even if I die.'"

By the end of the week *Time* magazine had ranked him among the greatest composers in jazz. "At the end of his gasser of a concert," raved the reporter, "5000 cats rose in a thunderous ovation they had not accorded Ellington or Dizzy Gillespie or even Thelonious Monk." Another paper compared his bowing to Pablo Casals and his compositions to Debussy. The *New York Herald Tribune* wrote that he had erased the memory of any other bass player in jazz. Mingus told someone else he was playing to love and to the spirit. When he came home he said he was playing to me. I didn't really believe him. I didn't understand the size of his feelings—for me or for anything else. I wasn't ready. His roar and his clatter were like the sound of breaking glass. I wasn't ready at all.

It hardly mattered. He paid no attention. He was bursting with ideas, shouting them over the phone, declaring it was time to start another record company, listing the crimes of every major label he'd had the misfortune to sign with. He described how they favored white musicians, how they withheld royalties. When I mentioned I'd been looking for a job, he suggested I help him organize a small mail-order record club that would offer *Mingus at Monterey* to the public. He said Frank Sinatra's office had called and wanted to release the music, but he'd decided to do it on his own.

"It's the only way," he shouted happily before hanging up the phone, "to get an honest count!" At the recording studio where he mastered the tapes and where I accompanied him, already hooked on a dozen plans for the future, he included three full minutes of applause. Someone talked him out of the remaining two.

Within two months, Charles Mingus Enterprises had set up business—the two of us, plus a post office address, one studio, and a variety of cafés. Soon jazz writers included our address in their reviews. Mingus himself created a comic-strip ad that ran in the press. "People will read it if it looks like the funnies," he declared one afternoon. With his usual priorities, the comic-strip ad was as aggressively concerned with alerting the public to rip-offs at the hands of crooked record companies, bootleggers, and thieves, as it was with the albums we were selling. He wrote his own liner notes and included passages from his still-unpublished autobiography. His oldest son, Charles the Third, a painter who had recently moved to New York, designed the covers.

One afternoon after work, we sprawled on a friend's tar roof in Greenwich Village while he improvised verbally on the Manhattan skyline. A skyline had been just a skyline in the old days, but Mingus reinvented everything in sight. From his bottomless briefcase, he brought out a bottle of wine, set two paper cups on a ledge, and began to expound on his autobiography, *Beneath the Underdog.* "I received a big advance for it—twenty-five thousand dollars from McGraw-Hill. But a senior editor, a guy who was about six foot five, called it the dirtiest book he'd ever read and refused to publish it. The worst part was I wrote the truth about powerful people and their names were still in the book when it was passed all over town. It went to *Esquire* and everywhere else. When I heard that I almost went crazy." He uncorked the bottle of wine, tasted it, and poured a second cup. Then he continued his story. He believed there were people who wanted him killed. He said he'd dreamed he was gunned down in a club.

"See that?" he cried out suddenly, swinging his head uptown as if someone were already stalking him across the tar. I turned around swiftly, but no one was on the roof. Instead, he was staring at the Empire State Building, whose familiar spire loomed above Fifth Avenue.

"What are you looking at?" I asked nervously.

"It's not a spire, you dig!" He laughed. "It's a hypodermic needle infecting the sky." He examined the Empire State Building as if it had just landed on the horizon. He said he had written a gospel tune for the junkies of the world, advising them to get a spiritual hit in their lives, not in their arms. He said he'd called it "Better Get a Hit in Your Soul."

"Look!" he shouted again. This time he waved his arm at some small birds that were poking about in the rain gutters. "Sparrows!" He contemplated the busy little creatures dredging up whatever they could from the detritus on the roof. "They're mongrels like me," he said. "Outcasts." He watched approvingly. "They know what to do, though. They're the sharpest of all. When the other birds have split, they'll be around."

He put his arm around me as I sat beside him and listened to the facts. He described a recent visit to the accounting department at Columbia Records, where he'd gone up on the elevator carrying a shotgun, intent on demanding his royalties. He was dressed in a safari suit and helmet for the occasion, which he'd charged at Abercrombie and Fitch. Columbia brought his royalties right up to date. He recalled another appointment at Bethlehem Records, where he'd gone to negotiate a contract. He'd taken along his drummer Dannie Richmond, who pulled out a knife on cue, stared at the company executive, and then casually cleaned his nails. Creative anger Mingus, called it, as he had that first night in the park. It got results.

Although he painted musical portraits onstage—tunes called "Self-Portrait," "Portrait in Three Colors," "Myself When I Am Real"—his own seemed never to dry. Long ago from my flat rock, I'd dreamed my way across Lake Michigan, imagining a thousand futures. Not one of them was close. Even the soothsayer-astrologer who had appeared at one of my mother's luncheons in Milwaukee when I was a teenager and had predicted for me a second husband "in the public eye," hadn't a clue. Not even a five-star clairvoyant could foresee with precision someone in my life who would write compositions called "Precognition," "Extra-Sensory Perception," or "Mind-Readers' Convention in Milano."

I've often wondered what it would have been like to know my parents as peers when they were in their prime, not as upholders of power or bearers of late-life compromises but as they were before me. If such magic had been possible, how much easier for Charles and me! After all, my parents' coupling was as unlikely as our own, their worlds as disparate. Surely they had set a precedent somewhere in my genes. But without a clue, some clarity or revelation, Charles and I battled out our differences as if they were happening for the first time. In the end I would repeat my parents' life as inevitably as if it had all been fashioned at birth. Their world of convention was only a temporary stop, one that assumed destiny could be subverted, character suppressed, or that all of us at home, my brothers and myself, would fail to read between their lines.

One weekend, while having a rare dinner in New York with my father during my senior year at Smith, a year after my Roman Catholic mother had died, he unburdened himself of something I already knew, that he was a Jew. One of my brothers had revealed scraps of family history earlier that year, but I was twenty now, not much affected by family news. I told my father I imagined my intelligence quotient had just jumped a notch. I said that despite my Irish red hair and hateful freckles, I might tan instead of burn. I saw him smiling in the candlelight, his face touched with surprise. We'd been taught at home not to display our feelings, but his pleasure and relief at my casual endorsement were visible after all the baggage he'd endured. He looked at me shyly and began to laugh. It was an extraordinary moment in a relationship that was so devoid of intimacy.

I remember that dinner for another reason—my father's rare look of respect and surprise when I offhandedly observed that Mom had a contrived innocence—a moment so exceptional in my memory that it still resonates. I imagine he did not think I held ideas. He did not think I reflected at all. Now, years after his death, I try to bridge the chasm at least in dreams where my father and I communicate as equals, where I am proud of his good looks, his intelligence, his snobbery, his past.

He had arrived in New York from England at age eleven, entered

Columbia University at fourteen, tutored graduate students in advanced math a year later, and remained an isolated prodigy, ignored by fraternities, intimidated by women. His remarkable talents peaked at twenty, I once heard him say, but his brilliance was evident in his inventions, the engineering devices he perfected and manufactured for the rest of his life.

As with most of my friends and their fathers, I was outside his orbit, the youngest sibling, female, removed from his intellectual concerns. He lived for his inventions and for my mother. He had no real friends, nor did he bother to learn the names of my mine: he called them all Mimi, though there was only one Mimi among them. I suppose he tried to joke his way through his lack of interest. He wasn't interested in much that Milwaukee had to offer, certainly not the social affairs my mother thrived on. He had little patience for society and amused himself at cocktail parties by taking contrary positions for the sake of argument. My mother never reconciled herself to this small perversity. Her enthusiasm for harmony and her need to circumvent the shadow side of life ruled our house. "Look on the bright side," she would tell us. It was close to a warning.

My mother and father had met at a military ball. He was a handsome young major in a cavalry unit intent on a military career. She was a young harpist fresh out of the exclusive Convent of the Sacred Heart, where she had once planned to enter the order and become a nun. Now she was doing social work in Washington, D.C., and engaged to another man. She was full of spunk and determination, brave and wholly naive. Once, locked in a room with a raving inmate while on the job at a mental institution, she kept him at bay with her stories and her warmth until the guards arrived. Once, bedridden with a swollen leg, she saw a purse snatcher from her window, raced down three flights of steps, and pursued him down the street, shouting, "Stop thief!"

Family stories.

My father courted her with poetry and boxes of dark chocolate and, in one month, won her heart. She had no intention of leading her life on an army base, and so they moved to New York, where he began his career as an inventor-engineer. Catholic and Jew, 1918. When she was introduced to his family, her new mother-in-law said only: "Please God, it may yet come out all right!" I'd heard the story as a child. I was twenty before I understood. Had my mother been alive for either one of my marriages, doubtless she would have said the same.

My mother's credentials were the ones extolled at home: her ancestor Thomas E. Stone, signer of the Declaration of Independence; his nephew, Thomas E. Stone, the first governor of Maryland; her father, same name, private secretary to Presidents McKinley, Theodore Roosevelt, Taft. We heard about her holidays at the White House, playing piano sitting on Teddy Roosevelt's knee in the Green Room. We heard about her childhood at the Convent of the Sacred Heart. She never forgot her vacations alone in the dark corridors of the convent while other children were sleigh-riding at home, her father on tour with one president or another while her mother rotted in a mental ward in solitary confinement. We didn't know our maternal grandmother had been placed in St. Elizabeth's Hospital in Washington, D.C. when Mom was three. Her own mother was twenty-eight when her husband signed the papers and she was erased. She never saw her three children again. I've searched the records and can't find her maiden name; not even on my mother's birth certificate, where it's just a blank. Everyone has a mother. Even the Immaculate Conception involved a mom.

My father's English-Jewish background, his intellectual accomplishments, his personal tutors at home in England (he never attended a conventional grade school), his family's wealth lost at his grandfather's death, their early days as immigrants at the turn of the century in Manhattan's Hell's Kitchen, none of it was discussed— only bits and pieces seeped through. At his death I found a Phi Beta Kappa key in a drawer and learned he was a Rhodes scholar. He had co-authored a book with his cousin, Ben Graham, an economist whose investment approach laid the foundation for Tweedy Brown, the largest brokerage house in London, and whose book *Security Analysis* is still taught at Harvard. Benjamin Graham is recognized as the father of value investing, later championed by his disciple Warren Buffett.

The early innocence and naïveté of my parents—persistent outsiders—allowed me freedom and muddied the conventional paths they had intended. If there was a lack of awareness of the real world, there was a lack of propaganda as well. At age fifteen I was full of certainties but didn't know the meaning of "schitt." Seven years later I went with two other Smith graduates to the big desk in the editorial room at the *New York Herald Tribune* in Paris where we all worked, to establish its meaning with the managing editor. No one spoke about the grotesqueness of innocence. In those days innocence was a plus.

Charles was standing on the rooftop watching the sparrows. I had just told him about the episode at the *Herald Tribune* in Paris when he remembered an appointment he had himself with a journalist from the *New York Herald Tribune* at the nearby Earle Hotel. He consulted his wristwatch, glanced at two additional timepieces in his vest, snapped his briefcase shut, and locked it with a key. Before walking across the roof to the tiny stairway below, he poured the remaining wine into the gutter "for the birds."

In other words, business with Mingus was a blend of theatrical derring-do, frequent time-outs, fits of brilliant imagination, and constant creative trouble. There were calls to the post office because, knowingly, he'd broken the rule and put two companies—Charles Mingus Enterprises and Jazz Workshop, Inc.—in one box and then pretended he didn't know, and everything was the fault of the post office or his lawyer or his manager or me or anyone else who stepped into the room at the wrong moment. Soon the world was full of people whose records had been paid for and not received, overdue press runs, unanswered mail, and an enterprise that was running out of cash. Worst of all, we were locked in icy moral confrontations over how to proceed. He insisted the business could go forward only at the expense of others who had to wait. It was preferable to fill 10 percent of the orders and let the rest go until later.

"I've always been honest," he protested. "I've never hurt people. I only stole somebody's lunch once when I was eight years old."

"I wouldn't ask you to write a piece of music that was half you and the rest a copy of the Beatles," I shouted. "You can't ask me to defy my principles and back something I don't believe."

"You are my enemy," he shouted back. "You aren't helping me when I need you."

That stopped me cold for a moment. "Well, maybe I am."

It was a reply that surprised us both. I didn't believe it—I had my moral position and he had his. My own discordant needs kept popping up, as urgent as Charles's, and I thought how easy it was to be misunderstood. A lifetime of innocent misunderstandings flew into my mind, all the way back to the first I could remember up in the art room in school when I must have been five or six years old. I'd climbed a lot of stairs to get there, very high up, and I wasn't sure where to go. When I found the room, I sat at a table, wearing my blue-and-white uniform, protected by a smock. The others all looked like me. We were silent together, worried about the teacher, buttressed in this strange and exciting room by our common silence—isolated spectators about to face a common enemy. The teacher entered with a warning: we were told we were never to say "I can't." Soon after, when she approached my desk and asked me to draw something a different way, I replied: "I am not able to."

She sent me out of the room for impertinence.

I thought about other misunderstandings, less innocent, the mind-sets you couldn't foresee. Charles had survived them all his life. They were the dangerous kind. But my own were distortions, too. I thought of Mrs. Goodenough, the housemother in my dorm in college. We had made fun of her name behind her back, at the large dark circles around her eyes, her impatience with our pranks, her mannish ways, and then we took turns sitting at her round table in the dining room as we were supposed to do. I liked Mrs. G. and sat there more often than my friends. I remember she once looked at me sadly and speculated on my life ahead. It was lunchtime, the sun was coming through the window behind her head, and I could hardly see her face. She looked almost pretty, the bags under her eyes barely visible, a halo of light around her hair. In a curiously sad voice she said, "I think you will leave a trail of broken hearts behind." It was a surprising, rather embarrassing and personal thing to say. I wondered whether she thought I might die young or simply have trouble connecting with Mr. Right. She didn't explain.

A mind reader at an entertainment convention once looked at me with the same sadness and told me I had suffered deeply in past lives, she could see it in my face. I began to notice that my face elicited a range of connections having little to do with what was on my mind or who I took myself to be. I resembled college roommates, former lovers, tragic heroines ("the woman who snatches her lover's severed head from the hands of his executioner and speeds off with it in her carriage" was one of the more flattering), younger sisters, Katharine Hepburn, somebody's shrink. I seemed always to be someone else. My face was misunderstood so variously that I began to feel it was not my own. I thought of Carson McCullers's deaf-mute in *The Heart Is a Lonely Hunter,* whose silences were measured and interpreted according to the needs of his visitors. Men in particular let their fancies wander.

That I was his enemy, I made clear to Charles, was just one more misconception. As I faced him I knew he was a fighter not because he enjoyed fighting but because he had learned how and it had worked. Nonetheless, I was no match for his training in defense, his training in offense, his quickness to spot trouble. I was no match for his expecting the worst, for growing up gifted and sensitive in white America. Eventually, anger became a device: intimidation kept people away. At the studio I'd watched him at the piano, a man who disliked violence and its physical risks, who didn't want to hurt his hands, a man who wished to compose and be left alone. A man with a vast appetite for every scrap of life.

"Be all you can, man," he told anyone who asked for advice.

I don't remember what happened after he called me the enemy. He was often theatrical. I might have opened the fridge and made a salad.

Despite our bickerings, we produced four albums and sold them through the mail. Along with *Mingus at Monterey,* we issued material from three other live concerts: *Town Hall Concert,* a sextet Mingus had assembled in 1964 before leaving on a European tour; *My Favorite Quintet,* recorded at the Tyrone Guthrie Theater in Minneapolis a year later; and my own personal favorite, the typically unwieldy *Music Written for Monterey, Not Played, Performed at UCLA,* which introduced an expanded group of musicians at a complex Mingus event that could have been recorded and released only on his own label. It included impromptu firings and rehirings of band members; his explanation of their flaws ("mental tardiness"); fiery lectures to the band; and the familiar full spectrum of soaring composition, personality clashes, musical ruptures, and, finally, resolution—all on record, all for sale to the public. If you were interested in process and those links that normally land on the cutting room floor, this was it, pure and unedited.

. . .

One day at work I told him about my mother's harp. It was a golden harp that stood in the corner of our living room throughout my childhood. A long mysterious crack ran along the gold-inlaid wood of the sound box below the strings and contained a secret I never learned, though I believe she pushed it over in an argument with my father. It is a difficult scene for me to imagine, because she was not a violent woman.

She had married my father when she was nineteen, barely out of the convent, giving up a possible career as a harpist or even a pianist—she was talented on both instruments. Once when Charles was tuning the strings of his bass, I remembered an afternoon long ago when I was a teenager, begging Mom to let me hear her play. I told him how Mom and I had been reminiscing together—she might have been recalling her days at the convent when music comprised a third of her life—and I had managed to persuade her to give it a try. As far as I knew, she had never touched her harp since she was in school. She sat down and began the arduous task of tuning the strings, an effort that at first seemed hopeless, given all those years of not practicing—and of course there was the crack in the sound box—but she finally tipped it back, arched her spine straight on her chair, and ran her hand gracefully and surely along its old familiar strings. Then she stopped. She had played for only a few seconds, but for a brief moment that late afternoon she had almost managed a luminous return to another time. Spurred by my excitement, she had been willing to try. And then it was over. I sometimes wonder what dreams lay concealed inside that royal harp whose ghostly presence dominated our living room for so many years, whose silhouette against the window marked my childhood without a sound.

Our grand piano, on the other hand, led an active life at the far end of the room. As a child I studied musical composition and performed in classical recitals for nearly a dozen years. Mom herself continued to play, mostly to accompany my father, who sang operatic arias at festive occasions. Sometimes, when there were intimate moments between them, they might sing together "Oh the Days of the Kerry Dancing" or "Pale Hands I Loved Beside the Shalimar," a sad story about an Indian man and an English woman whose love was doomed though even then I never did understand the problem.

None of this, however, prepared me for Charles—an artist for whom music was life itself, for whom everything he lived, all that he was, found its way into composition. The music that he wrote and played for the world outside was as personal as his love letters, as urgent as the messages he scrawled across walls or scribbled inside his books and Bibles, or left on his answering machine at home. He once told his friend record producer Nesuhi Ertegun that he was trying to play the truth of what he was.

"The reason it's difficult," he said, "is because I'm changing all the time."

He wasn't writing out music on paper when I met him. He said he didn't like "pencil composers." He wanted his musicians to sound as if they were making it up as they went along. He wanted them to communicate the freshness of composing on the spot. In those days he was more concerned with conviction than with accuracy, although sometimes there was no real choice. He changed his composing techniques according to the players in his band, adapting to their strengths as readers or as improvisers, writing more complex parts for those who read easily, shouting out the lines vocally for those who did not. Real life lapped around and folded into the music with ease. As an artist, he was in charge. Real life off the page was another story.

One afternoon while we were working at his studio, still adjusting to each other's needs, preparing a mailing for our record club, he insisted I stand beside him while he looked up postal rates. He needed my "full participation." Perhaps he only wanted me to stand close, but it sounded very much like an order and I was working on something of my own. We began to argue. "People don't stand still for others," I warned him, "I'm not a sideman reading your notes." And then a memory sailed into my head from the past—standing beside my own father as a grown woman while he read the meaning of words from three large dictionaries. I'd been visiting my father in Florida, sitting beside him in his breakfast nook on the Gulf, staring down at an early-morning perch that lay drenched in butter in a pan. My father's English childhood was still reflected in the way he began his day—fresh fish, kippers, or broiled lamb chops—and in his British handling of a knife and fork, despite Mom's lifetime efforts to change his grip. The small pan holding the fish rested on a three-legged iron stand. My father had just discovered I did not know its name.

"You really don't know?" He stared with disbelief at the black iron object before us as if he could conjure its name into my being before it was too late. I shook my head. I felt the sting of my faulty, insufficient vocabulary.

"It's a *trivet!*" he exclaimed.

His voice held the same astonishment I remembered from childhood when he learned that I had no idea of the meaning of "rhetoric" or, worse, that it was not taught in the private girls' school I attended.

Language mattered. He could never reconcile himself to what he considered its careless abuse in the country he had inherited. He pushed back his chair and beckoned me to follow.

"We'll look it up," he said with a stab at optimism, a refrain from long ago when not to care about the meaning of a word was not to care about your life. Although he was suffering from a tumor in his spine and it was difficult for him to walk, we inched our way down the long hallway to the library, past the casement windows that overlooked the Gulf. My father paused every few seconds, bent over and suffering, to relieve the pressure on his spine, my feeble arsenal of words sufficient cause to propel his body onward where he could set things straight.

"We'll look it up and you'll remember," he said, catching his breath before moving on.

Inside the library a complete set of the *Oxford English Dictionary* filled a shelf beside the door. Nearby, three large dictionaries lay open on their stands. We sought and found "trivet" in them all. Sometimes my father read aloud. Other times it was up to me.

Before retiring to Florida, he had manufactured variable-speed drives that regulated tempos in heavy machinery. Like Charles, he was involved with time. When he moved to Naples, Florida, he continued to publish a small monthly journal called *The Dial,* with articles about the products he had invented. His most beloved endeavor, however, was a column he called "Private Corner for Mathematicians," in which he published problems and solutions sent in by industrialists and scholars around the world. Each month he awarded a five-dollar prize for the most elegant problem and a five-dollar prize for the most graceful solution.

Besides mathematics and my mother, who was at the center of his reason for living, my father was defined by his love of Shakespeare, his love of opera, which included *Porgy and Bess*—American opera— and his love of pure song. I remember attending a Marian Anderson concert with him on a school night and going to visit her backstage. He sang "Bess, You Is My Woman Now" or "Old Man River" as ardently as he sang "Bella figlia del 'amore" or "Che gelida manina." He was an equal-opportunity songster before his time, although his openness in art failed to enlighten the conventions he lived by at home.

My father's uninhibited singing was at such odds with the taciturn, dignified, uncommunicative self he normally displayed to his children that his joyful forays into song filled us with unease. He was in the habit of breaking into song, for example, at the end of a meal at a fancy restaurant, gazing happily at the waiter, who would smile encouragingly while my teenage brothers sought to disappear from view. Years later, a teenager myself, I found his obliviousness to others, because of a need to sing, almost endearing—perhaps another window into the life ahead.

I still imagine that Charles and my father would have admired each other, that in many ways they would have gotten along: two angry men, purists, perhaps geniuses in their fields, outspoken, impatient with flaws, nourished by beauty.

Late one night Charles and I wandered through the city and ended up at a small hotel. It had been my idea. We'd gone from bar to deli to café unwilling to let go and, despite Charles's misgivings, had found a room. A bare ceiling light exposed the limits of our tiny chamber as clearly as Charles's uncertainties illuminated the obsessions and jealousies in his head, the demands he knew he'd be unable to control. He was in no hurry to make love: sex was not the issue; he had little interest in seduction. His abilities to engage a woman through passion were an old story. He wanted love, a shared location on the map. Despite our embraces and all the tumble of words, he was far more aware than I was of the trouble ahead. We dressed without speaking and then dawn crept through the window and extinguished the cold bulb, and shadows from the courtyard came and softened the uneasiness and we undid our clothes and made love again and banished any premonitions. Then as the weeks passed and our encounters became a passionate affair, he insisted he didn't want an affair, he wanted a life together, love with an address.

I wasn't ready for an address. As soon as I could afford some sessions, I went to an analyst recommended by a writer friend. They were expensive, inconclusive exchanges in which the analyst wondered if I was in love and I protested I was embattled, embroiled, involved—but in love? It was too early to know. I was coming out of a marriage and needed time. I knew only that I couldn't afford— didn't want—the answers if he had them.

.   .   .

Not long after, Charles and I met a woman who was full of answers. We were having dinner at a restaurant where we'd heard a famous numerologist was in residency. We'd had drinks at Peggy Hitch-cock's Park Avenue apartment earlier, and the discussion had centered on her skills.

"You don't look like what you are," the famous numerologist said to Charles as she sat down opposite us. She had just heard his birthdate—4-22-22—and was examining him across the table. Charles was skeptical. A waiter approached our table.

"What do you want to drink, sir?" the waiter asked.

Charles eyed the woman facing us. "Well, what do I want?" he asked her. I laughed out loud.

"I have no idea what you want," she replied haughtily.

Charles ordered a margarita. It arrived in a glass that was not rimmed with salt. Together, they made a great deal of it. Charles sent it back for salt. The numerologist agreed she had never seen a margarita served without salt. They had bonded.

Then she got down to business. "You don't look like what you are, I told you. What I meant was that you looked, when I first saw you, you looked gentle and passive. But you are a big man, you have a lot of weight. I don't mean your size. You are blocks and squares, you are very much of the earth, and you have great energy. Whatever you do, you do in a big way. You want to control, you are very domineering. You give a great deal to people and, in return, you expect a lot. But you should lighten up. Be easier with other people. You often create your own problems. Concentrate instead on yourself. Other people will try to put you down out of fear or envy. Don't pay attention to them. Big men always have enemies, people who are jealous. You should be close to nature, be outdoors, go to the country, or keep your windows open and breathe deeply. Everything will go well. It is a very good time, don't waste it."

Next she looked at my numbers, which added up to nine. She stared at me and shook her head. "Well, you're a mixed-up kid, aren't you?" she said. "You have quite a dual nature, don't you? You need to be loved and approved, to belong and be protected. However, you are also ambitious. But you have to make choices. It is very hard for you to make decisions, you are torn between things, two lives, or two people, or two worlds. You have to give up the old and make way for the new and the superior. You are also very strong in what you do. You would have great success in your field, as an artist, an actress, a writer, whatever you do. You create attention, you attract people around you. Also the lovers, the Don Juans—such people have your numbers."

Was she throwing me a bone? "As far as getting along with *him,*" she continued, "your natures are both very strong. You could have an extraordinary relationship if you used it properly. Or else it could be very destructive. You should learn not to fight him. Let him say what he feels, he'll find out by himself when he's wrong. Be womanly. And he must learn not to be so domineering, to lighten up. You need to have a cave of your own that you can go into and be alone, and he would have to respect this. If you had your own field, your own camp, you would get along much better. What do you want to do?" she asked me.

"I want to be whole," I said. She was annoyed with the reply. She wanted something more ambitious. Charles, full of margaritas, slipped her a large bill. We had more drinks at the bar, waiting for a private limousine he had ordered, extravagantly, as it was pouring rain outside. When he knocked over his drink at the bar and broke the glass, he pointedly ordered the next one "in plastic."

TWO

I t was the beginning of spring, 1966. Charles and I were headed north to the Hitchcock mansion in upstate New York where Charles was an occasional guest of his close friend Peggy and her brother Billy, who had turned over the family country house to former Harvard professor Timothy Leary for his experiments with LSD. According to the media it was Leary's decade. Kids around the country, including my nieces and nephews safe in the burbs, were tacking up psychedelic posters on their wallpapered bedrooms at home, whether or not they dropped acid, whether or not the swirling images meant a thing. On this particular weekend, Leary was studying the psychedelic effects of light. Late in the evening, he released a bucketful of frogs under flickering strobes onto the grounds that spread out before the main house, a prelude to the light shows that would soon proliferate across the land. I remember the wide colonial porch encircling the house and the beautiful longhaired boys and girls who were looking on.

The frogs had been captured at dusk by Mingus and my nine-year-old son, Roberto, who had gone frog-gigging together in a nearby swamp and expected to eat the frogs for dinner. Instead, the vegetarian crowd had voted for their release and, inspired, Leary staged a show. As the small creatures leaped to their freedom across the immense lawn, a cheer went up among the young people assembled on the porch. The frogs fled into the night, flickering off and on, transformed into a series of small, blinking, live snapshots racing along beneath the beams of a strobe light that was held by an assistant professor in the dark. At last, with their strange jerking forward motions, now luminous, now magically erased, they sprang into the woods and disappeared.

Charles and Roberto were cool about the dancing frog lights and the curtailing of their meal—they'd managed a heaping side dish in the pantry before the show—although they had spent hours together in a murky swamp, sloshing through the mud, Charles as bold and committed and full of pluck as if he'd held slippery bullfrogs in his fingers all his life. He and Roberto had shouted orders at each other, disputed technique, shrieked over the size and quantity of their catch, until it was so dark you could hardly see and they were so far away you could hardly hear. Finally, when my daughter, Susanna, and I noticed the pail was full, we called from our end of the pond that it was time to go.

One thing about that night was certain. When the strobe lights were extinguished and the show was done, Charles took an imaginary pencil and scratched down the whole idea in his mind. At the end of the weekend, following a routine dispute on our way back home, those frog lights went on flickering in our lives for a long time to come.

We'd gotten into the car the next morning and headed home. Charles and I were arguing about where our relationship was headed and why we weren't together under the same roof. My children were counting out-of-state license plates from their windows in the back-seat as Charles spun down the highway, driving a car he'd been forced to lease because his new torpedo-green Corvette Sting Ray sports convertible with the fabulous fuel-injection drive was, as usual, in the Chevy repair shop on Fifty-seventh Street. He'd just decided I was "too American," which, as he said, was the cause of our problems.

"I can't get to you," he was saying. "We have a different language . . . You're so American . . . you really are. You're the most American person I've known! I'm never going to try to love an American again." He reached for a cigarette from my pack on the front seat and lit one up, although he didn't smoke and looked completely bogus trying to blow out smoke as if it were natural while insisting that I was "removed from real life," "craved loneliness," "should have been a hermit," and needed "breaking in like a car."

"The way they break in a Rolls-Royce," he went on. "Cadillac doesn't do that. But Rolls-Royce and Ferrari, they take their cars out on the road and really break them in before they take them back to the garage. They drive them a thousand miles, they take them through all the shit, and then when they get back home they know they've got a car." When a man is not controlling you exactly the way he likes, he may tell you that you need breaking in like a car. I didn't bother to respond or to point out that he happened to be American himself. By the time we reached the Ninety-sixth Street exit of the West Side Highway in Manhattan, we'd worn each other out and lost whatever thread existed. With a minimum of commotion, my children and I got out at the curb and went the rest of the way home in a cab.

All that week Charles sent double-edged gifts by courier to my apartment on West Eighty-seventh Street. They were accompanied by assorted messages (a magnificent full-length antique mirror, for example, bore a note that advised me to "look at yourself for company, you can't get along with anyone else") or came without comment when the message was clear (a solitary china teacup and saucer). I acknowledged none of them. By late Friday afternoon he'd succeeded in renting a furnished apartment directly across the street. It belonged to an old girlfriend named Jo whom he'd run into on the block. She was leaving New York and he'd made a deal on the spot.

Immediately, he moved a few basic possessions into his rooms (tape recorder, music score paper, a twelve-inch round of Roquefort cheese, half a case of Château Mouton-Rothschild); purchased several large paper bags full of electrical fixtures, wiring, timing devices, and colored bulbs at a hardware store down the block; and went to work. By nightfall he was programming jump starts and delays, timing his spurts and tremors so that, hour after hour, from windows opposite my own, he flashed his own brand of light show, his own swaggering display. Psychedelic events were beginning to occur around the city. Light shows would soon become a nightly feature at Bill Graham's Fillmore East. Oversized kaleidoscopic machines would whir and flicker their colored slides across the ceilings of downtown bars and clubs. An odd contraption planted at the end of the bar at the Village Vanguard, where Charles frequently performed, already projected changing patterns, hour after hour, across its basement walls. But nothing was quite like the fierce and incandescent show that blinked nonstop outside my windows through the Upper West Side night.

Mingus's lights modulated, like his music, into themes and variations that flickered in perpetual change. They erupted into life or dimmed and vanished, according to his moods. Sometimes they splattered bright, rude, and incessant through the dark. Other times he gently staggered the rhythms of his bulbs. He invented fresh images, sacred and obscene: shining crosses, ejaculating phalluses. And all the while, beneath the wild activity of his window, the conductor lay concealed in his bunker behind the sill.

As days went by he began to receive letters stuffed in his mailbox from people on the block: "Dear Mr. Light Man, your show is *fabulous!*" "Magician, you're a *groove!*" There were no shades on my outsized windows, and it was impossible to ignore the display flashing nonstop from across the street, impossible to cross him out of my mind. All night long his lights threw their raging colors and quirky motions on my walls.

Daytime he parked his convertible beneath my windows, his radio blaring through the streets until neighbors called the police. One afternoon he invited the staff of the *New York Free Press,* the counter-culture newspaper where I worked, to his "wedding" a block away at the Marriage Museum on Broadway, a dusky archive of romance that had caught his fancy. His mysterious bride-to-be, he explained to friends, would be chosen among three or four "candidates" attending the ceremony in a sort of impromptu lottery of love. Afterward there was to be a sumptuous banquet at a restaurant directly under our offices. The escalating plans for his wedding ceremony were re-layed to me daily, hourly, in full detail by members of the staff. At the last moment, when the theatrics of his imagination were finally spent, to no one's great surprise he canceled the event.

Other times love came easy. We would run into each other on the street, make up, and start again. Down at his studio on East Fifth Street, he jabbed at lobsters in a boiling pot and called me over to watch the color change. He poured wine into new goblets, melted butter, cut melons, and stuck a piece of fresh celery in my mouth while he disappeared into the bedroom to write a letter to General Motors about his car. Soon he came roaring back into the kitchen, naked except for a Mexican robe swinging loosely over his stomach, shouting that plants know about death and hide themselves at night-time and crawl from the earth in the morning toward the sun. He said that people haven't learned enough not to die or how to stop the sun and keep it overhead, although God is waiting for them to find out because everyone, he said, has the power to keep the sun.

He went over to the piano and played a chord and said when he was young and loved a girl named Mary Ella, that chord gave him the knowledge that love and life went on forever. That chord, he said, held all the truth that people refuse to see or believe, people who still think they have to go to sleep at night or have to die.

He wrote a check to General Motors and grew angry thinking

about the part of his life that was money. Afterward on the street waiting for a cab, the spring was cold and he gave me his Mexican shawl and stood behind me, his stomach nestled in my back, and held me tight and shook and trembled in the wind with cold and turned the shaking into a rhythm and sang about loving me in the snow and melting the ice until we were lying in the grass and it was summer and we were hot and perspiring and the cab came along and we jumped in, already warm.

At the Village Gate, the band burst onstage like an explosion. Charles wandered across the platform like a man possessed, breathing down the necks of his musicians, shrieking orders, goading his men until they expressed the visions in his head. He shouted to his drummer, insulted his piano player, roared like a locomotive off its tracks—the huge angry shout of an original, contrary voice that would not be stopped. He tromped around the stage, his force and energy and fury and passion bringing the audience to its feet.

Afterward in the dressing room we had a fight about his drinking.

"I'm not drunk, baby, I just don't like waiters that fill up aisles . . . I didn't knock over all those chairs, they *fell* over 'cause I'm a big man."

"Go ahead," I said. "Destroy everything. Your job. Other people's acts onstage. Your musicians. Go ahead."

"I know what I'm doing," he replied. "I can play bass hanging from the ceiling. Up there onstage I know what I'm doing. I ain't destroyin' nothin'. I just had something to drink and I'm drunk, so what? Order me another margarita."

There were times when I wished I could have plunked down my money at the door, heard the extraordinary music, witnessed the prodigious event that was Charles, and drifted onto the street, a free woman. But I was caught in his struggle now, no longer outside, trapped in the middle of his vast appetites and imagination, his sexuality, his angry intelligence, his nonsense and his pain.

Sue's mother playing the harp at the Convent of the Sacred Heart in Washington, D.C., in 1915.

Sue and her mother in their garden in Milwaukee.

Charles in Watts, at age 5.

Sue with her nannies in Milwaukee, at age 5.

Sue at the Milwaukee Cotillion in 1950 (second row, third from the left).
Copyright © Milwaukee Journal.

Charles in 1950. *Photo: Bob Parent.*

Charles and friend: time-out during a European concert in 1964.
Photo: Robert C. Ragsdale.

Charles and his band on a European tour in 1964. *Courtesy Mingus Archives.*

Charles at Monterey in 1964.
Photo: Celia Zaentz.

Sue and director Robert Frank in 1963,
during the filming of Frank's film *O.K. End Here*.

Charles, in motorcycle gear, with bassist and childhood friend Red Callendar
in Tompkins Square, New York City, in 1965.
Photo: Teppei Inokuchi.

The Hitchcock
Estate in
Millbrook,
New York.

Roberto searching for
ticks after frog gigging in
Millbrook. *Photo: Sue Mingus.*

Susanna at home on
Tenth Street.
Photo: Sue Mingus.

Sue and Charles with the staff of *Changes* magazine, in 1973.
Photo: Sy Johnson.

Charles, Sue, Sue's niece Luciana, Roberto, and Alvin Ailey
watching a rehearsal of Ailey's *The Mingus Dances* with members of
the Robert Joffrey Ballet, in 1971. *Photo: Sy Johnson.*

His drummer, Dannie Richmond, entered the dressing room and the focus shifted. Charles was staring into worlds of his own. Suddenly he turned to Dannie and pointed to the floor.

"Whaddya see there, Dannie?" he asked.

"I see a bass on the floor."

"Who put it there?"

"Don't know, Mingus."

"See that table, see the split there in the middle a' the marble, what's in the middle a' the marble?

"It's a drumstick."

"Why is there a drumstick, Dannie? And why is there only one drumstick?"

"It was two drumsticks last night, Mingus. I saw 'em, they was two."

"Well, here's what happens to tables like this, split marble tables like I got in my own studio, when somebody plays games with me."

He hoisted up half of the broken heavy marble and dropped it, *wham,* so that it broke up into five or six pieces, the plastic glasses on top hopping up into the air and splashing water all around. Dannie gingerly brushed off his immaculate suit. He looked at Mingus coldly and said he didn't appreciate getting his clothes soiled.

"I didn't splash nobody," Mingus said.

"Yes, you did," I said angrily, wiping off my stockings. "You splashed Dannie and you splashed me. You splashed us both. It's not necessary."

Dannie turned around and went out without saying anything.

"Why don't you have some black coffee?" I snapped.

"Who, me? I don't need no coffee, baby. Call up and order another margarita."

Again, the set was fantastic. Mingus wandered around the stage, eying people in the audience, playing his "catching and throwing" game with himself or with some other self he had around, insulted the trombone player, shouted at Dannie, called out to McPherson, and blew everyone away. They were on to something, all of them, as he roared across the stage, whipping his musicians together, the familiar intensity and fury exploding full force.

At the end of the set he chased his piano player off the stage, shouting with disbelief: "Ain't that a bitch? I wrote the music and *he's* telling me it's wrong!"

Back in the dressing room he moved off across the room, lurched over to the sink, splashed water on his face, stared at himself in the mirror, made some grimaces.

"Well, as long as we're going to turn the page anyway, let's make use of what we have right now, here tonight," he said to the mirror. Then he walked over to where I was sitting.

"Come to me, baby. You'll see what you could have had, what I could have given you. I'll be cutting out in a few days, anyway. I know lots of broads without 'caves.' " (He was referring to the numerologist's suggestion that I needed my own world.) "One of 'em was here banging on the door for an hour the other night. I was right there on the couch, laying out. I didn't let nobody in."

Some girl was knocking on the door right now. He let her in. She said she was the wife of a musician, someone who used to play with Mingus, who had left for Paris last weekend and had told her to come by and say hello.

"*He* told you to come by and see *me?*" Charles said suspiciously, with disgust and disbelief.

"Yes," she said in a high voice, smiling. She looked so artless and naive I believed her. She hung around. She spoke of memories her husband had of Mingus. Finally he put her out. Then he spun around.

"I don't want no musician's chick coming around to ball me. I could have a million a' those chicks. I want me a woman, I want a home, someone of my own." He peed into a glass, studied it, sniffed it, and then threw it at a calendar hanging on the wall, where it dripped down slowly.

"That's the ocean," he said, indicating the painting on the calendar. "Now it's got my pee on it."

As the other band began to perform onstage, he suddenly did a little dance, pulled me up into his arms, and moved slowly across the room to the music, staring at the ceiling as he shrieked with delight at the top of his lungs four or five times as if he were almost coming, from the depths of heaven or of hell, and then continued his dance, laughing and listening.

"They got more than we do, they really playing together, listen to those motherfuckers."

He sped out of the dressing room, marched through the aisles, did another little dance, hailed the waiters:

"I got turned on by some a' that LSD or ESP or some a' that stuff," he said as he danced out into the night.

"You got turned on by yourself," I said, waving down a cab. I was ready to go home.

On his night off, after performing at a funeral for a young fan who'd killed himself abroad and been shipped home in a box, Charles stopped by my apartment. The boy's parents had asked him to play his bass at the service that evening, and he was still shaken by the event, although he'd barely mentioned it to me when I'd seen him earlier in the day. He had evidently stopped off at a bar on the way over and was now wandering about the living room, peering out the window, talking to himself or to that other self still invisible to me, and attempting to keep his pipe lit as he moved back and forth across the room.

Pipes were one of his many diversions in those days, smoking itself less a pleasure of the lungs than an enhancement of life through ritual and accumulation, one more outlet for creation and for art. Down at his studio I'd observed his assortment of tobaccos stacked in tins: Borkum Riff, Three Nuns, Bond Street, Eurasian Black Shag "hand-mixed with aged Virginia" (chosen for taste and innuendo), which he would combine into his own private blends. Personal and Revelation became another mix when he learned it was my father's. He had an array of Windsor pouches, a stately rack of meerschaum pipes, some lowly corncobs, and a dozen designer bowls shaped like wild-animal heads or bearded gods. They vied equally for his attention.

After a while he sat down in my new armchair near the window and stared straight ahead for several minutes without speaking. He was juiced. Eventually, he shifted his attention to the early American patchwork quilt that hung on the wall behind the couch where I was sitting.

"That's how I'd start off a movie about you," he drawled. "You sitting there under that, with all its pieces."

"All the fragments." I laughed.

"There's a part that's very womanly, but I won't tell you yet. I doubt that you see it."

"I see a lot in that quilt. I've thought a lot about the woman who made it. I envy her."

"It's a jack-off," he said. "She sat there all winter jacking off."

"No, it's not," I said. "She sat there knowing what she wanted and inventing stitches. Exquisite stitches. Look at them! Look at the love she felt that winter."

Charles sat big in his armchair. Silently he stared at the quilt and thought his thoughts. Bright silken threads danced across colorful patches of cotton and silk that were sewn onto a background of soft maroon velvet in a personal flurry of design.

"Bird was really somethin'," he said finally.

"What?"

"Charlie Parker. He was really something. And nobody even heard him. Do you know how many people there were who never even heard him?"

"Can I get you some coffee?" I asked.

"Nat Hentoff never heard him, or Louis Armstrong. Joe Glazer never heard him. Or Milton Berle. Ornette Coleman stood in the doorway, and he didn't hear him. Not even Dizzy. A few people did. Duke Jordan heard him, his piano player, but he doesn't count 'cause he's dead, or the same as dead. Gerry Mulligan heard him, that rich boy, and left his hometown 'cause he'd heard Bird and picked up his horn and followed him. Chet Baker heard him, another white boy, and Jimmy Knepper, all white boys. But his manager never heard him. They just heard *of* him, they heard he was good and so they made money off him. He was really something. He said it all. Where do you go when it's all been said?" He stared blankly from his armchair. He'd run out of steam.

Neither one of us spoke.

"Why did you think of Bird, looking at the patchwork quilt?" I asked finally.

"People expressing themselves . . ." He yawned.

"I'm going home," he said after a while. "There's nothing more I can do after today. I can't make love to you any better. I won't even try. Nothing goes beyond that. All I can do now is join a monastery." He picked up his black briefcase. "You don't know me, you don't listen. You don't even know who I am."

I sat on the couch after he'd gone, pondering his words, as certain of what I knew as he was certain of what I didn't. We knew different things, I'd told him the week before, or we knew the same things in different ways, different orbits around the same sun. If he thought I was walking on the surface of his planet while he was speaking from its molten core, well, I had my own planet, I assured him. Nonetheless, I could feel his gravity. It was pulling me away from years of privilege in the enemy camp. There was no way to explain it, unless an inscrutable design with its own mischief and demands could be sewn into our genes at birth—brought in from another life, like my quilt on the wall—and Mingus had been stitched into mine.

I believed some parts of me were shaped before memory, accidental messages from vibrant lives that once moved through the universe and left their trails. Other parts, I knew for a fact, were utterly my own, yearnings that took root as I swung free on cold metal rings in the park near my home when I was little in Milwaukee or perched high in the sky out in the country on the uppermost branches of a hundred-foot pine, staring down at tiny familiar figures whose warning cries and commands were blissfully inaudible. Those were the early yearnings that could draw you far from home.

Fact: for months I had been waking up regularly in the middle of the night with a hunger for salt and a fear of death. No one took it seriously. My friends shrugged it away. It had started when I was twenty-nine, pestered by uneasy or irritating details during the day and by raw fear at night. I would eat anchovies or sardines, write in a journal as I sat on the living room floor, and try to get rid of my thoughts. I kept the kitchen shelves stocked with olives and boxes of saltines. It was as if salt were keeping me alive, preserving me from decay.

Alberto, the father of my children, had once told me how his salt rations were withheld during the war as punishment for his insolence when he was captured by the British in North Africa. He was a teenager then, whisked out of architecture school in Rome and plunked down in the desert with an Italian regiment under General Rommel's command. He had spent all day blowing "pernacchios" into his arm—loud, smacking, vulgar sounds in protest for his life which he saw being snatched away. And so his captors took away his salt. It hadn't seemed like a big deal when I heard the story. But the blandness of food without salt was a minor irritant compared with the dehydration his body suffered as he perspired under a scorching sun. By the third day, when he ceased his pernacchios, his salt was restored—in time for him to be sent off to a prison camp in India for the rest of the war.

I hadn't thought much about salt since that story. Now it was becoming the center of my life.

Afternoons in my apartment, I watched an old woman sunning herself in a skimpy red sunsuit on the opposite roof. I was ashamed of her vitality, her persistence, her exposure. I wondered whom she was darkening her skin for or whether she was seizing the sun while it was still overhead. I sat at my own window, hungry for life with an urgency that grew like a tumor inside. My yearnings began with a need for salt and continued in the months that followed.

Despite regular collisions, our relationship veered on. Charles's changing personalities, his views, and vocabulary continued to be as exotic and baffling to me as the writer Ezra Pound's asides were to a college friend of mine who visited Pound regularly at St. Elizabeth's Hospital in Washington, D.C. The only difference, as my friend pointed out, was that Pound's wife sat beside her husband and delivered a running translation—from Sanskrit, Italian, spontaneous riff, or arcane text—into language my friend could understand.

There were times when trying to translate Charles seemed a hopeless task. Just when I was ready to accept everything he was, profoundly touched by something he'd done, he would disintegrate before my eyes into a stranger. Long ago I'd read a fable about a damsel forced to hold the hand of an enchanted prince as he changed into a snake, a beast, a monster—a fearful series of metamorphoses whose spell she could break only by never letting go of his hand. I too hung tight while friends clucked at my stubbornness, my unwillingness to move on.

Our love affair and our fights were as passionate as his jealousy, as unexpected as the taboos I broke nearly every day. When I inadvertently sat down at a restaurant table and faced the entrance, for example, so that he was forced to sit opposite me with his back to the door ("in obvious danger!" as he was certain I understood), I too became the enemy. When I sat with my back to the bar and spoke to someone in front of my stool, he explained that only hookers faced into the room. New and astonishing information arrived daily, some of it invention, some of it part of a culture that was not my own, some of it from an unstoppable imagination that reached staggering heights when it came to our affair.

Although I'd gone to Europe to experience life beyond Milwaukee, Charles was several more laps around the globe. I was still coming to grips with the racial insanities in white America as he described them. You could be a sports star if you needed a job, he would say dryly, although only certain sports were available. You could be a famous musician if you played the right kind of song. You could be a gangster, politician, preacher, pimp.

Preaching might have been a calling for Mingus, as natural as music, but the fantasy of pimping had intrigued him since he was a kid in Watts watching the cool guys take over the streets. He'd devoted countless pages, real or imagined, to the subject in his autobiography, *Beneath the Underdog,* in which he tried to come to terms with the contradictions of his fascination—a deep-seated puritanism raging with his craving for experience. Now he was trying with me. Except that his hopelessly competing needs—echoes of his early Baptist church days as a child, his spiritual morality as a man, the contrary demands of his art—led to various doomsday scenarios of his own making as he constructed moral tests, dares, or obstacles that were alternately demonic or pathetic.

One of his earliest premises, which he expounded one night in a bar, was that if he couldn't depend on a woman's faithfulness, he'd be in charge of her lust. He'd orchestrate his own worst nightmares. He'd play into her imagination, her weaknesses, her naive belief in his own illogic, all the while living out his own personal torments and fantasies. He'd send his woman to another's arms. At least there would be no surprise: he would be calling the shots. Truth was preferable to the bottomless well of his imagination.

I listened to his mad reasoning with an iron will of my own. I had no intention of being pushed around. I could hear the bravado in his words and didn't particularly believe the scenes he described.

His Proustian hells of sexual jealousy—the agonizing dramas he would construct in his mind, the excesses of his imagination, its precise details (based on invention or fact, it hardly mattered)— drove him to feverish explorations and the continual testing of possibility, at least inside his head. You were never certain where things might go.

One night in a wild Mexican border town, his fears and his fantasies came to a head. We had flown out to the coast for one of his concerts, rented a car, and driven south. The afternoon before we left San Francisco, we'd gone up to a famous rotary bar in our hotel so he could show me the view. It was off-hours at the bar and we were the only customers. Mingus ordered a Ramos fizz from the bartender—a drink made of whipped egg whites, gin, and orange flower water, traditional in New Orleans but a bartender's nemesis anywhere else. The man standing before us had no intention of satisfying his request. He announced, arms folded, that he concocted only large orders.

"How large?" Mingus wanted to know.

The bartender looked him steadily in the eyes. "No less than twenty-four," he replied.

Mingus ordered twenty-five.

As the city spun beneath the rotary bar, he downed them one by one. Triumphing over his adversaries, large or small, was nothing new. The week before, in a crowded waterfront jazz club in Manhattan, we'd barely seated ourselves comfortably at a table for four when the headwaiter hurried over to redirect us to a smaller table. The club couldn't waste two empty places on a Saturday night, he explained.

"I'm a big man," Mingus said reasonably. "I need room."

"That's your problem," the waiter snapped.

I stood up and reached for my coat. Mingus paused only a second.

"Bring two more place settings," he said. "I want four steak dinners."

As I returned to my chair, the waiter set up the extra silverware, goblets, and napkins. I ate my steak. Mingus ate the remaining three. He was used to the enemy. He had been in training since he was a child. The opposition, in whatever form—righteous, nasty, or simply misunderstood—rarely prevailed. There were times, as he doubtless knew, when it was not really the enemy before him. But he had grown so used to the challenge, to the anger or irony or comedy unfolding, that he couldn't always skid to a stop.

After traveling down the coast from San Francisco to L.A. the following day, we drove first to Watts where I met his stepmother, a quiet, gracious lady uncertain about yet another woman he was bringing home. We walked the neighborhood where he had grown up along Compton Street and made our way beside the weed-covered streetcar tracks he'd followed straight to school as a child. Eventually, we stood beneath the towers of Watts. He explained how he and other children had gathered shards of glass from broken Coke bottles and cracked Mason jars and brought them to the eccentric Simon Rodia down the street. It was the early 1930s, and Rodia was building three towering monuments out of concrete, steel, and glass in the dirt of his small triangular backyard, where we were standing. They might have looked like crazy tottering edifices to the kids, but they would be immortalized one day as the Watts Towers, pure and perfect in their construction, architectural wonders. Misunderstood in Rodia's lifetime, they were symbols, even then, that rose above the disenfranchised.

Charles was offering me his past, bringing me into his family history and his roots, into the quiet center of who he was, so that what followed later—the noisy contradictions he was driven to orchestrate, one side of himself warring always with the others, his obsessions racing downwind with their great sails fully extended—was all the more sad and unreal. We went on from Watts to Tijuana, where, late at night, we ended up in a raunchy club. It was the kind of place that gave this border town its name, the kind of no-holds-barred hangout that Charles had memorialized with his drummer a decade earlier, first in a chapter in his autobiography, where he claimed to have made love to at least a dozen women, and then in a series of scorching melodies on an album entitled *Tijuana Moods*. A tourist, I intended to witness the action like everyone else. Charles was wrestling with the usual dichotomy of his feelings: egging me on, sorry we'd come at all, suddenly angry at my curiosity as he sat in moral judgment, saint and Satan on a single barstool grumbling beside me. After a while we moved to a table near the stage. Two women who were undressing themselves descended into the audience to cavort among the clientele. An American college student seated at an adjoining table, who had attempted to flirt with me earlier and had unexpectedly come face-to-face with Charles, was now being led around by his long, limp, naked penis by one of the girls. Eventually he landed onstage. I felt sorry for him—he hadn't managed an erection at all and, I assumed, must feel ashamed to be led around so goofily by his unresponsive floppy dick.

On his own Charles had decided I'd been lusting for the young student from the start; that someone had planted him at the adjoining table; that the evening was a plot. He became loud and accusatory. He stood up and shouted. Within a few minutes he was in a state of blind rage. We were on about our tenth tequila. The two women had stripped completely and were beginning to perform a grinding dance together around the stage. Sex and nakedness had become commonplace, part of an elongated background blur. Everyone was partying. Everyone was having a drunken ball. Sambas, rumbas, mambos roared on without distinction.

For a moment I was nearly swept onto the stage, nearly joined the fray. I rose up from the table. Charles was yelling in the distance. He sounded faraway. And then some small distraction—a flick of my cigarette ash, a waitress's demand—abruptly returned me to the reality of the table where I stood, to the stained wooden surface beneath my hand, and the moment passed. I remember what little difference it made, how boring were the transgressions onstage, how ordinary and accessible and without mystery. As I sat down I could hear Charles howling somewhere through the club.

The dangers of his fantasies and his proddings, the consequences so casually avoided, the fallout of these private furies so painfully exposed in a border-town spree, were far more sobering than the lack of tequila on the journey home. The freedom and integrity of his music, with its boundless risks and explorations so integral to his art, had little to do with the woman he loved. That much was clear. Sexual jealousy and art had separate lives. Whether or not I agreed, it was one subject we no longer explored.

Back in New York, Charles took me to meet his former psychiatrist, Dr. Edmund Pollack. It was part of a continuing rendezvous with his past that he was determined to share. Like it or not, lovers, girlfriends, wives, and I were thrown together in an ongoing stew. He needed to spill out his flaws, his friendships, his secrets, which were never secrets for long. Exposure was as essential to his life as oxygen to his blood.

At the time of his sessions a few years before, he had invited Dr. Pollack to write some liner notes for an album he was recording called *The Black Saint and the Sinner Lady*. It was a unique request— asking your analyst to comment on your music. As people said at the time, it was typically Mingus. He wanted the public to know how Pollack saw him. (No guarantee, of course, that a month later he might not be somebody else.) Around that time he had spent several days locked inside Bellevue Hospital, where he'd talked himself in one evening, despite ample warnings from the night guard on duty that "inside" was not exactly a hotel. He'd explained to the guard that he was an insomniac, was exhausted with New York life, and needed some sleep. Personally, he believed that if he spent time in a mental institution he could obtain "crazy papers," as he called them, documents that would invalidate a contract a Mafia promoter had induced him to sign. An attorney had told him this, and he believed it was so.

Once inside Bellevue, however, he quickly found himself a prisoner in a ward. He was unceremoniously yanked from bed at dawn, terrifyingly at risk of a lobotomy, and dreadfully aware of his mistake. He wrote a short poem called "Hellview of Bellevue" and, after a few days, miraculously succeeded in calling his friend Nat Hentoff, who was able to help secure his release. Later, he recorded a composition based on the chord changes to the classic tune "All the Things You Are" and retitled it "All the Things You Could Be by Now If Sigmund Freud's Wife Was Your Mother." With a mischievous smile, he would repeat the title from the bandstand. Slow. Then fast. Then slow. Making sure the audience got it right.

Pollack was grave and cordial when we met, as uncertain as I was about why we'd been brought together. Perhaps Charles had some sort of validation in mind. (Celia, one of his former wives, once told me Charles never acted crazy until he started his analysis. She imagined he wanted to justify the sessions.)

I think he wanted Pollack to serve as a witness to who he once was. Or perhaps to all the things he still could be.

Three

One early evening Charles and I headed over to a prenuptial party for Peggy Hitchcock's friend Van Wolff at Peggy's new townhouse in Manhattan. When we arrived at her brownstone on East Sixty-fourth Street, a few guests were already assembled on each floor, waiting for the stylish forms of entertainment to begin: Indian dances, a jazz trio, African trance music, rock and roll. The couple who were to be wed the following day had not arrived.

On the second floor a dozen tables were set up for dinner. Someone's Infinity Machine hummed in the corner, projecting brightly colored patterns on the wall. When a rock band struck up, Charles and I headed upstairs, wandering from room to room until we ran into our friend the poet Allen Ginsberg, who had been wandering too. It would not have occurred to me to snoop through another's home, but Charles and Allen took such liberties for granted. Allen was in the library rummaging through its shelves, inspecting a large limited edition of Joyce's *Ulysses* with numbered prints by Matisse—my father had a similar edition at home. Other books were piled beside him on the floor.

"Marry us!" Charles said from the doorway.

Allen looked up. Without a word, he set down the volume he was examining, glanced around the room, drew up two straight-backed antique chairs, and placed himself before us on a stool. Then, accompanying himself with two small Indian cymbals inside his palms, he began to chant. Beating the cymbals swiftly together, shaking his hair and his beard with increasing passion, he slowly enveloped us with his meditation. We sat before him on our spindly chairs, his chanting low and insistent, fattening the air, blurring and erasing everything around us, until finally there was only his song, Allen chanting "Hare Krishna, Hare Krishna, Hare Rama, Hare Rama" as we sat transfixed before him.

A long time afterward he looked up and smiled. The ceremony was over.

Mingus, however, was not satisfied. He stared at Allen. "You married me, now marry her!" he said.

Allen looked surprised but immediately resumed his chanting. He stared straight at me this time, our eyes locked as he sang and clashed his cymbals: this brave man/poet who celebrated any whim, who jumped to any call. At the end, when he stopped chanting, there was a hush. We emerged slowly from our trance and found ourselves surrounded by members from the wedding party below. A dozen guests had come upstairs and gathered behind us during the ceremony. They had wrapped up presents from objects around the house and now were uncorking a bottle of champagne.

As glasses were passed around and the party picked up speed, Allen and Charles began to speak of other things. Allen had seen the poet Leroi Jones at an event the day before and reported that, after reading his poetry, Leroi had brought up a number of very small children onto the stage. The children had chanted together "We hate whites" and raised their arms in a black power salute.

"What do you think of that? Of his influence?" Allen asked.

"He doesn't have an army," Charles said.

"He has a voice," Allen said.

"Not on the streets of Harlem," Charles said. "He ain't got no guns, man. He just lets off steam, he shouts, that's all."

After a moment, Charles asked: "You ever married anybody else?"

"Leroi and I were married once," Allen said.

"Who did it?"

"Me."

"I mean, who else was there?"

"Oh, Peter was. He did it. I mean, you know, he put Leroi's hand on his cock and we . . ." Allen grinned.

"I like women, myself," Charles said immediately. "I mean I don't knock it. For you it's cool. But me, I believe in doors and doorways."

The room fell silent. Allen shrugged. There was an explosion and a cork flew past our heads: one of the guests had opened another bottle of champagne. Allen and Charles seemed startled. After a moment they reached across and hugged each other. Everyone looked relieved. Members of the party again passed around glasses of champagne and raised toasts to a long, uncomplicated future ahead.

Although a decade later we were married by a justice of the peace, it was the wedding with Allen—more difficult and intense, more charged and unpredictable, more like Mingus—that set the stage for the years ahead.

At 2 a.m. Charles and I left the cool elegance of Peggy's brownstone and headed up to Harlem for some grits and eggs.

Back at home, the phone had been ringing through my sleep. When I finally picked up, Charles seemed to be in the middle of a conversation about his stepmother. He had been talking about her all week, anticipating her death. She was the one who had raised him in Watts, stood up for him at family squabbles, put up with his father's womanizing, built a home. It had snowed the night before, unseasonably, and he was taking credit for it. He was connected not only to the supernatural, it seemed, but to the weather as well. "Sure it snowed," he was saying. "I pushed my weather chart to Snow last night, just to check my mama out. She's got powers, you know. She's been around a long time. And 'fore she goes, maybe she'll show me a thing or two. I know she's cuttin' out, I knew it even before I called. She was in the room with me last night. 'Course if I told Dr. Pollack that, he'd say I oughta be checked. But Mama know a thing or two . . ." Before he hung up, we made plans to drive up to Millbrook again, that weekend.

Despite the unexpected snow early in the week, the weather was balmy as we headed north, Charles at the wheel of his Sting Ray, which was—at least for the time being—out of the shop. Fired by its superpowered engine, we shot up to Millbrook at 115 miles per hour to visit Leary and his entourage. We might have outrun the New York state police, whose maximum speed was 93 miles per hour (as the rookie cop who ticketed us explained admiringly), if only we hadn't stopped to refuel on the road. The cop's head was down somewhere under the hood while Charles described the engine's features and tried unsuccessfully to offer him the car for the weekend. After filling the tank we tore off at a somewhat reduced speed, waving to our new friend, who tactfully turned his car and headed in the opposite direction.

In the sumptuous surroundings of the Hitchcock estate, Leary's followers included college professors, artists, poets, musicians, the beautiful, the spaced out, and the very rich. Although Tim once invited him to remain as a resident guru, Charles had declined the offer and never dropped acid, despite Tim's insistence that everyone should wipe their mental slate clean and begin again. "You've got nothing for Harlem, man," he told Tim on one of our walks. "Nothing for the workers, the people who go to their jobs, the people who get up at six . . ."

That night we were sitting as usual at a long banquet table in the main dining hall beneath flickering church candles while a musician from the Egyptian Gardens, a popular belly-dancing club in Manhattan, played the oud. (Charles and I went there occasionally, presumably for the oud.)

"I once went out of my mind with pot," I could hear Charles telling Tim, who was seated on the other side of the table, dressed in his white Indian robes and listening with amusement. "So why should I take LSD? I don't want to go crazy. I don't enjoy not knowing reality. Someone once gave me hashish and another world came in. I was dying, more or less, or trying to stay alive. And worst of all, the sun was falling into the sea." Tim nodded and smiled.

After dinner, on our way to the guest quarters, Charles said: "You know, it happened another time without drugs or alcohol . . ."

"What happened?" I asked. I hadn't paid much attention to his rapid-fire talk with Tim. Elaborate arrangements were under discussion at the other end of the table for a costume pageant and an outdoor staging of *Steppenwolf,* the following evening. Instead of going to our room, he suddenly took my hand and we detoured across the lawn. I was limping beside him in my heels, wondering why I hadn't changed to hiking boots and jeans. As we headed into the woods I stopped and removed my shoes.

"The same thing happened," he said. "Without drugs at all. Another world came in. I was controlling my heartbeat—I could speed it up or slow it down—and I knew I could will myself to death. I was prepared to die. And then a yellow bird landed on my window ledge. I knew it was Odel, my half brother back from the dead, who'd come to warn me. And so I stopped. But I knew I could reach those stages on my own." He held my arm tight and steered me down a path into the woods.

"And so I don't believe in chemicals," he continued. "Not like Tim. You've got to wait years and years and find your own way naturally. After I was confused with pot, I saw that my reality was to play my bass and write music. I saw that drugs were not going to help me do it. So I canceled that out in my youth. And now they tell me in my forties to 'take a trip' and describe how somebody goes running through the woods buck naked and how you can have these terrible dreams . . ."

We were making our way through those woods now, past bodies meditating, bodies dropping acid, bodies making love in the night. We sat down near the fountain. The summer moon was bright as a streetlamp. His face in the shadows was serious and handsome. It was also tense: a face prepared for action. As always, something about him resembled my father: the anger and intelligence, the dark impatience of the outsider, the power of the loner. Except at home Dad's anger was muffled, present in the shape of his mouth or in his silences. Desire, too, was an undercurrent, folded away with the linen. We were a formal and modest family, not like my best friend's, whose family members walked freely through the house half dressed. We never saw one another without clothes. The rawness of our bodies was barely acknowledged—soft mollusks safe inside our casings. I remember the shock of seeing my father standing naked and furious one midnight at the top of our staircase, one hand shaking his fist with rage, the other holding an open book that barely concealed his sex. His body was covered with thick dark curly hair. I was fifteen, late from a date on a school night and filled with terror at a fury that had led to such immodesty.

Charles took my hand and slipped it inside his shirt. "The first thing I wanted to do was fuck when I got high," he said. "I used to fuck to keep from going crazy. These people on LSD fuck each other all the time. Once when I was here I went straight to the piano like I always do, and they tried to get me to leave it by bringing in three beautiful girls. They couldn't understand that I wanted to fuck my piano. So the next time I went back they had three or four pianos there and they had taken off all the strings and the legs and turned them up against the wall. I know that was Tim Leary and I know he was saying that I was going through my karma with a piano as my guru."

We sat in the darkness. I asked why he'd gotten involved at all.

"One day I was in Boston . . ." he replied. "I met this tall handsome guy with gray hair. He introduced himself. It was Tim Leary. He said: 'I have this new thing that's going to straighten out the world. I want you to be one of my subjects.' I said: 'Man, I know I'm not perfect, but I don't want to play bass any different. I don't want to write music any different. I'm satisfied with what comes out.' He said: 'Well, stay with us a few weeks and see what you think about it. Meet some of the people.' So they gave me a room to stay in and I went . . . I never had too much faith, though. You know my analyst, Dr. Pollock? Well, one day he said: 'I hear you know Tim. I wouldn't trust him too much, he wasn't the best student in school.' And then you know what he said? He was Tim Leary's roommate!"

He laughed and pulled me into his lap. His hands with their familiar roughness caressed my face. I was used to them now. In those days the calluses on his fingertips were like hard-earned skin armor, the result of plucking skills that sent notes shimmering into balconies long before amplifiers made it easy. He'd explained how he needed those calluses, how they formed and hardened at the ends of his fingers as he played and helped to mute the sting. It took him weeks to rebuild his hands, he said, when he stopped playing his bass. Of course, it was a different sort of playing then, before electricity—more physical, mining notes from gut strings and sending them off to the ceiling. I'd heard him talk to students who came over to his studio about his calluses. He'd talk about technique and about music and then, in the middle of everything, he'd talk about love. He always got around to love.

"The piano doesn't kiss back," he warned a young musician who spoke too loftily about art. He wanted the priorities to be clear. It was important to understand the shortcomings of the piano. And yet the piano was where he composed, it was the heart of his existence, it was where he found his melody waiting for him on the keys. He'd go to the piano when the world failed him. It was where he found his peace.

He bit into my shoulder and held me still with his mouth while he unbuttoned my clothes and pulled me into the grass. Off in the distance, somewhere under the giant moon, we could hear Tim calling out his name.

In the daytime, Tim strolled through the mansion or out in the sun wearing his white tennis shoes, white Indian slacks, and white tunic, wrapped in the certainty that all was well. He believed people could shed their old neurotic imprints and begin again. Mingus was less interested in shedding his imprint than in changing the world's. His views and the anguish that frequently accompanied them were unleashed on audiences, night after night. Sometimes the nights ended badly. Other times, the anger, even the violence, turned to gold.

One crowded Saturday back in New York, on the stage of the Village Vanguard, Mingus leaned over from his stool between tunes and took a long swallow from a gallon of Christian Brothers wine that was perched on the piano. As he replaced the bottle, he contemplated the label and considered aloud the monks who made the wine. Then he delivered a rambling dissertation on religion in America, ending with a commercial grading system for the latest cult figures, including Billy Graham, Oral Roberts, and Robert Schaller. In the course of his monologue a listener took offense.

"Have some respect," a young man protested from the back of the club.

Mingus paused. He stared into the crowd. He began again. The young man yelled some insulting remarks, Mingus talked on.

"And your woman's a slut," the young man said.

Mingus stopped dead. He replaced the large jug of wine on the piano, walked to the front of the stage, and glared through the lights.

"Your woman's a slut," the incredible words shot again from the rear. Mingus wasted no time. Wielding the microphone stand before him like a lance, he charged through the packed audience to the back of the house just as the young man jumped up from his seat and bounded through the club. Leaping among the crowded tables until he reached the stairway up to the street, the young man ran out of the club. Mingus, still clutching the microphone stand, followed three steps at a time. Behind him raced the author Norman Mailer, who had been sitting in the crowd, fresh from a recent and much-publicized brawl of his own during his New York City mayoral campaign. I scrambled along at the end of the line.

As the four of us reached the sidewalk at the top of the stairs, Mingus whipped a paper napkin full of black pepper out of his shirt pocket—a defense tactic suggested to him one late night in a bar—and tossed it high in the air. The wind was from the north and the pepper flew in my face. Mingus scooped me up, screaming, and carried me to a restaurant across the street, where the house cook washed out my eyes in a sink. I recuperated on a stool. Mingus returned to the fray. When at last I joined him outside the club, he and the young man were hand-slapping and embracing on the street. As we descended below, they were making plans to toast their new-found friendship in an after-hours bar at the end of the night. They had traveled the familiar spectrum from foe to friend, a journey Mingus frequently took with his adversaries. Perhaps he needed a confrontation to clear the air—pave the way and make it safe for love.

One afternoon while I was listening in my apartment to a record of soliloquies by Molly and Leopold Bloom and Charles was writing out a letter to an insurance company, he asked me to lower the volume. He needed to focus, he said. He was describing in full Mingus detail his version of an accident with a crosstown bus, which I wasn't at all certain was the bus driver's fault. I'd been in the car too and had my own opinion of events but decided for once to let it ride. When he seemed to be through, I raised the volume. He began to listen without interest until he heard Molly Bloom describing her love for Daedalus and how she'd "like to take him in my mouth." Then he cocked an ear.

"Play that part again," he said. His interest grew simultaneously with a kind of jealousy and annoyance.

"So that's where you got that expression," he said accusingly.

"No one has a monopoly on words," I said. "That's my style, that's the way I talk, I'm not taking it from anyone. You speak your own style, which is not mine. So what?"

"I'd be embarrassed to hear that record in company. Someone once tried to play it for me."

"It's not a dirty record," I said. "There are a thousand thoughts running through someone's mind on that record."

"Is she a whore?" he asked.

"No, she's not. She's an ordinary woman waiting for her husband to come home. It's late and he's out with some other woman, maybe, she doesn't know for sure. But she's alone and she's thinking, she's imagining, she's remembering."

"She's imagining sucking somebody else's dick. Right?"

"Is that the only part you heard?"

"It was enough. He's just some dirty writer like everybody else. He sounds like a homosexual trying to imagine what women think."

"It's really impossible for you to hear anybody else."

"He doesn't have anything to say to me. He's white and he's not American and he's dead. Why don't you play some black writer for me, somebody from Watts?"

"Because Watts isn't the whole world. Besides, I'm playing this."

"Well, I can't hear it. I'll only hear it when I meet him, shake his hand, ask him how many times he fucks his wife, then I'll hear him and understand."

"Maybe if you listened or read him yourself, you'd find you liked him. Actually, you have a great deal in common."

"Listen to that record? To a dirty record put out by Americans who choose some sexy part of a whole long book so they can sell it to people who sit around in living rooms together and turn on?"

"Oh, forget it. You know who gave it to me? My sister-in-law. She's not a whore."

He thought about it. "Well, who knows, maybe your sister-in-law's a German madam like I thought she was when I first saw her."

I stared at him dumbfounded. He began to consider that possibly he had gone too far. After another moment he said: "Well, maybe if you tried to play it for me sometime when I wasn't working . . ." His voice was softer. ". . . when I wasn't trying to write a letter to somebody so I can raise some money to have my car fixed before this society takes it away." He paused. He thought about it one more time. Then he got his second wind. His voice rose.

"I'm almost bankrupt, I haven't made my car payments, and on top of that I'm trying to concentrate on a letter about a bus driver who crashed into me!" With a great deal of commotion and several false starts, he gathered up his papers and returned across the street.

Later in the day he cut his foot on some scissors in his apartment and went off to the emergency room at a nearby hospital. Before departing he left a message in block letters on the sidewalk in front of my building—I LOVE YOU—written in his blood.

Although he was performing that month at the Five Spot, he agreed to do a benefit at the Village Gate, a few blocks away, to help raise money for a struggling school uptown. The owners of the Five Spot—the Termini brothers, Iggy and Joe—had generously agreed to let him take a long intermission. The night before the benefit Mingus had a vivid dream in which terrible forces of evil were pitted against him. He couldn't identify them, but he knew very well the harm was real, as real as anything he'd experienced outside his dream. They reflected a thousand realities inside his bones. He couldn't get the dream out of his head.

The evening of the benefit I went before him to the Village Gate and was seated among a packed audience. The audience's respect and love were tangible. The room rippled with all the good vibes universally celebrated in those days. When Charles finally came onstage you could feel the groundswell of anticipation and support. The audience stood up and applauded. Charles stared from the stage. In the sea of faces before him, he examined, one by one in the dim light, the tormentors of his dream. He recognized them. For a long moment he glared into the packed room. Then he turned to his drummer, Dannie Richmond, and growled an order. Dannie began to solo. Charles marched furiously offstage. Dannie played for twenty minutes alone. Charles did not perform, nor did his other sidemen. He returned to the microphone only once, to berate anyone who might have failed to understand his music. He told the audience they got what they deserved. He was in a trance of rage.

Back at the Five Spot, after an angry and unprovoked scene, Iggy vowed one more time, as he had done on so many other occasions, never to hire him again. The next night Charles returned as if nothing had happened, the music roaring, tight, passionate, and unpredictable as always.

Occasionally he'd accompany me to the Port Authority, where I'd catch a New Jersey bus to my brother Bob's. He'd stand on the platform draped out in leather, his toes curled in beneath his bowlegs, his face intense and solitary under his oversized Mexican hat. He'd smile and wave through the bus window, where I sat surrounded by pale New Jersey commuters. The time was too soon, I'd imagine—any time might be too soon—to accommodate a man like Charles: a man so openly vulnerable, so openly aggressive, an artist of such urgency whose tent was staked out miles beyond anybody's backyard. There was no familiar small talk about him, nothing ordinary to grasp on to or compare to. His life loomed large and unpredictable.

He'd discuss his views on meditation as he roared down Park Avenue with the top down on a sunny afternoon. He'd shout about the sacredness of love in the middle of an angry quarrel. He wrote a book and the grammar and the spelling and the characters broke all the rules. It took months, years, to see the truth of a man whose packaging was so unfamiliar. His imagination, which on a bad day could appear either inscrutable or wholly out of control, was the source of his art and his life and was now part of my life as well. If one were able to follow that imagination—the inner dramas that loomed so immense compared with the slight incidents that provoked them—one could see how reality itself was just a fraction of the show. How small, how limited and inconsequential it appeared, in contrast to the endless carnivals inside his head.

I was reminded of Sartre's short story about a father's visit to the chambers of his daughter, who is married to someone going mad. He hopes to bring his daughter out of the dark room full of monsters that she and her husband inhabit together, although her husband alone perceives them. As the daughter stands in the doorway, blinking at her father in the bright daylight, she looks back suddenly and manages, at last, to see one of the monsters in the room. It is a moment of triumph. Impatiently she bids her father farewell and returns inside.

I began to understand how the ever-expanding scenarios that were woven together so ingeniously—one real event leading to another and still another, which then continued on, just as vividly, in his head—held him captive in their overlapping webs. Tenses, past or future, were hopelessly mingled. The subjunctive was as vital to him as plain fact.

Above all, he tried to express everything at once without interruption. He was so worried he might fail to express something on his mind that he was compelled to state it instantly, examine it, get a reaction to it. Perhaps he was afraid of carrying the burden alone, afraid to hold his feelings in privately where he was not always sure what they meant or where they might take him. He needed other people in on it who could share the responsibility or the pain. It was his way of surviving, of keeping his sanity. Sometimes I thought if he failed to express himself—every fact raging inside his head—to the world around him, he would go out of his mind. He wrote, talked, played music, made love, endlessly. He had to get the sperm, the sounds, the words, outside his own house, his own cage. It was a constant throwing out.

And still I was hooked on his life, his music, his imagination, his passion and attention, his tall tales, his fury, his lies, his caresses, his extravagances, his lack of caution, his tenderness when he loved me and believed. I held on to that intensity without wrapping it up and sending it somewhere with a name and address.

For years he would not forgive me for refusing to give our love an address. It was the source of every fight. I was from my hometown more than from Italy or Bohemia. I couldn't shake Lake Michigan. I'd chosen him because he was different; now I couldn't live up to that difference. I would stand in front of that antique mirror and wonder if I was going out of my mind. Was I in purgatory because I couldn't reconcile the disparities of my life? Or because Charles looked at a glass of beer and saw paint or pee or poison or plots?

Briefly, I went to an analyst, worried about my children. The analyst reported that my children were fine: I was the one with problems. Things appeared reasonable enough to him: my kids attended a Greenwich Village school; I was co-publishing a counterculture newspaper called the *New York Free Press;* I was separated from my husband, who, despite our differences, was my closest friend. The kids saw him regularly. However routine our home life may have seemed to the analyst, he didn't have a thousand lightbulbs exploding across the street from his apartment.

A more endearing lightbulb was the one Charles picked up in front of a movie camera during Tom Reichman's filming of *Mingus* in his studio in the winter of 1966. He had been talking about love, delivering a complex, Joycean, poetic, warlike Mingus version of it, when he spied a lightbulb on a table nearby and reached over for it. "You see this bulb?" he said. "All by itself it ain't nothing. But when you find its component . . ." He held the lightbulb in one hand, placed it inside a socket he'd picked up in the other, and with a magnificent smile into the camera, said: "... You dig? *It lights up!*"

After ten years of marriage, my husband Alberto had told me I didn't make a man secure. He could not allow the part of me that claimed a life of its own, any more than Charles could allow it. It was a need I barely understood myself, tearing at the old Victorian ways instilled at home. Alberto took it personally, called it willful distancing, an innocence out of control. Out of his control. Only a few weeks after Alberto and I were married, the trouble began. I'd had a life before him, an affair in Paris with a Brazilian journalist, but worse than that, I was without regrets. I had no sense of transgression. What distressed Alberto most was my failure to suffer the sins he suffered on my behalf. It was my loftiness, he said, the safe distance from the reality of guilt or pain, that he couldn't bear. He suffered his sins. He suffered them dreadfully. He couldn't accept that I didn't suffer mine.

"You could go through Sodom and Gomorrah and come out unscathed," he said. Even his evaluation was a mix of awe and disgust. And then one evening during the first months of our marriage, he decided I should be baptized into real life. He could no longer stand the disparity between the gentility and detachment I seemed to embody and the rough world below he felt I didn't acknowledge. We climbed into his little Fiat Topolino and headed for Via Flaminia, where the hookers walked late at night. He had challenged me. I had agreed. He was my new husband. I was twenty-three, he was thirty-six. I was frightened, but I called his bluff. If this was necessary to make our marriage work, I was prepared. We cruised the streets. He rolled down the window as, one by one, the women looked over at me and shook their heads. A wife? Finally an older woman around forty got into the backseat of the car. Perhaps they were friends, I couldn't tell, my Italian was still new and unreliable. We drove around while they discussed money and plans. This woman, too, examined me as I sat, more or less removed, in the front seat beside him. Then, like the others, she shook her head. Perhaps she felt protective. She told him it was not a good idea. She turned down the gig. He invited her to join us for coffee instead, at one of the espresso bars on the street. The three of us drank cappuccinos and chatted together at a round metal table on the sidewalk, and that was that. I had come out unscathed.

Although I'd tried to shake Milwaukee and to shed the rules, the dice generally came up Lake Michigan. True, I had escaped the tight-fisted grip of the nannies. But something fended off any dramatic change. That was my crime: keeping my self in the face of someone else's notion of real life. Especially when that self was at odds with a man who was offering his love.

It was past midnight at Mingus's place after one of our usual unresolved conflicts: my refusal to live together in the same house; his insistence that I was defying the rights of love, coupled with every racial spin he could conjure. My own position regarding personal freedom was paltry and wormlike in comparison, lacking the scope and dignity of a crusade. "I'm going back to the garage now," he'd sighed before we parted, a continuation of his analogy concerning women and cars. "I'm going back home where I started. I've had a long trip and so have you. We're broken in. I mean, I know things can go wrong, flat tires and windshield wipers and all that. Oil changes and grease. Some things aren't always perfect." He was shifting gears slightly. "But when we've had tensions like tonight . . . well, I'm going back to the station. I'll lose weight, that's what I'll do first, I got to lose this belly. Maybe you have to get out in the open air, you're not a city girl, neither am I. Get outside and feel the air and walk in the park and be by yourself. And if you ever feel you aren't loved, well, think of me." I sat in my chair and let him talk. I had made up my mind and so had he. Still, his words lingered on like his music. They had an annoying way of settling inside my head.

"Oh, I know I kicked the lamp over today," he went on, "but I knew it wouldn't hurt you. I only wanted to shock you out of your thing. I can't get to you—even that way. We have a different language. You're so American . . . Oh, I know we've made beautiful love, sure we have, we've made some beautiful scenes, but you were looking on, you were on the outside, you weren't really there. Right now as you sit on that chair in the kitchen, there's a rim of mirrors around the wall. I mean—not that you're narcissistic, I don't mean that, but you *want* to be lonely. If you could only get on the outside and look at yourself sitting there, at what you really are, and understand . . ." It was the same old story, I thought: wanting to connect, wanting to be allowed a life apart. That was how I saw it. Men saw it a different way.

After downing a large quantity of wine from a flask of Chianti, Charles walked me home across the street. "I'm going out and earn me some money," he went on. "I wasn't born with a golden spoon in my mouth, maybe that's the biggest difference. I know I could be, I could be rich. But I never thought that's where it's at. I've just been here loving you. Now I'm going back where I started."

At home I settled accounts with Mr. Connelley, our Irish baby-sitter who lived in the building, and went into my children's bedroom. They were not in bed. They were standing at the window peering down at Charles, who, instead of returning to his apartment, was marching oddly up and down the block, piling mattresses and chairs and anything else he found on the sidewalk in the middle of the street. The wine was having its effect. He was making a lot of noise. He had found a pair of crutches leaning against a gate and was shouting that somewhere a cripple walked. Soon he was making predictions in the night, calling out the visions in his head, visions that were as vivid and real as the melodies that claimed him from the keys whenever he sat at the piano to compose.

"I hate him," Susanna said from the shadows. Roberto had already gone back to bed. I lay down beside her. "He always comes over and plays his stinky old records."

"He's many different things," I said. "Very good and sometimes bad. Right now he's very drunk." I couldn't think of anything else to say. Justifying Charles was seldom an easy matter.

In the morning the crutches were stashed on the fifth-floor hallway against our door. My children were not judgmental. Their notion of reality was still in flux. Except that now the woman next door, whom we called the Bird Lady and whom my children frequently visited to play with her parrot, had changed. My son understood that she did not like loud minorities driving Corvette Sting Ray convertibles with the top down and the radio up. He remembered that when someone broke into the Bird Lady's apartment and stole her bird—one of the neighborhood smart alecks—she had told everyone it was the superintendent's son from San Juan. My children were born in Italy and were beginning to understand that the Bird Lady was a mix: you could count her pennies and feed her bird, but her take on humans was unreliable. She also called the police whenever there was a neighborhood disruption. Most of the disruptions that year occurred in the vicinity of Charles's new apartment.

As usual, everything was entirely different by the afternoon. Charles was calm and beautiful during a televised interview for Channel 13 and spoke objectively about such personally loaded subjects as pop music, Bob Dylan, and homosexuality. Neither of us had had any sleep. I was so tired all the rough edges were gone. His calmness, most of the time, depended on his sex life. Not so much his heart as his glands. ("I want to lay my heavy gland on you.") We had a big dinner with the children at home and he fell asleep on the couch, his records playing on the phonograph.

It was either hell or high water, as my mom would have said. We had become too close, made love too many times and too well, to look at each other, even during our fights, without remembering everything in our bones. Sometimes he was moved by so little, it touched my heart, like the time Fritzie, our German shepherd, put her paw over his ankle and kept it there possessively while she slept; or when Susanna called him into her room—"Charles, come and look!"—he was so delighted, so pleased. And it was after that terrible night when she had watched him on the street and heard him yelling up at the window and kicking at the door.

He forced so much, beat up on people so much. He expected mountains from people and was prepared to give the same in return. It was as if he could only love or hate, nothing in between. On occasion he was so wise and quiet and fair, so balanced and deep. When his richness found an equilibrium, he cut everybody. He had lived more, created more, dared more, than most people in one lifetime. But I didn't want to be a slave to him any more than he wanted to be a slave to society.

The hours with Alberto and the children were civilized oases of peace. On Sundays at Sheepshead Bay in the cold sunshine I remembered how to be considerate, generous, quiet. The battleground was far away. One Saturday, Roberto ran down Eighty-seventh Street toward a weekend with his dad, a hunting trip, dreaming of wild ducks and wet boots and the sound of rifles. As we headed toward the drive a sudden gale struck without warning, forcing both of us to our knees. Roberto crawled with his suitcase against the wind, laughing, while an old man clung to a tree and shook his umbrella angrily, trying to hail a cab, and delivery men stood flattened against the back of their truck. We were so bold and gay. The wind swept away everything except the sun.

"Mommy, do you like life?" Roberto was back from his hunting trip. He walked into the kitchen in the afternoon and posed the question before returning to his drawings of explosions and missiles and big fish swallowing smaller ones—lots of red now, though his favorite color was black. Black is strong, he said. Later he said: "I know Daddy thinks you want to marry Charles and he feels bad." He was matter-of-fact. He didn't want to take sides. Both of us knew there was nothing I could say. They were things one could barely manage to express. Charles expressed himself at every moment and declared he was always changing and his music reflected that. I was changing, too, and what did it reflect? Artists get away with their ambiguities and immoralities because they leave something behind, maybe not to their own children, but to the world. The rest of us leave our children behind, whose judgment will add to our own.

When one of Charles's children, a twenty-three-year-old son named Charles the Third who barely knew his father, arrived in New York, he brought over one of his paintings as an offering: an abstract canvas full of color. Mingus studied it gloomily. After a few minutes he looked up.

"Go paint an apple," he said gruffly.

"It's a gift," I protested. I rarely understood the rapport he had with his children.

"It's a painting," he corrected me. Then he turned to his son. "You can't improvise on nothing," he said. "Study reality before you improve on it."

I knew very well that although he refused to sacrifice truth to sentimentality and his words could sting, there was an underlying humor and irony to his toughness that people often missed. I hoped his son knew that too.

Once, when the great French writer Jean Genet came to hear Mingus perform in a scruffy club called Slug's on East Third Street (Genet was staying with Charles the Third and his Swiss girlfriend, Marianne, who had known Genet for many years), the writer hurried over to introduce himself. Although Genet was as cynical as the entire population of Manhattan's Lower East Side, he was also an orphan who had created for himself a fantasy notion of what a father-son relationship might be. With an expansive grin, he approached Charles.

"I know your son," he announced.

Mingus looked over without smiling at the improbable, bald-headed stranger before him.

"I know him too," he said and walked away.

Much later Charles the Third told me that his father once said to him, when they were discussing his career as a painter: "You have to decide what you want. Nobody asks you to make art. You are responsible, yourself, if you make it. You don't do it for the rewards." Then he'd asked more pointedly: "What do you want? The respect of your friends, or their money?"

Charles the Third laughed. "Dad was something else," he said.

I was now co-publisher of the *New York Free Press,* a counterculture newspaper or underground rag, as such journals were called in the days of student demonstrations, assassination conspiracies, Vietnam War protests, and *Screw* magazine. As I entered our offices one morning, a fight was in full swing behind the closed doors of the editorial sanctuary. In the main room it was business as usual: Jim Buckley was hunched over the typesetting machine; Al Goldstein, his eventual partner at *Screw* magazine, maverick porn publisher and inventor of the Peter-Meter grading system in film criticism, was rummaging through his desk. The art director, Steve Heller (future op-ed page designer for the *New York Times* and student of the great Jean-Claude Suares, who liked to brag that he'd designed the covers of the *New Yorker* and *Screw* magazine the same week), examined his layouts. In the offices of the managing editor (my old friend Sam Edwards), something like a heavy table struck the wall. No one moved.

When the door flew open, the managing editor was visible hanging the publisher outside the window by his feet, three stories above

Seventy-second Street and Broadway. Some members of the staff ran to intervene. Others shrugged. It was one more ritual episode that would run its course, one of the frequent macho encounters—power contests on the floor, arm wrestling against the wall—that constituted the lunatic bondings required by our chief.

During the week I covered events that occurred, or more often did not occur, but were only rumors, on the Lower East Side where I lived. I'd moved to Tompkins Square with my children, who were attending Downtown Community, a school nearby where folksinger Pete Seeger had taught music a decade earlier. At the moment my kids were away at camp. Tompkins Square was in a Slavic neighborhood that, seemingly overnight, had become the heart of the action of the late 1960s. Concerts wailed outside our windows, and groups like the Grateful Dead and the Fugs drew mobs of peace-and-love kids all night long. Storefronts on or near the square included the Psychedelicatessen; Ed Sanders's *East Village Other* newspaper; a heavily integrated bar that had become a serious hangout called the Annex; and Bunch's soul food restaurant across the street.

It was now August 1968, the long hot summer that followed the assassinations of Martin Luther King, Jr., and Bobby Kennedy. New York City was on edge. Nervous officials believed that certain neighborhoods, particularly our own, were waiting to explode. Down the block someone was accused of plotting to blow up the Statue of Liberty. Suddenly city buses were provided to transport impoverished children to the beach. Community centers opened. A "University of the Streets," temporarily stationed in a dilapidated building on Avenue A, offered summer courses to the poor. Militant block associations sprang up and, to their surprise, received funding for their dreams.

Alberto died of a heart attack that August. The last time I saw him he was standing inside the elevator of his new apartment building and I was in the lobby; we were staring at one another as the doors closed between us. I had just told him that I would not wash his socks. It was a statement of rights, I suppose—after all, we were no longer living together—but the memory still hurt. I imagine that satisfying exchanges at the end of life are few, even when the end is expected. Mine have been flawed or filled with regret.

Soon I was no longer speaking to Charles. I walked the streets of the Village early one morning, alone under a cold sky, and my step was light, my feet barely touched the pavement. Life itself was turning into thin air, a vapor as empty and meaningless as all our jealous quarrels. For a terrible moment I felt free and exhilarated, stripped of connection, reduced and removed, as bright and insubstantial as the flakes of sunlight sparkling on the cement under my feet.

Four

When their father died of a heart attack on the stairway to his studio, my children and I regrouped away from big-city life and settled on a small lake in New Jersey off a narrow country road called Lake Shore Drive. My kids called it by its initials, LSD. It was the 1960s and cool to be living on LSD. When he wasn't reading at the library, my son spent the winter months drawing arrowheads, searching for fossils in the frozen ground, and ice-fishing on the lake. When my daughter wasn't sitting at a small sewing machine making clothes, she danced. Every child in our small New Jersey hamlet that year appeared to flaunt wildly sophisticated, state-of-the-art musical equipment somehow affordable to normal parents. Huge speakers, a tangle of microphones, entire sound systems, and, of course, instruments—mostly electric guitars and drums—were lugged after school to one another's homes. Our own was not spared. Barely teenagers, they were on the cusp, and they played music all afternoon and danced. Their parents lived in small homes, drove long cars, voted Republican, and had no idea their seventh-graders were experimenting with drugs, sex, and New York City. For most parents, although it was only forty miles away, New York City was as exotic and charged with danger as Soviet Russia.

We had an old red Chevy station wagon with a shiny black door defacing the driver's side—the original red door was mangled by a careless driver at a local filling station and a kind attendant had hustled up a black replacement, cheap, tying it on with heavy rope. Now, when I picked up my children after school, I swerved in adroitly on the far side of the street so that only the good passenger-side door of the Chevy was visible. My children were beginning to care about form.

At night the wind blew cold air through the window cracks, and I sat in the kitchen near the oven while the children slept. We lived in a big house with an upstairs we never used, bunched together like orphans at the end of a hall off the kitchen, three of us in two rooms, a bedroom and a library, though we didn't have to share, we could have gone upstairs. I climbed to the attic once and lit candles under the rafters and tried to summon Alberto. Another night when a black dog with yellow eyes appeared and remained three days, we considered it a sign. I'd seen a black dog when my father died, too. It had stared at me crossly from a pet store window with the sharp eyes and angry expression of my father, and I'd felt oddly close to him—though closeness was not something I normally felt toward my father. Now I see him in my dreams and am free to tamper with the facts.

The following year my children and I returned from our rental on the lake and moved into an apartment belonging to the photographer Diane Arbus. It was on Tenth Street opposite St. Mark's-in-the-Bowery Church, three blocks away from our old apartment. Like some other churches in Manhattan, St. Mark's had become a cultural center for poetry readings, dance programs, and theatrical productions, a few of which were directed by the playwright Sam Shepard, who shared an apartment with Charles's son Charles the Third, or

Tertius, as we now called him. I was still co-publishing the *New York Free Press* and had also started a small advertising agency called Vulture, which supplied ads for much of New York's underground press, including the *New York High School Free Press,* a spin-off of our own paper, run by students living in a firehouse off Tompkins Square.

I called my agency Vulture because I was aware that earning a commission by making a few phone calls to moguls in the record industry to help friends who ran heartfelt enterprises was a loathsome profession. I was sucking away part of their income like a large repulsive bird. I had become the underside of bird life, no longer song and freedom but beak and claw. Still, an income was necessary, and Vulture continued its attack. Steve Heller, our new teenage assistant art director at the *Free Press,* whose beard was a delicate fuzz and whom we called Militant Heller, created a seedy-looking, dejected vulture for my logo which I stamped on invoices and correspondence.

In the spring of 1969 I ran into Charles at a dinner in his son's apartment in New York. I don't remember how the dinner came about or what combination of events or tall tales were orchestrated that led me into his trap. I had no intention of becoming involved with Charles again. Within a week we were back where we started.

That winter, the *New York Free Press* threw a benefit at the Fillmore East to help pay our printing bills. Charles played bass for the first time in three years. He had been given an electric amplifier by Ampeg, and although he loudly maintained that "electricity plays you," he reluctantly used it the night of the concert. Other performers included the author Norman Mailer, Peter Yarrow of Peter, Paul, and Mary, and Ed Sanders of the notorious Fugs, who was now running a bookstore on Tompkins Square called the Hungry Eye.

Rock and roll had taken over the music scene. In jazz clubs where

the audience was thinning, people talked louder than ever and cash
registers, if less full, continued to jangle impertinently over the music.
In protest of a fickle and disrespectful world, Mingus had long ago
dropped out. He'd stopped playing music and stopped composing.
He wheeled around the East Village on a seven-speed bike, carried
five or six cameras slung about his neck, and shot arrows from a
longbow into a target propped up against the wall of his rented studio on East Fifth Street. His friend Jo had returned to her apartment
on Eighty-seventh Street and he had settled, full-time, into his studio
downtown. The neighborhood was so run-down that even the Con
Ed electric company across the street was missing two out of five letters on its blinking red sign.

"I should never have left the post office and gone back to music,"
Charles said early one afternoon when he was feeling miserable. "I
was doing just fine."

"You worked at the post office?" I asked. We were hanging out at
his studio while the kids were in school. "Back in the fifties," he said.
"I got a job as a loader boy, loading mail on a belt. That's where
Charlie Parker called me. He called me at the post office and wanted
me to go to Boston with him."

"And you went . . ." I was stacking up old record jackets in the
corner, left over from our record club, which was now defunct.

"Well, he asked me, 'How much you want?' and I said, 'I don't
really want to go, Bird. I'm making more money here than I made in
a year.' He said, 'How do you know, you ain't asked for no money
yet.' I said, 'How much can you pay?' He said, 'Two-fifty.' So I said,
'I make a hundred seventy-five here, Bird. And in time I'll make two
hundred. Why should I go?' He said, 'Because you're a musician,
motherfucker. You can play. Your heart is in music. You're not supposed to work in the post office. You're supposed to come play with
Bird.' So like a fool I quit. He had Arthur Prysock with him and a
couple of dancers. They'd make up things to Bird's solos. Anyway,
when it was time to get paid, Bird was sitting in a chair with just the

whites of his eyes showing. If you said something, his eyes would come up, then they'd go white again." He was silent, remembering. "What happened?" I asked. I was beginning to recall the story myself as he spoke. The details in a Mingus event were always changing, expanding like the music itself, taking on additional, sometimes contrary, meanings, the point of view shifting to include newly considered or more urgent facts. "The whole band was there," he continued, "and Bird says, with his eyes up, 'Talk to Teddy Reig, he's my manager.' So Teddy says there's nothing left. He gave it to Bird, who shot it all up. Here I quit my job, spent money to go to Boston, and ended up with nothing. Teddy gave me the money to get home on, and that was it . . . I never worked with Bird again."

"Well, he got you back into music," I said.

"Oh, yeah," he replied.

Charles bought Japanese mats and slept on the floor of his studio. He discarded the mats and constructed a Moroccan tent out of spreads. He dismantled the tent and ordered a loft bed built by a neighborhood carpenter. He bought a Steinway grand piano on Fifty-seventh Street, which he had wanted all his life and which soon became a sad artifact gathering dust in the center of his room, the action too stiff, his mind too unsettled. He landed a one-night gig as a photographer at a theater two blocks away. He went crazy. After only a week in the psychiatric ward of Mount Sinai Hospital, he was released when a pyromaniac, who shared his quarters, set fire twice to the room. "I'm safer outside," he grumbled to the doctor as he was packing to leave. He fought in Village bars, from Casey's on West Tenth Street to the small Ukrainian bars where he lived on East Fifth. He insulted friends, other musicians, total strangers. He rigged up an answering machine in his studio which he changed hourly and which reflected every nuance of his suffering consciousness. "It's Christmastime," the machine reported one afternoon late in December, "and I'm going for a walk. No one gives a damn about me. The lights on my tree are out. And all you motherfuckers out there who are threatening my life, I know who you are! You can take this as a warning: I've got a surprise in store for all of you!"

Word got around and strangers called up just to hear the tape, hanging up afterward, adding to his uneasiness. He said the world he was forced to live in was destroying his mind. And not playing music—no matter what he said—was making him ill. Then one day the phone rang and a call came in that would end his retirement. It was about a concert that was to take place in Berkeley, a tribute to Duke Ellington—the man he loved most on earth. That concert, at which Duke played Charles's composition "The Clown," was the beginning of his return to music.

At the tail end of the 1960s my daughter was fourteen. Girls her age were dropping acid, someone she knew was pregnant, and although she spent the year following her father's death at a small school run by friends in the mountains of Switzerland—the École d'Humanité—the hiatus only delayed by a year the action back home.

Around that time a nervous middle-aged man entered the offices of the *Free Press* with a beat-up black suitcase. He opened it in the main room in front of everyone. Inside, like a street vendor's wares, was a display of prophylactics and birth control devices, stark and unapologetic. Here was an overt and shameless call to arms, a demand for self-protection, sexual freedom, the will to take charge. Such messages were hardly common then. Although a decade earlier my sister-in-law had headed the Milwaukee chapter of Planned Parenthood (resigning after conceiving her fourth child in four years), the message then was population control: diaphragms in the States, bead counting in India, whatever worked. It had not been a feminist call to grab the wheel. (Although macho rumblings might have been expected from Charles, he supported, by nature, intelligent change.

The first feminist poster I ever saw was in his studio—a defiant housewife with a broken broom.)

I looked over at Jack Banning, our editor, who shook hands with this rumpled street pioneer and promised our support. I suppose it was a harbinger of things to come. Not long after, the sexual revolution in publishing, spearheaded by *Screw Magazine,* exploded in this very room. By the middle of 1967 the new sex papers were flourishing, the first of them having mobilized in the typesetting corner of our front office. Al Goldstein and Jim Buckley, formerly in charge of the machines, had created *Screw,* which—as a result of lawsuits they eventually won—changed the nature of publishing. Although Sam Edwards followed soon after, replacing the *New York Free Press* with the *New York Review of Sex,* the soul and spirit of everyone on the staff belonged to political change. The *New York Review of Sex* quickly became ashamed of its limited role, despite its determination to champion any sexual freedom you could possibly invent. By common agreement, and several stormy staff meetings, it changed its name, to the zany, conflicted *New York Review of Sex and Politics.*

The sexual revolution in publishing was now taking its toll on the underground press. Papers dedicated to political and social change, with their tiny budgets and limited readership, understood that sex papers offered the possibility of quick money, which, eventually, might fund their political agendas. In rapid succession the publication *Rat* became *Kiss* and the *East Village Other* became *Pleasure.* In 1969 our office splintered into four different, not to say warring, factions. In a move that only a perversely comic divinity could have engineered, all four groups angrily moved out of our Seventy-second Street office only to discover themselves on four different floors of the same building in a new complex on Fifth Avenue just below Fourteenth Street. Unpredictable elevator encounters posed a daily test of endurance and self-restraint.

Meanwhile, *Rolling Stone,* the new rock publication on the West Coast, was doing well. Before we left our uptown offices, a New York newspaper distributor approached Jack Banning, the former publisher of the *Free Press.* "I have five thousand dollars. How long would it take you to come up with a rock paper?" Jack replied: "I'll have one for you in a week." That exchange was the beginning of *Changes* magazine. I flew out to the Coast to line up advertising from the major record companies, all of whom were eager to lend their support. Soon we were in business. For the next seven years we published first a weekly and then a monthly paper that gradually evolved from a rock publication into a counterculture journal of the arts. Charles was an occasional contributor, with outspoken essays like "Open Letter to the Avant Garde" or, more confrontationally, "Open Letter to the *New York Times,*" directed at John S. Wilson, the music critic who had given his comeback concert at Philharmonic Hall a mixed review.

In those years Charles tied up a lot of loose ends. His autobiography, *Beneath the Underdog,* which McGraw-Hill had shelved a decade earlier, was finally published by Knopf in April 1971. Although friends and fans, including Norman Mailer, had regularly approached publishers on his behalf during the intervening years, none had succeeded in making a deal. Charles rejected them all, convinced that every editor he met would whitewash his book. Only after his first bout with hospital drugs—when he was momentarily operating on half a cylinder and uncharacteristically amenable to any project at hand—did the powder keg his book had become find a home and an editor he approved. *Underdog* came out at about a third of its original size. Enough of the voice and holler remained, however, to salvage its intent. Even the original version had been lopsided, missing much of the musical life and commentary Charles would later set down on tape.

Nineteen seventy-one proved to be a banner year. Charles collaborated on an hour of *Mingus Dances* with Alvin Ailey, who was choreographing for the Robert Joffrey Ballet. He received his first Guggenheim grant and was the holder of the Slee Chair in Music at the University of New York at Buffalo, where he taught a seminar in composition during the second semester, flying back and forth from New York. In March and April, Tom Reichman's documentary *Mingus,* filmed during his eviction in 1966, was shown on national television. A Mingus album called *The Great Concert,* recorded live during his 1964 European tour, was released in France and won the Gold Medal Award in that country (although the music itself was pirated and became the material for my first Revenge Records album, twenty years later). He also installed a big band in a new, experimental venue called the Mercer Arts Center, located inside a large red building on Mercer Street in the Village, which provided concert space and private studios for himself and other artists like the actress Viveca Lindfors and the French playwright Arabel.

Charles's son Tertius was collaborating with Arabel at the time and invited us to attend the premiere of a play called *They Handcuffed the Flowers.* To prepare the audience for the atmosphere of the play and to evoke the terrors and abuses of freedom under tyranny, we were guided into the auditorium through a dark makeshift tunnel inside of which arms and hands shot out of nowhere and flailed at us for the several seconds it took to reach our seats. Charles created such a stir, fighting back at whatever came at him in the tunnel and shouting out threats at the top of his lungs, that Arabel rewrote the play for subsequent performances. The gigs ended for everyone after only a few weeks when the building behind the Mercer Arts Center collapsed and the Mercer itself had to be demolished.

Later the same year Charles signed a contract with Columbia Records and recorded one of his seminal albums, *Let My Children Hear Music.* It would be released in 1972 to coincide with his comeback concert at Philharmonic Hall, a sold-out performance called "Mingus and Friends." Columbia recorded the event, emceed by Bill Cosby and featuring several guest musicians. Afterward, when we gathered at a long table in a restaurant to celebrate the occasion, Charles, who had remained silent throughout the meal, was asked his opinion of the concert. Without raising his eyes from dessert, he summed up the evening in three short words: "Too many friends."

Regarding the new electrical amplification of music, he told an interviewer: "It's like replacing your feelings with a machine. You can't control the dynamics, they control you. It's for people who aren't sincere about how they feel. If I'm not sincere when I'm playing, then I'm not alive. If I'm hollering, I feel it, I'm not pretending. I've found if you put your heart in it, everyone will respond. I've always been able to tell how the audience feels. I'm pretty perceptive about that. I always had the knowledge of how to please an audience—which I don't do."

The simplicity of rock and roll and its execution, instrumentally, were not very interesting to someone who had spent his life challenging himself musically. What disturbed him even more was the way in which rock had pushed jazz off radio and television, diminishing its audience. Jazz had lost a whole generation of potential players. Good young musicians who were coming up and who once might have gone into jazz, now saw rock or fusion as an easier path to gain and glory. Amplified musicians were ruining music, he thought. "They play so loud it's wrecking people's ears."

One night, without much enthusiasm, Charles accompanied me to one of Miles Davis's early fusion concerts at the Beacon Theater on upper Broadway, where rock concerts were frequently held. At intermission, Miles's manager, Jack Wittemore, approached Charles in the lobby.

"Well, what did you think?" Wittemore asked Charles.

"About what?" Charles asked.

"About the concert. What did you think of Miles?"

"Miles?" Charles looked at him with surprise. "I didn't hear Miles."

We didn't stay for the second half of the concert.

As for "the new thing," although Charles appreciated Ornette Coleman's ingenious sense of composition (if not his intonation on his horn), Ornette's early abandonment of chord changes and conventional structures was incompatible with Charles's own musical vision. He wanted schooled players who knew the rules and how to break them, musicians who could travel both ways. When I took him to hear Ornette confidently scratching music on a violin at the Fillmore East, Charles's only comment afterward was: "His mama sure loved him."

He considered musicians who were playing completely free, like Archie Shepp, Pharaoh Sanders, Albert Ayler, and others, at the very least, incomplete. "You don't do anything *all the time*," he said. He regularly used group improvisation and free sections in his own music within the larger context of his compositions, not as something in itself. "I don't know whether they were trying to con the white folks or whether they were conned themselves. I think they were trying to cut Bird. They were trying to say this is a new movement. But you don't take an inferior product and put it in place of Vaseline and say this is better than Vaseline, because everybody knows it's not. They may be serious, but the seriousness hasn't gotten through to me yet.

"Music has to have some form, to come from some historical music created by a people. You just can't have guys making up different lines. If you study music you're able to do anything, to have variety in what you do. When every piece sounds just like the last one, that's no fun. I enjoy playing something where everybody's creating together and where there is some ensemble. I want to have different meters, different chord changes, or different music with no chords at all. But to just play free, to have no sense of where you're going or where you came from . . . I mean, if I'm going to have my appendix taken out, I want to be sure the doctor can retrace his steps."

Annoyed as he was with free jazz, he had begun to joke with musicians like Dizzy Gillespie and Clark Terry and Thad Jones about getting together to do an "avant garde" or "new thing" date themselves. The point was to show what would happen if musicians who could really play the chord changes, who could play time and not get lost, were to improvise and play free. The idea was to show how they could cut everyone.

In the fall of 1972, Charles was among a contingent of musicians invited by Yale University to receive "Duke Ellington Fellow" honorary awards. A fellowship program had recently been created to "perpetuate the many dimensions of the Afro-American musical heritage," as the letter of invitation explained. On the day of the event Charles had an opportunity to draw Duke aside and discuss his idea. In an article Charles later wrote for *Changes* magazine, called "Open Letter to the Avant Garde," he described their conversation. It went like this:

"Duke, why don't you, me and Dizzy and Clark Terry and Thad Jones get together and make an avant garde record?" Duke's reply was very quick: "Why should we go back that far? Let's not take music back that far, Mingus. Why not just make a modern record?"

"And so that appeared to me to be very funny," Charles wrote. "Because Duke was saying just what I was thinking—which I didn't have enough nerve to say. My main reason for wanting to make this record was as a joke, calling it 'Avant garde by Duke, Mingus, Diz, etcetera.' But Duke dropped out, because he considers what they call avant garde today old-fashioned music. And it's true. It's old fashioned because it's played by beginners.

"So don't tell me Duke and Mingus can't play avant garde or incoherent music if they wanted to. It would be the *most* incoherent. . . . We would cut everybody playing bad. Duke could sit down at the piano and play a composition that would sound like a Symphony of

Wrong. . . . I mean, what Duke said about modern music was so funny. A man almost in his eighties, and he's saying 'Let's not go back that far, Charles.' That's funny."

One night, as I was leaving Charles's studio, I waved goodbye from the curb and grabbed a taxi home. The cabdriver had a baby face, long, shaggy, blond hair, and was wearing a studded shirt with the sleeves cut off and a visor cap. "I'm going to Paris next week," he said angrily. "Going to finish my novel and produce my film." He paused. "And publish my three plays." I did not respond.

"I've been working on my film all summer," he continued. "I'm the hero and also the director and the producer. It's a fantastic film. I wrote *Scorpio Rising,* but Kenneth Anger stole it from me and got all the money. I was the actor, but all I got was my salary, not even a percentage of the film."

"That's some shirt you've got," I said.

"Yeah, it says SCORPIO RISING," he replied. I looked at the studs again and saw that it did. "I'm going to have both my arms tattooed. A skull with a flower and heart on one side and a—"

"I hate tattoos," I said. "Bare arms are more interesting."

"But they're *symbols,*" he explained. "They're important, they mean something . . . My film opens with me lying in bed. See this? It's a Nazi flag, I just picked it up." He held up something in the front seat. "I'm going to be lying under a Nazi flag and it'll look like I'm dead. There'll be intercuts of the war going on, bombardments and all that. Also I'll be sleeping with a shoe, Cinderella's shoe, next to me. The Righteous Brothers will be singing a song. During the marriage scene I'll have Bob Dylan's music playing. I'm going to show the world the way it is, motorcycles, rock and roll, bombs. They ask me what I think about the war in Vietnam. I say it's like any war, both sides lose. You know what I mean? I learned everything I know in the last ten years, I'm self-taught. I read Dostoevsky,

Kierkegaard, all of 'em. I'm like Kierkegaard, I'm an existentialist, sort of, but I believe in God. I studied all the religions, the theologies, the philosophies. When I get back from Paris I'm going out to Big Sur, going to get a cottage and get me a chick with some head, and then I'll do my paintings and write poetry . . ." He talked on.

"I'm glad you don't drive like you talk," I said.

"Oh, I'm relaxed tonight, I ain't in no hurry." A few moments later he said again: "I'm going to have both my arms tattooed." His words hung in the air. When we reached home I gave him an extra dollar tip by mistake. He must have thought I meant to. As I got out of the car he looked back and said gently: "I'm sorry I sounded so angry."

"That's all right," I said. "Most of the people I know sound angry."

Ten minutes later Charles showed up, although it was already 3 a.m. He said he came because of the cabdriver. First of all, because he thought maybe the driver wouldn't bring me home—he thought it was suspicious the way he zoomed off and Charles couldn't catch his name. Second, because he thought I might be digging him. "Oh, I mean I didn't think you'd climb over into the front seat to be with him. I mean, did you?" he asked, only half joking.

"My God," I said.

"Your eyes are shining," he said suspiciously. "You look good. Why are your eyes so bright? What have you been doing?"

"I've been at your studio for five hours," I said. "Also I'm immensely tired."

"Yeah, I guess so," he said and nodded. Then he went home.

One day my son showed me proudly how he had cut out a square in the middle of one of his books and made a stash for a small, mostly smoked marijuana joint. It was the early 1970s and Susanna, now at a private school in Brooklyn, had recently reported that she had paid a school chum to pick up a pack of chewing gum and, when he forgot the gum, he gave her a tab of acid instead (went the story). She said kids left school at lunchtime and went to different homes to turn on. Their dealer was the school librarian's son. I marched over to the school and confronted the principal. I did not finger the librarian or her son. When the principal denied there was a drug problem at school—refusing my suggestion to have a recovered drug user (I had a perfect young candidate on my own newspaper) talk to the kids about his year in rehab—I withdrew my daughter in the middle of what was now her senior year. She completed her studies at a makeshift experimental school called City as School.

In the summer of 1972 I took her to Europe with me for a week during Charles's tour. Roberto was away at camp. Once more, Charles and I were reaching a point of no return. His hijinks had become so constant and excessive that I left in the middle of the week with Susanna and told him that he and I had come to the end. It was Susanna's presence, finally—the growing and absurd shenanigans that I saw filtered through her eyes—that sent me home.

Meanwhile, back in Europe, en route to Ronnie Scott's club in London for the final gig of the tour, Charles spent a week at a club in Copenhagen, that climaxed with a famous headline in a Danish newspaper: MINGUS RUNS AMOK ON STOGET! The article described a "shirt scandal" that had taken place on Stoget, a strip of elegant shops where, in his usual fashion, Charles had purchased twenty-four shirts at one of the stores. When he returned to his hotel, someone told him the price was not right, that he'd "been took." He hurried back to the store where one thing led to another, a series of "colorful threats" was exchanged, the police were called in, and Mingus went briefly to jail. The British newspapers got wind of the story and ran their own headline. As a result, Mingus, whose English booking agent had arranged for him to perform on an ocean liner back to the States following his engagement at Ronnie Scott's, lost a gig he'd wanted all his life. The managers of the cruise ship were not about to risk a cruise having any surprises.

His mood was dark. Emotionally, things had gone from bad to

worse during the tour, and now the ocean liner gig had been sabotaged. He spent a whirlwind series of days in London at the club, fighting about the music and recording some of the most exciting music of the tour, thanks to Columbia Records and their mobile sound trucks. Although I had broken up with him in Italy and was now back in the States, I eventually returned one of his many calls from the club. Ronnie Scott himself answered the phone.

"I can't talk!" he shouted. "Mingus just threw the tenor player, Bobbie Jones, down the stairway and I think he broke his leg!" He hung up the phone. When I called back an hour later, Ronnie again picked up the phone. *The music is incredible!*" he said. "It's utterly fantastic! I've never heard anything like it in my life!"

"How is Bobby Jones?" I asked. "Is he all right?"

"The music is unbelievable!" he continued.

"The tenor player," I asked again. "Is he okay?"

"Bobby? Oh yeah, Bobby's fine. He's back on the bandstand. They're blowing away the crowd! It's completely out of sight." He hung up. One of the musicians told me afterward that Bobby had been drinking heavily, tripped on his way to the dressing room, and then drummed up the story, which later was reported in the press.

When Charles returned home he had a nervous breakdown in Central Park. He threw off his clothes and scattered hundred-dollar bills in the wind. The pressures had been building for a long time. The balancing act of juggling his artistic sensibilities, the white world around him, the personalities onstage, and his own persistent demons had finally given out. The police took him around the corner to Mount Sinai Hospital. The following week a psychiatrist at the hospital called to report that Charles was concerned about a paper bag.

"What sort of paper bag?" I asked.

"A paper bag he says he left with a bartender the night before his . . . his episode in the park," the doctor faltered. He explained that Charles had told him he'd been drinking at a small bar on

MacDougal Street in Greenwich Village called the Kettle of Fish. I remembered it as a folkie bar where Bob Dylan used to sing. I told him I had broken up with Charles but promised I would try to locate the paper bag.

The bartender was absent when I arrived at the Kettle of Fish the following afternoon, but I was able to reach him on a pay phone at the bar. He remembered the paper bag. He thought he might have placed it on a hat rack near the door. I hung up the phone and rummaged through some old newspapers on the rack until I found the stained and crumpled bag stuck between some metal rungs. Even on the edge of a breakdown, Charles had crafted a perfect disguise. Inside that rumpled bag was ten thousand dollars in cash, the proceeds of the tour. It had sat, unremarked, on a rack before an open door of a busy bar for more than a week.

With time, Charles and I once more began to adjust and to close the gap between our lives. He had run into a brick wall, survived, and found a measure of calm—at least temporarily—in the following months. In 1973, when my children and I moved out of Diane Arbus's apartment to a larger apartment a few blocks west, Charles moved with us. For the first time, our love had an address.

From the moment he moved in, life was as peaceful and productive as I could possibly have imagined. Our confrontations were over, easy as pie. It had taken only eight long years of growth and misunderstandings to work things out. Charles was now a member of the household. When he was not on tour, he spent his days composing at the piano in New York or, on weekends, in Woodstock. At home, there were large communal dinners, often with a half-dozen members of the *Changes* staff around the table.

Two phone calls from those days are etched in my memory. One came after Charles's album *Let My Children Hear Music* was released on Columbia. Chock-full of new music and rarely heard compositions from a decade earlier, it was performed by a large ensemble, with a special section that included six of the finest bass players in New York. Charles was enormously pleased with the result. He had written an essay that accompanied the album—liner notes that described not only the music but what it meant to be a jazz composer. Among other things, he had written about an astonishing "spontaneous composition," as he called it, with a typically expressive Mingus title, "Myself When I Am Real." Alvin Ailey renamed it "Adagio ma non troppo" for his dance program, which was how it was called on the album.

When the phone rang on this particular morning, the sun was shining through the kitchen window as I prepared breakfast and Charles waited impatiently on the living room couch. I picked up the receiver and heard an excited voice from the record company: Charles had been nominated for a Grammy Award for his liner notes to *Let My Children Hear Music.* Instantly, I relayed the good news to Charles, who looked up from the couch with disbelief. When he finally managed to respond, his words exploded from the couch with a lifetime's worth of pain and indignation.

"My *liner notes*?" he sputtered. It was the only Grammy nomination he had received in almost four decades of music, and it was not for his music.

Twenty years after his death he was honored with a Grammy Lifetime Achievement Award. I imagine if he had been alive he would have sent it back. He was in the habit of returning jazz awards from magazines like *Playboy,* whenever he won their polls, along with letters that went more or less as follows: "Polls are nigger contests. They don't have polls for classical musicians, they don't ask who is the best violinist—Yehudi Menuhin or Isaac Stern or Salvatore Accardo—they don't ask who is the best conductor. After you win a poll you can only go down, and when you're in third place, promoters aren't interested. I know fifty bass players as good as I am. The system puts one nigger at the top and keeps everyone else scrambling."

TONIGHT AT NOON   113

The other phone call came from an airline-magazine reporter who was writing an article on creativity. Specifically, she wanted a definition of what creativity was all about. Charles responded immediately: "Anybody can play weird, that's easy. What's hard is to be as simple as Bach. Making the simple complicated is commonplace. Making the complicated simple—awesomely simple—that's creativity." Those spontaneous words would be repeated over the years, not only in the airline magazine but at an IBM Science Awards presentation, in the opening statement of an Apple Computer annual address, in *Sports Illustrated, Reader's Digest,* and countless other places, I imagine, where creativity is still honored.

In the spring of 1973 the jazz roster at Columbia was dropped by its president, Clive Davis, in a scandalous surprise housecleaning that only Miles Davis survived. Not long afterward Charles accompanied me to one of Clive's lavish record parties for a new rock group, a routine event like many that, in my role as a member of the press, I frequently attended—gatherings that were of interest to Charles only insofar as the buffet table might offer an imaginative spread. Clive Davis never did forgive Charles for drawing up a chair at the banquet table that evening—a heaping plate of food before him—and consuming his meal among the platters as if it were his own private place setting.

The good news for Charles, in his sacking by Columbia Records, was that he returned to his beloved Neshui Ertegun at Atlantic. Another plus was that Columbia returned to him the extraordinary tapes they had recorded, live from their mobile trucks, at Ronnie Scott's club in London, during that weeklong engagement the previous fall.

Neshui Ertegun was one of the most cultured, sophisticated, and generous men in the industry. His warmth and friendship for Mingus lasted a lifetime. He had understood and supported Mingus from the beginning and, now once again, gave him not only a home on his label but complete artistic freedom. Neshui had always come to his rescue without question when Charles needed a friend—bailing him out of jail if he'd gotten into a scrape, advancing him money whenever he called. Once, after one of our fights when I'd run down the street to my brother Bob's apartment in Greenwich Village and Charles was hollering outside that he loved me—imploring Bob to open the door, from the top of a parked car where he'd climbed in order to get closer to the window—the police had arrived, summoned by the irate car owner, handcuffed Charles, and carried him off to jail. Early the following morning Neshui arrived at the station to secure his release.

As for the social and political changes taking place in the sixties and early seventies, Charles had been speaking out for years from his own soapbox, usually the stage, about civil rights, Vietnam, the uses of language, artistic freedom, and the inequities of the music industry. The Lower East Side, where he lived from 1966 to 1973, was bustling with creative and political activities that included Booker's New Breed fashion statements, Black Panther militancy, peace and love concerts, and the various crusades of the underground press. Charles knew everyone and joined no one. His music was not for sale. Although Tim Leary was a friend, Charles refused an offer to collaborate on an album at the height of Tim's popularity. He turned down Allen Ginsberg's invitation to record William Blake's *Songs of Innocence and Experience.* The Black Panthers' minister of information was a fan who came regularly to hear him at the Village Gate, but Charles had no time for the party agenda. Although he frequently tacked on titles to his compositions after the fact, like "Remember Rockefeller at Attica" or "Remember Cell Block F, T'is Nazi USA," and although he wrote a handful of vocal pieces like "Don't Let It Happen Here," "Fables of Faubus," and "Oh Lord Don't Let Them Drop That Atomic Bomb on Me," his music itself was not at the service of his political beliefs. He was too much of an artist for that. I never saw him compromise a note in his career.

The early seventies were times of interior change as well. The cauldron of Charles's vast imagination occasionally spilled over into the old Mafia conspiracies, the rival lovers, the noisy furies of his past, and I would consider bolting from the nest, wondering whether I had actually invented the man I thought I loved. But then the other Charles would reappear, full of the vibrancy of life and love, the Charles who ran to the piano with excitement to illustrate some point like a schoolboy, full of pure joy.

Often staff members of *Changes* would join us for large, family-style dinners at home that were really extended editorial meetings. Charles would sit at the head of the table focused on his meal while the children excused themselves to do their homework and writers and editors at the far end swapped ideas about the next issue. One weekend, a few *Changes* staff members, along with Charles, flew to Paris to attend a show of political drawings at the Louvre. The show, called "Art of the *Times*," had been assembled by Jean-Claude Suares, *Changes'* current art director, who had published a book by the same title while he was working for the *New York Times*. It featured drawings by artists he had hired to illustrate pieces for the op-ed page—an exciting and innovative idea then—illustrations by living artists rather than old prints.

Like Charles, J. C. Suares had an artist's appreciation of invention and embellishment. The going joke was that if J.C. had a tuna sandwich for lunch, he would, in principle, tell you it was ham and cheese. The show in Paris, according to J.C., was the first show of newspaper art at the Louvre in a century, since Daumier. We all stayed at the Hotel Élysée Star on the Champs-Élysées, which Charles, in principle, called the Elsie Star—part of the spin he regularly put on language. (I remembered when Whitney Balliett interviewed him for a *New Yorker* profile years before at a bar on Second Avenue, Charles ordered bottle after bottle of Pouilly-Fuissé, which he chose to call Polly Foose (stepsister to Elsie Star?). The name Polly Foose surfaced more than once in Whitney's faithful rendering of the facts. The week the *New Yorker* article came out, Bill Cosby promptly sent a case of Pouilly-Fuissé to Charles at the club where he was performing.

When we arrived at the main lobby of the Louvre, J.C. rushed over and, in an inspired display of family love, bumped stomachs with Charles as a form of greeting. It became their signature hello from then on. Theirs was a natural coupling. They enjoyed outsized celebrations, had bellies that hung over their belts, and shared a similar sardonic understanding of life's ongoing comedy. Charles's humor and his irony were something most people missed—forever to his disappointment and surprise. He was astonished that people took him so seriously. He expected them to laugh, though many were too intimidated. When Charles and J.C. first met in the long corridor of our apartment during a party and Charles noisily confronted him with some issue on his mind, J.C. looked him in the eye and laughed out loud. A new friendship was born. It was J.C. who turned Charles on to cigars. Together they became connoisseurs, procuring illegal Cubans from one of the most distinguished suppliers in Switzerland. Soon, whether playing bass or relaxing at home, Charles was seldom without a cigar in his mouth, as the photos from that period attest. Eventually he fashioned special containers and phony cigar rings that allowed him to smuggle his precious Cubans through border customs while on tour.

In 1974 I accompanied Charles on a concert tour of South America. The political climate in Brazil, Uruguay, and Argentina was so outrageous, the governments so oppressive (even children's improvisational theater was suppressed in Brazil), the police and customs officials so menacing, we were eager to return home to the land of Richard Nixon, whatever its flaws. In Brasília—a strange, otherworldly capital carved out of the dense jungle that surrounded it, miles from the teeming life of ordinary cities—government officials who formed most of the population were joyless, living in a state of exile, waiting only to be sent home. This cold, empty city with its abstract buildings and vast concrete plazas was oddly devoid of anything green or living, despite the proximity of the jungle. It might have tumbled down on a windy night from some other universe. It reminded me of old Buck Rogers comic strips with their early space fantasies.

The casement window of our hotel room overlooked an unpopulated, dimly lit square below that seemed to stretch out like a concrete sea. The first night following Charles's sparsely attended concert, I dreamed I was standing at that casement window, staring out at a pale young woman with long dark hair drenched in water who had risen from the sea below. She was singing a lament of such extraordinary beauty and perfection that I stood at the window transfixed. She was singing her song to me, a tale of sorrow, describing how she had drowned herself for love, how she was filled with regret, how she passionately longed to live again. She hovered above the water and implored me with her eyes, gazing wretchedly across the sea.

I was aware that Charles was calling to me, shaking me in bed, trying to wake me up. I opened my eyes and saw his agitated face. "There was a woman," he said urgently, "standing beside the bed." He looked across the covers. "She had long black hair."

In 1975 we planned to be married in a ceremony at my place in Woodstock, outdoors under the thick grapevines that had never sprouted grapes. (Roberto called me to the porch one day and pointed to a clump of purple grapes that hung from the lattice of the arbor we had so optimistically constructed overhead. After my initial shriek of excitement, he admitted he'd tied them on with a string.)

We planned to order a bus to transport to the country friends, musicians, and the entire staff of *Changes*. Charles's children and mine were planning the fancy wedding outfits they would wear. The importance of food was frequently under discussion. And then the week of the celebration, Charles returned home from a tour with an injured back and went straight into the hospital. Weeks later, en route to the airport where I was seeing him off on another tour, we headed on the spur of the moment to City Hall. We already had our papers. Now, instead of Allen Ginsberg chanting with tinkling cymbals inside his palms, we joined a queue of fifty newlyweds in the narrow corridors of the Municipal Building in a ceremony about as engaging as waiting in line at a bus stop. As it happened, I was carrying a newspaper under my arm like a commuter, although I complied when the officiating magistrate ordered me from his podium to set down my *New York Times* on a chair. "Madam," he said reproachfully, "you are getting married."

I suppose we'd felt married for a long time.

For five happy years we lived at 39 East Tenth Street, a bona fide couple. Charles was touring regularly: Japan, Europe, South America, the United States. I'd observed his sidemen on tour, some married, some footloose, and had learned a thing or two. "Do what you like on the road," I told him coolly. "Just don't let me find out." Things happen. It's life. I hate confessions. I remember calling his room in Canada and the hotel clerk telling me that I'd forgotten my gloves at the front desk. When I asked about it later, Charles described an interesting interview he'd done with a girl from, I think, the *Toronto Star*. Or it might have been the woman from Atlantic Records who had brought the latest schedule to his room. I imagine it was true. But no matter. If there was fudging, it didn't touch what we had. Our pantheon remained vibrant.

. . .

Around the corner from where we lived was Bradley's, a unique
gathering place for those who loved jazz, a slightly mad late-night
haven that felt like a living room and bore the stamp of Bradley Cunningham, its aristocratic owner from New England. Cunningham
loved jazz piano playing so fiercely that, although he was not good
enough for a career in music himself, he did the next best thing: he
fashioned a place where every night of the year you could find the
best jazz piano in the city. That was how the great George Shearing,
who had his own special table whenever he showed up, character-
ized it one evening. Normally, a bass player and a piano player held
sway, and late at night—very late—Bradley would lock the doors,
usually around 4 a.m., and the real heart and soul of the place would
grow large and intense. Eventually Bradley himself would land at the
piano, hunched and passionate, ready to swap chord changes with
any of the hordes of musicians who congregated after their own gigs
were over or who just fell by to enjoy the atmosphere and the music.
How many nights Bradley and Charles hung out together at the
piano stool, I can't even imagine.

I remember leaving Bradley's at six in the morning, three or four
hours before the *Changes* office would open, walking arm in arm
with Charles, the birds chattering as we mused about ending the day
while for others it was beginning, and the sun shone past the still-lit
streetlamps and the early morning heat was already in the air and I
wished I could go to the beach instead of grabbing two hours' sleep
before the workday began. Charles talked about a dog that was
being walked by a doorman, a rich man's dog, he said, whose owner
didn't have to get up at six. I said it didn't look like a rich man's dog.
Charles had nothing more to add, having made his point about social
disparities and not, like me, entirely euphoric about the dawn.

During those years, his albums *Changes One* and *Changes Two*
were released on Atlantic Records. *Changes One* included "Sue's

Changes," a piece written the year we were married that was originally titled "Sue's Moods" and was an extended work full of gorgeous melodies, danceable tunes, and collective, frenzied noise. Chaos and climax, he would say. Naturally, it's one of my favorites. He'd hoped to have Sarah Vaughan sing the lyrics to "Duke Ellington's Sound of Love" on the same record, and although his band had recorded an instrumental version for her to sing over, it was in the wrong key and Atlantic wouldn't return to the studio. When Charles and I visited Sarah in her hotel room after a performance in New York, she suggested using her own trio on Charles's album, but nothing ever worked out. "I never heard such a voice, man," Charles told an interviewer not long after, describing the first time he'd heard her sing. "Billie Holiday and Sarah. Sarah's a singer; she vocalizes. Billie was more human. She almost talked her lyrics—it was like a poor man talking. She wasn't really singing, just talking her lyrics. Living her lyrics. Sarah does it in a singing way. She's the greatest singer going now."

His next recorded album was *Three or Four Shades of Blues,* whose title tune he prefaced, while performing it in clubs and concert halls, with long narrative explanations that so amused and delighted him that they seemed to grow longer with each performance. In condensed form they went something like this:

"The next piece is called 'Three or Four Shades of Blue'—or 'Three or Four Shades of *Blues,*' if you like. But there are more like six or seven. The first section is something I call 'Super Bebop Blues.' It's what Bird might be playing now if he were still living . . . Afterwards comes a black, Puerto Rican, Afro-Cuban, basic blues structure with East Indian overtones . . ." (Pause to see if the audience was paying attention.) "Then comes a 'Count Basie Blues,' followed by a Duke Ellington two-chord arrangement of the blues, followed by a Mingus Blues . . ." (Another pause.) "At the end we close out with something I call the Caucasian White Folks' Blues— American white folks, that is—I don't know anything about European white folks . . ." At this point his piano player would step into a little Irish lullaby, stiff as a minuet, with Mendelssohn's "Wedding March" as a prelude. One way or another, it was all the blues. Blues were the center of his soul.

Around that time the British rock star Jeff Beck recorded "Goodbye Pork Pie Hat," perhaps the most famous blues Charles had written. Columbia Records sent over a copy of the album, which I played for him the same afternoon. I asked what he thought it sounded like. He answered immediately: "It sounds like money." He was right about that. He made more money in a month of royalties from one tune recorded by someone else than he had on any of his own recordings.

One late-summer weekend we headed out to the Hamptons. Our small group included Charles, Roberto, our friend Myra, who was a writer and cat lover, me, and our two German shepherds, Muttley and Brunhilda. On a whim, no doubt similar to Charles's need for fresh lobster—when our family once took an impromptu night flight to the Caribbean—we had rented a small cottage on the water for three days next to the home of a famous Greek architect.

When we arrived in Amagansett that Friday night at dusk, the door to our cottage was locked and the rental agency was closed. While the rest of us wasted time discussing options, Charles hurled a rock through a glass pane in the front entrance and opened the door. In the few minutes this required, Brunhilda wandered across to the neighbors' porch and killed their Siamese cat.

No one was home next door, and there was another Siamese cat still alive on the porch. Charles suggested we put the dead cat in the middle of the road. "It could have been hit by a car," he said. When his idea was vetoed, he suggested buying a brand-new cat and leaving it on the porch. Instead, Roberto scooped up the dead cat and tried to revive it under a stream of cold water in our kitchen sink. It was incredibly hot outdoors and the cat was not reviving. Charles suggested storing it in the salad compartment of our refrigerator so it wouldn't, as he said, decompose before its owners returned. Myra was already wailing about retrieving milk for her morning coffee above the remains of a dead cat.

At ten o'clock a car pulled into the driveway next door. Soon we could hear people murmuring on the lawn. I left our cottage, marched up the road, and announced to everyone in the dark that we had killed their cat. I was standing alone at their gate as the Greek architect, who appeared to be hugely tall, hugely angry, and surrounded by moaning family members of all ages, raised his fist above my head.

"Where is our cat?" he hollered. His entire entourage was now keening in the night.

"Back at the cottage," I said, trying to break free, hoping to race ahead and retrieve the cat before he arrived. But he strode with long steps directly behind me and, when Roberto indicated the refrigerator, snatched his soggy cat from the salad compartment himself. As he hurried off into the night, he announced that he was getting out his rifle to shoot our dogs. After a series of late-night calls to local kennels, I found one that was open and sneaked the dogs into the car. They spent the remainder of the weekend behind bars. Through the windows of our cottage we could hear the neighbors crying in the night.

Most of the time Charles ignored what seems to be a basic human need for definition, for categories and time frames, anniversaries and recollections. The normal incremental signposts we live by, the twentieth of this or the tenth of that, were of little interest to him. Time was a continuous sweep he entered and left on his own. As for holidays, he created surprises and occasions all year long, an unexpected gift, a sudden banquet. Christmas was a day like any other, made for sleep or celebration, it hardly mattered.

One Christmas he gave me nothing. We were gathered in Woodstock with visiting friends and relatives. Under the tree, for the dogs, were bloody dripping raw beef bones in tinfoil wrapped with red ribbons. My children had their usual green money from Charles hanging from branches (a hundred-dollar bill, a fifty, whatever excess Charles's whims dictated). The only person he had overlooked was me. Words were unnecessary as I walked out into the snowy night.

Three days later I was awakened before dawn by a circle of beaming, wide-awake faces that escorted me down a long hallway where, while my daughter snapped photos, I viewed a transformed state-of-the-art kitchen that now contained a brand-new stove, dishwasher, washing machine, dryer, and a huge refrigerator. Charles, in his usual fashion, had warned the appliance store and its delivery men that his purchase depended on a predawn surprise. My children had led the workmen through the woods in the dark, and they had labored feverishly in the kitchen to set up the appliances before dawn. Although I would have been happy with just a book, our household was ecstatic, proud of Charles, glad for holidays.

Off and on Charles made a stab at dieting. Briefly he went to the Pauling Health Manor (Roberto called it the Appalling Health Manor), a diet clinic located between Woodstock and New York City near the Roosevelt estate in Hyde Park. He spent two weeks drinking a lot of water, eating salads, and fingering mantra cards that read "I am developing a distaste for those foods I know are harmful to my health and my diet" or "I find it easier and easier to stick to my reducing diet." Meanwhile, as we discovered later, he was ordering pizza from a pay phone down the hall and calling taxis to pick up leftovers from the Cordon Bleu Cooking School up the road.

Another stab was a two-week visit we made together to the home of comedian Dick Gregory, who was renting two hundred acres in Plymouth, Massachusetts, from the Liggett-Meyers estate. Dick, his wife, and his ten children lived in the main house up on the hill. Our own quarters were in the boathouse below, where Dick frequently held press conferences and meetings on nutrition, diet, and ways to combat world hunger. For eight days Charles stuck to his water fast.

When we returned home, Charles described his downfall to his friend Booker: "I was just on water and I lost a lot of weight," he said. "But then Dick had a cook there, a guy who cooked every day and night in the boathouse, and he finally got to me. A big guy with a beard. He cooked everything you can imagine—barbecued chicken, baby-back ribs—he was unbelievable. Dick could walk around and not touch anything. He called it garbage."

When we left, Dick Gregory gave me several complex diet recipes for Charles's meals in New York: nuts to grind, dried fruits to blend, soups to simmer, all of which I faithfully prepared. And then, one night after Charles had consumed his usual diet dinner at home, I went to join him at the Village Gate. I asked a clerk at a food concession in the lobby if he had seen Charles following his performance. He replied that he had, but that after consuming two heaping orders of roast beef at his stand, Charles had gone around the corner to a Chinese restaurant. Which was where I found him.

During that last year of health, we had a memorable party on Charles's fifty-fifth birthday in 1977, and, at Christmas, an eggnog bash with members of the jazz community, beat writers, artists, and promoters representing an era that was nearly over.

Our friend Daniele Senatore, the Italian film producer, was working on two films, one with director Elio Petri called *Todo Modo,* about a weekend retreat outside Rome at which members of the clergy and the Christian Democratic party were killed off, one by one—the film's conceit was similar to that of Agatha Christie's *Ten Little Indians.* The other film was about the drug culture in Colombia and its counterpart in New York City. Charles wrote music for both. The subsequent album on Atlantic contained one long piece on each side: "Todo Modo" and the new piece, "Cumbia and Jazz Fusion," based on authentic rhythms taped in the jungles of Colombia by a friend of Senatore's in what now became a merging of styles and cultures, Latin rhythms and jazz—wholly and magnificently Mingus. Soon Charles was performing it on tour in Europe, North Africa, and in the American Southwest.

And then, without warning, it was over.

Five

"I don't think I'm sick. I think I have a severe para-
noid illusion . . ."

—*Mingus*

"You see, they were talking when they played. They
were telling stories about their lives. And that's
what we do. We represent a long line of facts."
—*Mingus talking to Nat Hentoff about Fats
Navarro and Bud Powell*

In the early days he used to brag he couldn't fall. Even when I
barely knew him, he would repeat the phrase from time to time in
a signifying way. "I can't fall, you know," he'd say out of the blue,
marching down the street or on his way backstage. He didn't boast
about his music or his talent on the bass, but something dark and insistent about not falling was on his mind. He once read me a poem

about a monkey that signified things that were either too obvious or too precarious to say straight out, a signifying monkey with codes to skirt the danger zones. Sometimes the object was privacy and other times it was merely hip, but most of the time it was ways to talk around Whitey—insider poetry that if you had to ask, as Dizzy said long ago, you didn't know.

But there were other forms of signifying that belonged only to Charles, visions that issued from darker regions of the soul and could not be explained away. Some of them nourished his art and others were full of dread, but all of them carried meanings that wound like shiny eels around ordinary words and squeezed them into new shapes and intentions, making it difficult for me to know exactly what was vision or what was code or what was just my own language suddenly restored.

In those days when he couldn't fall, he might streak down the block after a cab or race another musician up the street—"swift as a string of Art Tatum arpeggios," someone once said. They were marathon sprints that Teddy Curson, the young trumpet player in Mingus's band at the old Show Place club, could have described firsthand—legendary nights when Charles would chase Teddy down West Fourth Street during intermission, hitting the sidewalk with a catapulting leap down the front steps of the club and then off around the block, the two of them shouting about the music as they ran, arguing about whatever had gone wrong during the show.

And though Mingus rarely danced, we all watched from our seats late one night in a Harlem ballroom as suddenly he was gone— spun off from our table like a flying hubcap, his feet below moving faster than anyone could follow, speeding across the length of the dance floor. It was 1975 and we were celebrating uptown with the drummer Olatunji and some African musicians and Mingus was feeling good. Normally he displayed an uncharacteristic reserve when it came to dancing—the only concession I saw him make to his size—but this night his feet were the fastest in the house. They were as fast as his fingers on bass. His feet could have cut his bass that night.

And then one afternoon in the spring of 1977 I went to pick him up at Gallagher's Steak House, where we'd had our first meal together. We were on our way out of town, headed up to Woodstock, where he was designing a recording studio and where we thought we might move full-time. When I arrived to pick him up, the manager of the restaurant and several witnesses were standing at the door. They told me he had fallen. They said he had taken a waiter and two loaded trays down with him when he fell. They said he had made a terrible scene and had blamed the waiter for getting in his way.

When we left the restaurant, he threw the crumpled Gallagher's bill on the front seat of the car. The bill was a tabulation of the colossal quantities of house specialties, beef, and imported wines he had consumed that afternoon, plus whatever went down with the trays. Then he shouted his legs into the car. "*Feet!* Get movin'! *Feet!* What you think you doin'?" He forced his heavy right leg into the car, ordering and supplicating it while people looked on with curiosity. "*Feet!*" he said one last time.

Speeding along the New York Thruway, we argued about his health. He was searching for reasons, anything that might clarify the crisis that seemed to be emerging from the folds of some early premonition. He remembered that Norman Mailer had once recommended a doctor I'd never called. He reproached me for it now. He wondered why I hadn't started a publishing company for his music long ago. He complained there was no food in the car.

I reminded him that for seven years I'd published *Changes,* a time-consuming newpaper of my own. I said there were apples in the backseat of the van. I assured him that Mailer's doctor had moved to Florida. I stepped on the gas. As we sailed through the night, he suddenly shouted, "*There!*" and pointed to a large white sign that was blinking out of the darkness on the right side of the road. In bold black letters the word CHIROPRACTOR shot by. "If you cared about me you would take me to that doctor. *There!*"

I U-turned in the middle of the highway and swung up on the grass. Without a word I marched ahead of him across the lawn to the lighted porch of an old clapboard house and knocked on the door. After a while a white-haired man appeared who spoke to us from behind the screen.

"It's late," the man said calmly, looking us over with a friendly nod. "It's after ten. I've just returned from the South." I was staring past the door at some autographed pictures, evidently his patients, which were framed along the vestibule walls.

"But if you come back tomorrow, I'll be happy to see you." He was kind but firm. Behind his head a few favorite photos were gathered in a special shrine. And then Charles and I both noticed.

In the center of the shrine was the face of Norman Mailer.

Charles put his arm around me. We said good night to the doctor and stood for a while outside the screen door watching the moon. It seemed natural enough that his recommended doctor had materialized in the night—one more collision of contingencies, one more chance encounter that, as always, seemed to reflect the inspired or dreaded events in his head, little windows of prophecy that rivered along through his life like a dream, or shot out of the darkness like a bright white sign.

I remembered years before when he had stood nervously in my living room on the Upper West Side of Manhattan and stared angrily at a white wicker wheelchair that was filled with plants.

"Why are you taunting me with that chair?" he'd asked.

"My plant stand?" I replied with surprise. I had known him for only a few months and was still adjusting to the personal, unexpected ways he interpreted whatever was going on. The beautiful old-fashioned wheelchair he was referring to was a prop from a Monty Woolley film, *The Man Who Came to Dinner*. It now overflowed with avocado plants and leafy ferns.

"Where I come from it's a wheelchair, baby," he said in a tight voice.

"It's a movie prop." I laughed. "A friend of mine bought it at a Hollywood auction." In fact, it had belonged to the young producer of Robert Frank's film in which I had participated. He had given away most of his possessions when he returned to California, and I had lucked into the chair.

"Wheelchairs are for cripples!" Charles said, his voice rising. "It's an omen. I know things. I'm a warlock. Get it out of my sight!"

I thought of the crutches he'd found leaning against the gate in front of his apartment that same year. I could hear his noisy proclamations up and down the block, shouting in the moonlight like Cassandra, that somewhere a cripple walked. Next day he told me that the crutches might have been a threat or warning to himself.

There were few simple answers when you were forced to guard against the alien world around you; when your head was split with imaginings; when you were cursed with a clairvoyant nature and the messages were seldom clear.

The following day and for the next six months he submitted to a nutritional program designed by Dr. Jack Soltanoff, who was currently dividing his time between Florida and Woodstock. Everything that ailed him began to disappear—his excessive weight, his indigestion, his insomnia. Everything except the strange weakness that medical experts on three continents had been unable to diagnose for over a year. The virus we still knew nothing about was lodged deep inside him, eating away at the circuits of his nerves.

By the end of the year he knew he was booked.

When he realized something was wrong, he went directly to bed. The man with perpetual insomnia, who had written a haunting ballad entitled "The Man Who Never Sleeps," now spent all day lying in a dark room in the back of our apartment nursing his health. One evening when a club-owner friend turned him on to cocaine, its sharp stimulation revitalized his body. Or he believed that it did. And so for the rest of the year he snorted coke like a drowning man gulping in air. He overdid his blow as he overdid everything else. In Woodstock, where he was writing music, I could hear him wheezing in the bathroom down the hall.

"Are you doing coke?" I'd ask.

"Nah," he'd reply, "I gave it up."

During the week a dealer who came by the house suggested to Charles that it was necessary to be high in order to compose.

"Bullshit," Charles replied instantly. "If I needed coke to compose, I wouldn't be a composer." When a traditional medical expert finally warned him that cocaine could harm his condition, he stopped in a day. "Drugs are in the mind," he dismissed them.

The last time we saw the dealer he was walking along the street. He stopped for a moment to say hello. "If you sober up, you have to have a plan," the dealer said with a shrug. "I don't have a plan."

A few weeks later, we discovered we had no plan, either.

It was the day before Thanksgiving, 1977, when Dr. Greenspan, a psychiatrist filling in for the head neurologist at Columbia Presbyterian Hospital in New York, informed me that Charles had amyotrophic lateral sclerosis—also known as Lou Gehrig's disease, after the Yankee ballplayer—and that he had from three to six months to live.

Dr. Greenspan was holding a pointer in his right hand, which he ran across a green map of the body tacked high on the wall, indicating the nerve sites, like military targets in a war, that would soon be destroyed. Only a month before, on Charles's final tour in Arizona, we'd stared up at a lobby TV set in our hotel and watched Reggie Jackson hit four home runs for Lou Gehrig's team. Beside us was a green map of Arizona with a "Mingus Mountain" to the north—

rumored to be full of ghosts and Indian massacre sites—that we planned to explore next day.

Instead, as he inched his way across the stage of the State University Theater in Phoenix, Arizona, that evening, he received a standing ovation for what turned out to be the last concert of his life. Arizona was the state where he was born. To the south, fifty-five years earlier, on an army base in Nogales, Arizona—a dusty outpost on the periphery then, and little more than a shantytown now—his ailing mother had given birth: 4-22-22. It was a date hailed by witches and mystics all his life, like the numerologist we encountered at a trendy New York restaurant a decade earlier.

We canceled the tour and flew home to New York. With the help of friends, he entered the prestigious Neurological Center at Columbia Presbyterian Hospital. Its chief resident neurologist, I told him, was the physician summoned when Bobby Kennedy was shot.

"Bobby Kennedy died, didn't he?" was all he said.

When bass player Red Mitchell visited the hospital a few days later, Charles asked him to play a bass that had just arrived from California. It was leaning untouched against the wall and was one of his favorites—the French Lady, he called it. Red tuned it in fifths like a cello, as he did his own, and played "Body and Soul." The following morning, Charles tried himself, standing up without the walker. I closed my eyes across the room and prayed. He plucked a few notes. Then he dropped his hand from the strings and handed the instrument back to the nurse. He never touched it again.

All that week I traveled from our East Village apartment to the hospital uptown on the A train, weeping into its dark reflecting windows, riding the legendary subway train to Harlem that Duke Ellington and Billy Strayhorn had turned into an anthem in the world of jazz. "Take the A Train" was Charles's theme song; it was the way he ended his late night sets at the Five Spot the summer we met. Now, as the A train shuttled north each afternoon, I thought of the years of struggle, of the largeness of Charles, and how, finally, we had made our two lives work; and now the largeness of death had appeared and no logic or embrace or screaming fight would make a difference. I turned from the window and wondered if the woman staring at me was miserable too and stared back at her despite my tears and thought about Charles and tried to imagine how I was going to tell a fighting man he didn't stand a chance.

I called Sonny Rollins, the tenor player, who was our friend. He said the doctors didn't know Mingus; they didn't know his spirit. My religious brother referred to a higher power; he said the doctors could be wrong. When I called Celia, one of Charles's former wives, she replied without hesitation: "The Mingus I knew fought for the truth." Still, I couldn't tell him. It took me more than a month to speak out.

In December 1977 we flew to a fashionable clinic in Switzerland where prominent figures, including Charles de Gaulle, Winston Churchill, and Charlie Chaplin, had received cell injections from the organs of unborn lambs. A New York doctor had recommended the visit: the injections wouldn't cure ALS, but they might fortify Charles's system.

We were aware that prominent figures make mistakes like the rest of us, but we were desperate and the idea had the ring of folk wisdom through the ages: treat an ailing organ with a healthy one. Eat it. Inject it. Whatever works. The doctor suggested that Charles's heart and lungs could be improved. It was enough, for the moment, that we were taking action. The circuit of help to the terminally ill was kicking in: the serious new experiments and the frauds.

On the third evening at La Clinique de la Prairie in Montreux, Charles received a dozen injections from the organs of an unborn lamb. Lamb liver cells. Lamb heart cells. Lamb kidney cells. Lamb pancreas. We shared a room with separate beds. Charles was becoming paralyzed. The nurses arrived regularly to change his position with a pull sheet.

The morning after his operation, I awoke early. The sun had not yet risen above the spectacular mountain range outside our window. In the semidarkness I watched him as he lay in bed. He looked crucified. He could barely move his body. He had been pierced with needles full of lamb cells over a period of three hours the night before. I realized his eyes were open and that he had been watching me as well. Suddenly his mouth quivered and emitted a long, low sound: "B-a-a-a-a-a-a-a-a-a-a . . ." he said.

We returned to New York the week before Christmas in time to move into our new quarters in a government-subsidized high-rise luxury artist ghetto of three thousand actors and musicians. Hundreds of airy apartments similar to our own offered sweeping views of the city. Ours overlooked the Hudson River on one side, and straight up the red arrow of lights on Tenth Avenue to the glittering George Washington Bridge on the other.

Looking for a place to die in was no different from normal apartment hunting in New York except for the importance of an elevator for Charles's wheelchair and, if we were lucky, a view. From our new windows on the forty-third floor we surveyed a nearly bankrupt city—a city whose failure to build a cultural center nearby had forced the developers of this luxury building to negotiate a government deal. The good news was that the scruffy community of performing artists and musicians had unexpectedly lucked in. Instead of an open fire hydrant spraying on the streets of New York in the heat of August, we had an Olympic-sized swimming pool and five tennis courts just an elevator ride away. Two former sidemen in Charles's band had already settled there, and saxophonist Dexter Gordon moved in when we did, two floors below.

When Charles looked down from his "chair in the sky," as Joni Mitchell would soon describe his wheelchair perch, he could see the rehearsal halls and small theaters that were springing up beside artsy luncheonettes and espresso cafés all over the neighborhood. A new culture was replacing the drug action, the candy stores with their late night sugar fixes, the seven-foot transvestites stalking Ninth Avenue, and the bustling pleasure trades.

Home was now Tenth Avenue and West Forty-third Street, down the block from the *New York Times*. I couldn't help remembering that my English grandfather, who had lost his fortune at the beginning of the century and resettled in the States, had begun the long path upward somewhere in the struggling tenement life of Hell's Kitchen, perhaps directly beneath our windows. Seven decades later I'd spun the family history backward three generations, returning its destiny to the very same cookeries of hell.

Although we had moved into a new apartment, unpacked our things, and were situated solidly above the city, Charles and I no longer belonged to its time or purpose. We had entered an order of our own.

At his studio on East Fifth Street, where I went to pack away his things, time snapped briefly into place. His collection of watches ticked on, spread across a table now covered with dust. There were only a dozen watches, not a real collection, just an exaggeration. Almost anything of interest to him became an exaggeration of some kind: he admired size—the outsized—and quantity. He overdid things intentionally. He understood the value of going too far. Had he been alive, he would have approved Christo's draping of the Reichstag or his scattering of umbrellas across Australia. Someone once said everything Charles wore or did was marked "Large."

Here in the studio where once we spent so many hours of love, the shades were drawn tightly, blocking whatever dangers lived on. I discarded a musty old plastic-and-cloth bass case (his cases now were leather, custom-designed, sharp) and saved the camera bags he used to toss over his shoulders a dozen years before when he rode his slick collapsible bicycle (an innovation then) across the Lower East Side taking pictures, landing a professional gig as a photographer, telling everyone he met why, in 1966, he was giving up music.

A soft leather case full of arrows still hung from the wall, a relic

from the bow-and-arrow period when he tramped nightly across the
Lower East Side armed with black pepper, an unloaded shotgun,
and his bow—on a take-no-chances reconnaissance of what could be
enemy turf.

Scattered everywhere were whims from the road: a waxed parasol
from Japan (1971 tour); gaudy beach towels from a Puerto Rican vacation by the sea (1973); a hand-sewn African tribal cloak from a
craft shop run by some black sisters on St. Mark's Place (the 1960s);
an ancient oriental blade, ivory-sheathed and engraved, from a flea
market in Paris. And here was the blood-stained wooden KKK stick
with notches for every Negro lynched that tenor player Clifford
Jordan had left behind one afternoon. Above the mattress where
he slept on the floor was tacked a 1972 Christmas calendar from
a Harlem warehouse where the belongings from his 1966 eviction
(filmed and televised by his friend Tom Reichman) were stored.

I remembered the night we went uptown for Peking duck with Tom
and his young film crew, Charles grumbling about being with a
bunch of children. After dinner we'd piled into Tom's open Jeep
and shot down to the Village Vanguard to hear Miles Davis, Charles
still grumbling about being bounced in a Jeep like a kid. Although I
was beginning to agree with him, I kept it to myself. I'd decided
not to let his mood step on the evening. I was still adjusting to behavior that was unsparingly consistent with feeling. Unlike the rest
of us, who took our parents seriously and learned to live with a measure of control, his behavior came direct and unedited. If it ever
appeared enigmatic, it was only because it was unclear which feeling in the immense spectrum held sway. Humming in the background there was also his imagination, which ran full-throttle at all
times.

He looked at me suddenly and said, *"Raise!"* as we hurtled downtown.

"I beg your pardon?" I said.

"*Raise, baby!*" he said again, his eyes flashing. "Get up off it." I had no idea what might be objectionable in my conversation with the crew, so I continued my discussion. Although he was sometimes jealous, his outbursts were usually fleeting, like a child's.

When we arrived at the Vanguard he saw his friend Nell King, a writer who had once arranged a high-paying job for him and Dave Brubeck. They were hired as music directors for a daring British film called *All Night Long,* a modern version of *Othello* with Richard Attenborough and Ian McClellan. Nell King was sitting with three young men.

"She's always with young people, too," Mingus mused. "I wonder if she feels lonesome like me." Nell maneuvered her way over unsteadily and kissed us both hard on our cheeks. Miles Davis came over, wiped Charles's face with his hands (wiping his own blackness onto Charles's mongrel skin, as Charles later explained), and tussled his hair. Then Miles headed for the bandstand.

Charles smiled happily. "I don't feel lonesome anymore," he said.

On the studio wall were tacked other Christmas cards from 1972: one from Robert Joffrey, whose ballet troupe had performed *The Mingus Dances,* choreographed by Alvin Ailey, at Carnegie Hall that year; one from tenor player Sonny Rollins and his wife, Lucille; and a gift subscription to the health magazine *Prevention* from Farwell Taylor, whose hospitality in northern California had once inspired a Mingus piece, "Far Wells, Mill Valley," and whose recent death was honored with another, "Farewell Farwell." A card from Father Gerry Pocock in Montreal was signed (with homage to Duke Ellington) "In a Mellotone." Another card contained greetings in German to Charlie Mingus from someone named Eva.

Scattered on the floor was still-unopened mail addressed to Charles Mingus, in care of Charles M. Holdings (a pseudonym he'd borrowed from his own title "Once Upon a Time There Was a Holding Corporation Called Old America." a composition written in 1965). Other unopened mail was addressed to him, in care of Ronnie Scott's club in London, where he'd performed in 1971.

Also tacked to the wall was a headline that read: HOLD PASTOR FOR DEFENDING HIS CADILLAC WITH A SHOTGUN. A sign below said "Whether you're rich or poor, it's nice to have money" and had Charles's signature at the bottom. Alongside it were letters from his editor at Alfred A. Knopf about the publication of *Beneath the Underdog,* and a response to his request that his life story be bound in leather and emblazoned with gold lettering like the Bible: the promotion department had other plans.

In a corner covered with dust were the handcuffs he once used to lock together Michael Harrington and his wife, who were hosting a fund-raising cocktail party in Greenwich Village. Mingus had admired the white activist, who was involved in an Equal Opportunity project uptown, but once inside his apartment he became so offended by what he considered a racist painting on the wall that he retired to his hosts' bedroom and lay flat on their goosedown comforter until he could regain control. When he reappeared in the living room, he pulled out a pair of handcuffs from his pocket and snapped them on the wrists of the activist and his wife.

In that moment the normal cocktail party ended and another one began. The couple made the best of it, moving graciously among their guests, he accompanying her to the kitchen to refill the trays, she standing by him as he poured the drinks. An hour or so later, as Charles and I drove the couple uptown to Charles's apartment where he'd forgotten the key to the handcuffs, we were stopped by the police for running a light and taken to headquarters in a group. The couple crab-walked through the station door—their left wrists bound together—but once inside the courtroom, Charles was unable to convince the judge that the circumstances and the events leading to them made sense. In the end we were all released. Charles received a scolding from the judge and a ticket for running the light.

His mechanical "Laughing Bag" was still beside the phone, a high-pitched cackle lasting a minute and a half which he occasionally attached to his answering machine, briefly replacing his own urgent messages. A box of oversized black silk matching "bibs"—once commissioned from a tailor to button over and protect in style the custom-designed black silk shirts he wore at his nightly Lucullian feasts—recalled his sartorial savvy long before the fashion world discovered bibs for babies to match their expensive clothes.

I found and saved a Carnegie Hall Tavern matchbook, perhaps pocketed after Alvin Ailey's performance of *The Mingus Dances,* waiting together with Alvin at the Carnegie Tavern for the Clive Barnes review in the early morning edition of the *Times.* It was hardly worth the wait: a disappointing review that acknowledged the music but panned the show.

Sources of protection, physical, spiritual, and literary, were still scattered about the room. A brand-new "adult life vest" wrapped in cellophane lay unopened. Some printed instructions for a "St. Charles Hunting Quiver" (naturally he bought that one) were stashed in a corner beside a lanyard with a metal whistle, a huge leather Everlast "crotch protector," and several tall candle jars assembled for his nightly vigils. Inside his leather arrow case, besides his bow, was a stash of books that included lectures by Swami Vivekananda, the New Testament, and several versions of the Bible (the margins full of penciled commentary), as well as *The Passover Plot* and an Italian-American pocket dictionary.

The Mafia surely figured in the mix. For years he'd signed his business letters with the name Dominick Antonio Monia, convinced that an Italian name carried more clout. He had rented the name from its owner, the real Dominick Antonio Monia. I met Monia by chance, years later, bartending opposite the Public Theater in Manhattan; he confirmed that Charles had indeed paid him $150 in the early 1960s for the rental of his name.

.   .   .

His appreciation of excess and exaggeration still rang from every corner of the room. A twenty-foot American flag lay beside an entire rack of knives purchased directly off the wall of a hardware store where he'd gone to buy a single knife. A large cardboard box containing sixty (sixty!) boxes of IBM pencil leads recalled his marathon bouts of composing. And here was the empty booklet of hat coupons inspired by an encounter in the early 1970s with a suspicious haberdasher on West Thirty-sixth Street. The proprietor of the store had refused to change the five-hundred-dollar bill Mingus offered him for a hat. Mingus promptly suggested he keep the entire bill in exchange for a booklet of "hat coupons" at $35 a ticket—a solution he invented on the spot. From then on, whenever he took a liking to someone—the owner of a restaurant, the driver of a cab, a fan at the club—he would flip open the booklet from his pocket and lavishly dole out a coupon for a hat.

And again: a cellophane envelope for a "wrestling knee pad," extra large. A giant box of Kleenex, "double area." Reams of custom-designed yellow manuscript paper stacked beside boxes that still held the empty album covers for *Mingus at Monterey* and *My Favorite Quintet* from our mail-order club, long ago.

As I was about to discard a single black leather glove with the index and last two fingers oddly Scotch-taped against the palm, I discovered on closer inspection that the glove was giving the finger to someone.

Inside an old maroon hardcover book, one of the thickest in his collection, I noticed that the middle pages of the book had been cut out in what was unmistakably the shape of a small revolver. The name of the book was *Personal Magnetism;* it was Charles's secret pocket for a gun.

His plaques and awards were covered with dust. He never put them on display. The only time he brought one out, with its flat hard shiny surface, was for cutting a rock during the few months he was doing cocaine.

An old 1967 bill from the Savoy garage in Brooklyn, where he stored his Cadillac limousine before giving it to his sister, was stuck to a leaflet advertising "Charles Mingus at Pookie's Pub" that same year. Pookie's Pub was a small Hudson Street bar down the block from the Half Note where Mingus had wandered in one night after the Half Note owners refused him a gig and talked the young owner, Pookie, into supporting live music. Two weeks later a new jazz club was born. It featured the Charles Mingus Quartet with his longtime drummer Dannie Richmond, alto player Charles McPherson, and Lonnie Hillyer on a trumpet. He invited the press to a party and for the next three months successfully played the door. Then late one night an argument with Pookie about a funny money count, followed by a threat concerning the smashing of whiskey bottles, followed by a miraculously agile flying leap over the bar (during one of his many diets), brought the experiment to a close.

A magnetized King Tut in a miniature coffin rested beside a broken ceramic nun doll that still held a lock of my hair. When all else failed, as it invariably did that year, he resorted to witchcraft, using strange devices he invented on his own. Voodoo was one more choice on the menu, one more means of seduction or attack.

Over the kitchen stove a Quotation of the Day by Leopold Stokowski: "A painter paints his pictures on canvas, but musicians paint their pictures on silence," to which Mingus added: "We provide the music, you provide the silence!"

A note once pasted on his bell: "To Mingus Ringers: Leave message if you care to—whoever you may be. I am out looking at my loneliness that has to go before it takes me."

As I was sorting papers, a shadowy figure knocked repeatedly at the metal gates of the studio window. It was a bartender from the bar across the street reporting with agitation that Charles had "phoned from Europe." He said it was "urgent" I return his call. For a moment I was thrown back into the time slot I was sorting on the floor. Then I remembered Charles's sly uses of "emergency."

From the pay phone at the bar, I reached Charles at our apartment in New York, where he reminded me sheepishly to pick up two quarts of ice cream on the way home.

That evening our friend Daniele Senatore, the Italian film producer who was now in California, called to suggest that Charles write music for T. S. Eliot's *Four Quartets* and that Joni Mitchell rework and sing the lyrics. Warner Bros. was interested in the idea. Daniele's own film projects had been offbeat and original: he produced Lina Wertmüller's *The Seduction of Mimi* and Elio Petri's *Investigation of a Citizen Above Suspicion,* which had been nominated for an Academy Award.

Joni was wary. "I'd sooner paraphrase the Bible," she said via someone at Elektra Records.

January 22, 1978. In the middle of a snowstorm, thirty musicians assembled in the Atlantic recording studios while Charles watched from the corner in his wheelchair. I was wearing summer whites under my old raccoon coat, a useless protest to the weather and to everything else. Julie Coryell appeared wearing a fur coat and summer whites and in a foul mood as well. Perhaps that's how new styles begin: everyone angry on the same day.

The musicians included two bassists, three drummers, two baritone saxes (Gerry Mulligan and Pepper Adams), the Brecker brothers, and others associated with Mingus's music through the years. Guitarist Larry Coryell and Charles discussed "Farewell Farwell."

"It's a beautiful tune," Larry observed.

"Yeah, it's simple. Direct," Charles replied.

"D flat. It's my favorite key. All black notes and C and F. That's how I think of it." Charles and arranger Sy Johnson looked on silently.

Producer Ilhan Mimaroglu gave orders to the alto player, Lee Konitz, over the loudspeaker, as Lee kept stopping to redo his solo:

"That's all right. Just keep playing. I already have some good solos of yours. We need another bass solo. Yours doesn't matter."

"So I don't need to play?" Lee asked.

"You just don't need to play good," Pepper Adams drawled from the baritone chair.

As I sat in the back of the room beside Charles, I tried to remember that no one is truly close, in order to feel less new and lonely. When the two bass players who were replacing Charles took their solos, battling each other at the session, I tried to ignore my tears, conceal them under my hair and focus on the whole community of loneliness and grief in the world instead of my solitary feelings at home. The thought of a community raced through me like an electric current, sobering my excesses and my rage.

During the lunch break, I overheard an Italian waiter say that life takes hold of you and breaks you in half like a breadstick.

A few days after the recording, our new nurse, Daphne, was busy preparing Charles's clothes for the difficult trip into the living room. Each morning we observed the ritual and importance of dress. Before traveling from the bedroom to the living room, Charles changed from his nightclothes into a clean shirt, newly polished shoes, and whatever trousers he had selected for the day.

"If I eat this goat cheese it might keep me from . . ." Charles eyed Daphne sheepishly and corrected himself. "From running off at the bowels."

"That's better than saying shit," Daphne agreed.

"Yeah, Daphne. You're like church. Isn't Daphne like church? Maybe if I stop cussin', my legs'll get better. You think so? 'Cause I'm a sinner . . . I've been all the things there are to be, the rats, the snakes, and the bees. Next time I want to be in the sky. You could wake up and be anything . . ." He looked again at Daphne. "You could be a star."

Daphne moved the wheelchair closer to his bed for the descent. "Only six more weeks of winter." She tossed her head, dismissing any notions of rebirth as she pulled on his brown flannel shirt. "The groundhog came out yesterday and saw his shadow."

"Who saw *him*?" Charles asked immediately.

Daphne stood in the center of the room and frowned out the window. "The weatherman must have seen him," she said.

"The weatherman saw the groundhog see his shadow!" Charles shouted. "Now *that's* some shit!

"Call Paul!" he said suddenly. The recording date was still on his mind. It had been on his mind all morning. "Tell Paul to come over here."

An hour later he and Paul Jeffrey sat together in the living room listening again to the tapes of the Atlantic recording, which eventually would be called *Me, Myself, an Eye.* They were discussing the performance of the two bass players.

"They don't swing at all," Charles said without enthusiasm. "They don't phrase any notes. They only play up high. They don't play the whole range of the bass. They don't make any intervals— those wide intervals . . ." He looked at Paul gloomily. "And dig this, man. Up high they ain't playing anything. They ain't playing any ideas . . . Trouble with the young cats today, nobody looks at the past. They start out like it all just started. Don't they know if you want to play bass, you have to play like Jimmy Blanton? You have to play like Oscar Pettiford. You have to play like Charles Mingus. You have to play like everyone who ever went before, and then, when that's over, you get around to playing yourself . . . You know, I used to want to be a piano player. But the day I found out I couldn't play like Art Tatum, I quit!" He looked over at Paul. "Turn it up, would you?" Paul went over and turned the tape machine even louder.

"The bassoon and the bass clarinet . . ." Charles was shouting over the tape. "They're supposed to be as strong as Harry Carney is on Duke Ellington. It's not Guy Lombardo's band! It's not Glenn

Miller! It's supposed to stand out like a *sore thumb!*" He was yelling at the top of his lungs. "I want the bottom notes *stronger!* You should hear the bass, which is the leader, at all times. You hear Duke all the time. You hear Harry Carney all the time . . . *Daphne!*" he thundered. "Daphne, come over here and fix my arm."

Daphne ran into the living room from the kitchen and began to massage his limbs. Charles and Paul turned their attention to music from another recording date, a section from "Todo Modo" on the *Cumbia and Jazz Fusion* album, which was only now being released, although Charles had recorded it the previous year. (Atlantic had just sent over a sample of the cover. It was underwear pink, and in the foreground sat a black man ten shades darker than Charles, against a backdrop of jungle-pink leaves. The man was wearing dark pants, a white shirt, and a black belt. He looked like someone we knew but he didn't look like Charles. When I asked Charles what he thought of it, all he bothered to say was "The belt's too thin.")

"Todo Modo" was an extended classical work that took up one entire side of the record and which Charles now listened to every day. It had become Daphne's favorite.

"You see!" he called out triumphantly one afternoon when she was humming a complex section in the kitchen. "You see! It's not the music that's difficult! It's the disc jockeys and the record companies! They keep us off the air. Listen to Daphne! If people heard our music every day they'd hum us like the Beatles."

The phone was ringing. Daphne ran back to the kitchen.

"My arm started going a little bit right on that date," Charles said to Paul. "I noticed it." In the background George Adams was playing flute while Charles bowed his bass in the final section.

"Mr. Sonny Rollins," Daphne called from the other room. Charles brightened. He spent a long time on the phone.

"I never got to know you too much. I just liked you," he was saying. "I heard you knew about Charlie Parker . . . Remember the time we both were booked down at the Five Spot together? I was honored to be there with you, man . . ." When their conversation was over, Daphne wheeled him back into the living room.

"You know, they don't respect our music," he said abruptly to Paul, as if the two of them were still in the middle of their talk. "The white world doesn't respect it. And you know why? Because of where it came from."

"From black people?" Paul asked helpfully.

"Not from black people but from what was done to black people and the pain they endured. And black people still lived through it. You know, if the average white man had been brought over to us in the same way, he'd have killed himself. Because suicide is a very simple thing . . . I learned that from this friend of mine. I looked at him one day and I knew he had a funny gleam in his eye, like a big joke to pull. Always when he was writing about me, it was like a joke. But he really wasn't making fun of me, he made fun of himself by blowing his brains out. That's what he did, he shot himself in the head. But he didn't kill me, man, 'cause I ain't gonna kill myself." He looked over at Paul. "Death is something we all got to face."

"I hear you."

"And so they don't respect our music," Charles continued. "They don't realize that jazz might be as good as classical music. They don't realize it might be better or that it may even have kept classical music living . . ."

Paul was pulling out some other tapes from the session. "You know," he said, setting them down on the table, "one time Monk wanted me to do a lead sheet on a tune for his daughter." He was sorting out the tapes as he talked. " 'Boo Boo's Birthday' was the tune, and I couldn't hear the changes. So I called him up to ask, you dig—I mean I ain't gonna guess. 'Cause the way Monk voices, man, he's the hardest cat to hear in the world."

"I know he is."

"And you know what he told me once? He said, 'Nobody's got

perfect pitch.' And you know what he said? He said, 'I can fuck them all up.' "

"On the voicings!"

"On the voicings. 'I can mess them all up,' he said. And then—"

"You know, there used to be a piano player in my band," Charles interrupted. "John Foster. He had perfect pitch. But you put E natural on the bottom, E flat next to that, and another E flat on top of that, he's lost!"

"He's gone!" They both roared with laughter.

"His perfect pitch is gone! Not only that," Charles said, still laughing. "Nobody's got perfect rhythm. 'Cause Monk can mess you up on that too, can make you think he's changing time. And Bird! He could make you think he was somewhere else entirely. He'd be phrasing a bar ahead of time and catch you later on with that bar he missed! No, man! Ooooh! Where are all those musicians, man?"

"They're gone! Gone!"

"You should have been with me at the Open Door club, it would have made you cry. 'Cause Monk knew how to play behind Bird. Bud didn't play right behind Bird. Bud played too many changes. But Monk said *ping . . . pinky pinky ping . . . pink . . .* and then maybe a chord . . . *poom* . . . and I'll be walking, you know, he gave me freedom, man . . . He didn't care, he knew where he was . . . *ping . . . ping* . . . Shit—you should have been there, baby! Hmmm. The Open Door on Second Avenue. We used to play there all the time.

"Bob Moss owned it," Charles continued. "He'd have these concerts with Ben Webster, Coleman Hawkins, Lester Young. He'd line them up all together, you know, and then say he wanted a loud bass player 'cause Ben Webster said, 'If you ain't got a loud bass player, I ain't gonna come!' They had no mikes in those days. No mikes, and that was right up my alley. I was with Lionel Hampton. I could run my tone right out front, project my tone out. Yeah, man, once you learn how to do it, you pull it hard and you get big blisters on your hand. I used to run my tone out, man, and Ben Webster fell in love with me that night."

"All the cats today, they've got their amps." Paul laughed.

"Yeah, they don't know how to get a tone," Charles said. "They don't know how to get a sound!"

"They can't get a sound!"

"They ain't got no chops for it!"

"No chops for the sound!" They laughed until they could no longer speak.

"Just going *pluck, pluck, pluck, pluck . . .*" Charles was still laughing. He turned his head around as far as he could move it toward the bass rack at the end of the room. "See that one over there?" He eyed the last bass in the corner. "That motherfucker has been through hell! Been through Nat King Cole. Been through Art Tatum, Charlie Parker, Lionel Hampton. Been through Duke—not long—but it went through Duke. Bud Powell . . . sheee-it!"

"Damn!"

"I bought that one myself long ago. It was the second bass I had. I've had more expensive basses but not like that one. Bill Cosby paid over ten thousand dollars for the one he gave me. It ain't played for me yet. It don't sing."

He closed his eyes for a moment. Time-out. Paul relaxed in his chair.

Off and on he had been composing lines, singing melodies into two different tape recorders and calling out the chord changes. Paul took notes; he wrote down everything Charles said. When Charles took a short nap, Paul transcribed one of the new compositions. He was making a piano arrangement so that when Jimmy Rowles came over that night he could have a shot at it.

"The Bird would have just *tore that apart*! He would have loved it! That's a bitch, man!" Jimmy Rowles was in our apartment, seated at the piano, talking to himself, trying (and having trouble with)

Charles's music. At the moment he was playing the chord changes to "Window (Chair in the Sky)," the tune Joni Mitchell was working on at home.

"Hey, gimme another chance at the channel. Now, watch it, Jim!"

Jimmy stared hopelessly at the score draped over the piano.

"Hi there, Music! Big City, I'll lick you yet!" Jimmy looked over at Charles. "Ain't it nice to be crazy?"

"It's safer," Charles agreed.

Our favorite nurse, Mr. Mackie (whose persistent optimism and homilies were beginning to wear thin, at least on my side of the aisle), massaged Charles's limbs and told him how strong his legs were.

"Push down, Charles. Push against me. See how strong you are. My God, come here, Sue! Try to bend the leg there. See? See how strong he is? Do you want to do it once more?"

Charles, pleased, pretended it made no difference. "I don't care," he said.

I got up and walked out.

Mr. Mackie insisted: "The more exercise and massage, the better off he'll be . . . It could be a miracle."

During the night, after turning Charles one more time and read-justing the position of his hands, Mr. Mackie said with satisfaction, "Solid!" I awoke enough to ask him where he had gotten such a hip saying, one so related to the world of jazz.

"It's an expression," Mr. Mackie said instructively. "It means okay. We use it when someone's done something right."

"It doesn't mean okay," Charles said haughtily in the darkness. "It means 'very well.' "

Soon they were cackling like two old hyenas over the enormous-ness of Charles's pajamas. The pajamas had been recycled from some leftover cotton Indian pantaloons fashioned long ago at the Hitch-cock estate in Millbrook for a costumed procession. Charles had marched regally in his pantaloons with the band of revelers as it snaked through the woods to a grotto where a theater event was to take place. The *I Ching* was thrown, mystical verses were chanted, and the sheer long dresses of beautiful young women moved in the breeze as they stood aloft like living statues on marble railings high above, holding tall candles that flickered in the night. Tim Leary read from Hermann Hesse's *Steppenwolf*, actors moved across the stage, and the shadow of our German shepherd Muttley loomed wolflike over the proceedings. A *Life* magazine photographer snapped pictures for the following week's edition.

What remained of that pageantry now were only the elephantine white pants created in the sewing room off the kitchen of the mansion at a time when it seemed to all of us that we were at the center of things. Now Charles and Mackie croaked uncontrollably over the width of his trousers.

In the middle of their revelry the phone rang. It was our friend Daniele Senatore calling from Rome. It must have been long after midnight his time; perhaps he'd been drinking. He said the Russians had discovered a treatment for ALS and that three people had been cured. He asked for the name of the disease in Latin and spoke of medicines he would bring. We agreed to suspend hope until we knew for certain. Nonetheless, my heart lifted. All night long I smiled. It would be a miracle, of course, but people have been snatched from the mouth of the beast before. Why not us? Now I could tell Charles the truth and there would be a happy ending.

The next day Daniele called from New York. His voice sounded fast and nervous. "I have good news," he said. He began to talk about the recording date with Joni Mitchell. I realized there was no miracle.

"That's great," I said, my voice cold and forced. "And what about the other?" I asked in Italian.

"They will send medicine," he said.

"But is there really a cure?" I asked.

"They have a cure for three kinds of sclerosis," he said. (Last night he had said three people were cured.) "There are ten different kinds."

I was so depressed that even Charles questioned me as I sat on his bed.

"Are you pooped?" he asked.

"I guess so," I replied.

"You'll feel better tomorrow," he said.

Tomorrow I told him the truth.

Six

"Relax your body, tighten your mind and be cool."
—*Hambone, a bebop trombone player*
from California

It was late March, 1978, almost spring. We sat on our balcony staring at the sun as it hung bloodshot over the river like the eye of Medusa, paralyzing the city, lighting up a thousand skyscraper windows in a final blinding moment before dark.

"I had a dream about all the witches," Charles said from his corner of the porch after the horizon disappeared. "Mamie Pleasant and Hazel Scott. They wanted me as a warlock." He sat in his wheelchair, his head leaning over his neck brace. His shoulders under the black cloth of his African robes were becoming pointed and bony, tucked around his neck like the wings of a large sleeping bird.

"Did you go with them?" I asked. I knew the singer Hazel Scott—

she'd come by recently with some magical amulets and three kinds of ice cream—but I wasn't sure about Mamie Pleasant.

"I was too old for them," he said. "I don't mean in age, but in births and deaths."

He had just told a friend over the phone that he was "waitin' on Godot"—that his dreams were full of all the witches, devils, and saints; that he felt great inside but not being able to move was like being in handcuffs.

"They were bad dreams," he went on, after hanging up the phone. "Planetary wives under the earth were trying to claim me. I joined the voodoo cult once with Katherine Dunham here in New York. Hazel Scott was one of them. My dreams . . ." He paused. "When life first began, I was there. I know that now. I'm short of something here on earth that I missed. I keep coming back. All those mixtures—one-quarter Chinese, one-quarter West Indian, one part black, one part white, all those mixes. My identity is mixed together with Beethoven, Bach, and Brahms. It may sound crazy to you but I'm all right. I'm waitin' on Godot . . ."

We sat together in the dark. I heard him hum a little in a cracked voice. Just a little.

"You look relaxed."

"I am. I have good people around me."

"Yes," I agreed, thinking of the nurses, thinking perhaps he meant me.

"Oscar Pettiford. Duke. I saw them today," he continued. "Out in the other room. I'm not afraid anymore. You know, when I was up at Yale for that honorary event before Duke died, he looked at me a couple of times. In a special way. Once when he was being carried up a back stairway—he couldn't walk up stairs then. Well, he looked at me again today in the same way. And I saw Butter. And Harry Carney. And Ray Nance. And Bird . . ."

"I love you." I put my arms around him.

"Roses to you." He smiled.

. . .

Next morning the ghosts were back at the bottom of his bed. He treated them with the familiarity of his muse or of his melody, which had always waited for him on the keys whenever he awakened in the middle of the night and felt his way to the piano to compose. At least that's how it had been before his illness.

His bass playing, though, was another matter: the eight hours a day to strengthen one finger, the mastery, the virtuosity—he took credit for that. But the melody, he said, came from God. I imagined the ghosts in our apartment were just part of that connection.

"Boo," he called slyly from the other bed. "Want to come over?" I slipped into the rented hospital bed next to my own before the morning nurse arrived and wrapped my arms around his thinning shoulders. The nurses, like the ministers and physicians, kept their distance; they'd learned not to get involved. I, too, in the daytime, was straight up and sturdy like the nurses, keeping my feelings in the closet. But at nighttime, I imagined ways to murder Charles. For example, I could have taken him, motionless and strapped into the van, to Woodstock, where I would clean Roberto's hunting rifle and it would go off in his face. Like the French girl in Aspen who killed a skier and got six weeks in jail. I would explain it to the judge, my moral position—why the world owed Charles an easy death. Or I would tell Charles that we could avoid the loneliness-of-death syndrome the psychiatrist had warned us about last week by sharing it together, getting into the van and simply driving off the road.

"I'll stick around for the pussy, Mama!" His voice sailed through the apartment, full of Mingus life. *"Can't let go of that, Mama, no way!"*

Or I could provide him with pills, I imagined—provide his means of suicide. But then I thought of the restless souls they say stalk the earth and remembered how Charles himself once called out from the bedroom, as I sat working on some galley proofs in the kitchen late at night, that a woman spirit was disturbing his peace and his sleep in the adjoining room. Later we learned that a woman down the hall had thrown herself from the roof, long ago. Now she was back: one of those resilient, restless spirits who could not sleep either.

"Call Dizzy!" Charles's voice rose from the bedroom one more time. I went back to tell him Dizzy Gillespie had already phoned and was coming to visit later in the day. Charles beamed with delight.

They'd spoken together the week before.

"You better not go anywhere 'fore I get there," Dizzy had warned over the phone. "Don't start no shit . . ."

"My big toe went dead," Charles had told him. "And then another. And then my whole leg. And my arms. It's a nerve thing." He didn't mind discussing the facts with Dizzy. "Some people think there are things that can help."

"It's slowly making you immobile . . . you can't use your hands . . . I'd better hurry and see you, motherfucker, before you check out," Dizzy had said. "You travel in a wheelchair? You bad off, nigger."

"I go out if there ain't too many stairways."

"How's your weight?"

"I ain't got too much appetite, anyway."

"You got a juicer?"

"Yeah . . . How's your wife?" Charles asked.

"She's real good . . . I'll be in this week."

"I love you."

"Don't start no shit," Dizzy said.

Charles smiled to himself. He remembered a concert in Europe long ago when Dizzy was playing on the bandstand and he was standing below, some distance away, thinking about Dizzy's importance and hoping Dizzy would live forever. Although his back was turned, Dizzy swung around suddenly and asked out loud where all the love he felt was coming from. Then he looked straight at Charles.

"You really do love me, don't you?" Dizzy said. "I felt just then like I was in heaven!"

I thought how I, too, could sense Charles's gaze, how I could feel a lifetime's worth of courage and stubbornness pushing past the obstacles, the terrible paralysis, and warming me with his strength. The force field around him was like Jupiter's, a friend once observed, and it hadn't diminished with illness. Even in a wheelchair, at the mercy of a buzzing fly or a sudden stab of sunlight, his resolve did not falter.

The week before, when a friend who was suffering from depression called from her third-floor loft to announce she was throwing herself off the terrace, his reply was immediate.

"Tell her to come over here," he said. "We're forty floors higher up."

Roberto added his view: "To threaten suicide is in bad taste. It's an attempt to inflict guilt. It's in bad taste."

Not much sympathy from our side of the tracks. Arranger Sy Johnson pointed out how upbeat things appeared when he came over to do an interview for the Smithsonian. "I was feeling like hell," he said. "Mingus cheered me up."

Charles was as tough on his son, who'd threatened suicide years before, firing off a long letter to him that listed various options— advising him, for example, of the strongest rope (number 29) if it was to be a noose and observing, finally, that his paintings would be worth more money after his death.

He'd removed the stinging impact and drama of it and turned it into a paltry event. It worked.

At the graveyard, which seemed to be indoors, we looked for his slab on the ground. The church service was in full swing—the house was packed. Someone was shouting at me. Perhaps Charles weighed too much for the coffin. But they insisted they had fit him in easily, bent him right into place.

In the half light I awoke from my dream and looked across the room. Charles was staring at me.

"That chlorohydrate ain't worth shit," he said. "We should tell Dr. Aldin it don't do nothin'. I took eight of 'em the other night, I tried to kill myself and nothing happened. I didn't even fall asleep."

"They didn't work?" I asked in a hoarse voice, coming out of the stupor of sleep. Did he really try to kill himself? I felt the relief of disaster avoided. I also felt resentment. He hadn't thought of my own feelings, hadn't considered me at all. My future or anyone else's was not on his mind. I tried to treat the resentment as something to hang on to for company if I was left alone, something to break the fall into sheer loneliness.

"So you tried to kill yourself?" I said at last, as I knew he was waiting for me to do. "Why did you do that?" I knew that if fifteen Doredons hadn't done him in (he took them, in the old days, as a matter of course to combat insomnia), then eight of these milder pills would have proved ineffective. I was certain he knew that too, that he hadn't really tried to kill himself, only considered the possibility. He was holding it in reserve as an escape hatch, trying the idea out on me now for size.

"My hands have gone," he said simply.

His dying is severe and dignified, as steeped in reality as Camus. When I mention that a minister had called and might stop over, he was silent. He used the Bible recently only as a weight to press the damp thermo heating pad closer to his skin.

"Maybe I'll get well," he said. "Or the opposite."

"One or the other."

I approach and touch him, put my head on his knee, bring him grapes. I have ordered the Hoyer lift again and the sling. Daphne and I can no longer handle him, he is turning into deadweight. Still, he gives the commands, calls out the numbers, the time, the beat: "One, two, three," as he used to on the bandstand. On the count of four, Daphne or Mr. Mackie and I lift him to a standing position, our shoulders under his armpits.

Paul and Charles discuss the music continuing, whether or not Charles himself performs.

"After all," Paul points out, "what did Stravinsky play?"

"He played pencil." Charles laughs.

Today he sang out three new tunes—a blues and two ballads. He used a metronome to keep time.

Yesterday, in a moment of frustration, he fixed his attention angrily on my birdcage in the living room, complaining that it was dusty, full of feathers, and interfered with his breathing. As a result, my doves were exiled to a tiny cage in the back room beside my desk, where they resumed their life, one sitting as always on her infertile eggs, the other perched on a wooden rung. Like Charles, they have adjusted to their new quarters, to the limitations of their movements, to the murderous and senseless attacks on their well-being.

Last night for a brief time I visited friends in the building after midnight. Their guests included a black actress with big tits and flamboyant shoes, married to a wealthy playboy from Rome; a manager of a New York jazz club; one or two musicians and/or actors; a hostess with a lot of coke who kept making lines, passing a rolled bill, offering fat joints of grass and waiting for her husband to come home who never did. Every time I looked for matches on the table I upset somebody's stash. I barely spoke to anyone. Real life, hip or ordinary, is now as removed from my current existence as someone else's dream.

On the phone, Max Roach said: "Stay strong." I told him when anyone talks about a drummer, Charles always says, "Yeah, but he's not

Max Roach." I asked if he could find commissions to help keep Charles busy—Charles always wanted to write for a symphony orchestra. I left similar messages for Gunther Schuller, Zubin Mehta, Seiji Ozawa, Leonard Bernstein. Bernstein's office was the only one that returned the call. I talked to someone at the New York Philharmonic. I tried Alvin Ailey. Things, as they say, don't happen overnight. One of the chamber groups I approached called to say they would make an offer next September. I told them now or never. The Cuban Mission to the United Nations called to arrange a tour for next October. I said they were a year too late.

His heavy arm like an anchor against loneliness is wrapped around my waist; his deadweight, his warmth and uneven breathing, cover my back like a life preserver. We lie together in the dark morning as the nurse adjusts the sheet or cranks the bed, and I arrange myself among the pillows in a way that will ease the pressure of my shoulder against the cold steel of the bed rail or soften the weight of his lifeless arm across my stomach. I lie in the dim light keeping watch over the metal and chains and bars that hold together our precarious embrace in this tomblike room. How natural it seems already! The trappings of his disease have become ornaments that sparkle among the plants and Sicilian folk art, the shiny Hoyer lift as ordinary as a hangman's noose for the executioner. Only six months ago I wanted to disguise the metal lift, throw colorful spreads around the bed steel. Now even the ministerings of the nurses on the periphery of our intimacy are as far from our consciousness, as familiar and ignored, as the shifts of light that flicker through the window curtains.

On my desk, a confusion of faith, surrender, and day-to-day plodding ahead: names to invite to Charles's birthday party on April 22 (if he's still alive), a note to buy silk pajamas (he once said he wanted to be buried in them), a note to call a certain friend and ask him to replace the two dozen Doredon he once borrowed.

When he gives up, perhaps I will shoot him. Or else he will need a bucketful of pills.

On April 2, Charles threw a surprise party for me, organized it secretly from his wheelchair, and got me something I'd wanted all my life—the complete set of thirteen volumes of the *Oxford English Dictionary*. It was one of the few times I lost control. At the party Roberto read out loud before the assembled guests what Charles had asked him to inscribe. Roberto printed it himself in block letters inside the first volume, as Charles could no longer write or hold a pen:

TO SUE

THE GREATEST FRIEND I'VE EVER HAD

LOVE CHARLES

I burst into tears in front of everyone.

Charles dresses up as usual every morning in clean, immaculate clothing, shiny shoes, pressed shirts—selecting the colors or matching outfits he fancies that day in order to travel in his wheelchair from the bedroom to the living room. Who would have imagined a day when the high point would be belly-laughing through *All in the Family* on television? Who would have imagined that this sitcom could make anything, even his own recovery, seem possible? Except for watching some old Victor Mature gladiator movies with my son during Roberto's teenage years, he never turned on the tube. He went straight to the piano. But here he was, Charlie Mingus, looking forward to afternoon reruns of Archie Bunker.

I remembered when monster movies and horror flicks were too scary to watch. Now nothing bothered me. The worst had happened. It was liberating, like a high wind that blows everything away. When you've watched your husband go from being one of the most physical, dynamic men you've ever known to being a cabbage in a wheelchair without losing his magnetism or his passion or his desirability, then nothing seems strange any longer. You cease to think in terms of injury or aberration. The unthinkable is something ordinary, part of the day, like breakfast.

On April 22, three weeks after mine, Charles had a birthday himself. Early in the morning, before he awoke, we decorated the apartment with grapes, Charles's favorite snack. I'd ordered seventy pounds the day before, big black grapes and green seedless grapes. Our living room quickly turned into a living jungle as we sneaked around at dawn to prepare the event. His visiting children, Carolyn and Eric, his nephew Henry, our nurse Big George, all of us hung grapes from the birdcage, the wine rack, and the lamps. We strung them along the wooden frame of the bass stand like a grape arbor. Grapes spilled out of plants, piled up inside pots, filled baskets and bowls. They towered above the speakers and the liquor cabinet. They transformed the dining room table and the piano. They dangled from the base of the wooden statue and hung from the candelabra. Even the windows sprouted grapes from their handles.

When Charles entered the room he laughed out loud and ate grapes for a whole hour, indicating to Big George the different bowls or platters or plants from which he wanted grapes next—even though they were all the same—munching seriously and contentedly.

Then, at 6 p.m., the surprise birthday party began. Guests who had been waiting outside in the corridor filed through the door all at once, laden with food and gifts and flowers and wines and an enormous strawberry-and-whipped-cream birthday cake that rose like a monument from a huge piece of Sheetrock covered with tinfoil, created by our artist friends Mel and Jeannie in their loft downtown.

Charles was in the living room watching TV with the kids, Big

George, and Muttley. The sun's rays still lit up the enormous green plant on the piano as they filtered through the terrace windows. Charles looked up with his beautiful smile. Under his breath he said with delight, "That bitch planned a party!"

When he noticed Izzy—one of the regulars from Bradley's, our old hangout—standing uncertainly in front of his wheelchair, he grinned. "Aren't you going to pick up my hand and shake it and say hello?"

The party lasted until 3 a.m., with a few musicians, Daniele, and some Italian stragglers winding out the final hours as we played Debussy and Prokofiev and Beethoven and Mingus and consumed three cases of champagne and quantities of white wine and liquor.

As I walked Muttley in my old fur coat in the night after the party, my mournful face obscured in the dark, someone called out from a passing car: "Got anyone to go home to?" I wondered if I would bite down on a line like that one day from the bottom of loneliness. Muttley and I headed up Tenth Avenue, the weather almost balmy, snow melting through the dismal streets of Hell's Kitchen, where my father had walked seventy years before past some of these same buildings. Now the streets were lined with pinball-machine concessions, pirate recording companies (I recognized the names), pirate record distributors, a Greek printer, drab little delis. I thought again of my English grandfather, with his innocence and impracticality and refinement, struggling in the tenement life that lined the avenue. He was starting a new life then. Seventy-five years later, I was ending one.

"My soul was carried into my body by birds when I was born," Charles mumbled as I lit a candle in the room and he prepared for sleep. He had taken seven Doredons. "Carried by birds like angels," he said. "I remember."

All night he talked on in the dark. He dreamed two birds had carried off his soul to hell. Later he asked me what half men–half horses were called. I told him they were centaurs and belonged to Greek mythology.

"Oh, they're real, baby. I promise you. They're real."

"I was talking to a Korean," he reported when he awakened next morning. "I met him and could speak with him in his language. He said *"tee an ke la ke la ke la he n'."*

I was reminded of Gopi Krishna, an Indian clerk, who experienced Kundalini and subsequently spoke several languages, wrote volumes of poetry and philosophy, and, according to authorities on such experiences, hooked into a universal mind-consciousness that feeds the elect: the poet, the saint, or, more democratically, the dying.

"It's like that." Charles nodded.

Meanwhile the machinery was grinding for our trip to the White House to celebrate the Newport Jazz Festival's twenty-fifth anniversary. George Wein's Festival Office had cleared Roberto so that he could come along to help. Roberto, home from college for the weekend, was singing in the bathroom, weighing himself on our hospital scale in his white suit and inventing imaginary exchanges with the president. He has grown more exultant over his impending trip to the White House with each passing day. Yesterday he searched for brown-and-white wing-tip shoes at Church's and McGreedy's and Bloomingdale's to wear with his white suit. He imagines shaking hands with President Carter in the receiving line—a sock or shoe stuffed inside his breast pocket to unnerve the Secret Service behind Carter's shoulder—and then, when the agents frisked him, pulling out, with a debonair flourish, the hidden shoe.

"Always carry along an extra wing tip, you know," he said briskly.

I felt no exultation, although it was not the worldly disregard of

Daniele who plops ice cubes into his Dom Perignon with ennui while others toast; it was the failure of power, even a president's, to reverse the tide.

I have become a recluse of illness. Driving across Greenwich Village on Sunday through the crush of strollers jamming the sunny streets, I sat high above the crowd in the big Chevy van, as removed as an airplane pilot, perched in the oversized four-wheel drive that Charles pretended he bought "for the band" last year when he showed up proudly one afternoon behind the wheel.

Still, one hangs on to the normal progression of time: someone is coming with his trumpet at 2 p.m.; a California script must be read; Sunday is Mother's Day; today, a street fair. I priced a secondhand Ambulet to buy next week for $2,500 in case there was a next week, and then called my friend again to whom I once loaned twenty sleeping pills—his wife used them up before she died—and ordered him crossly to get more. After which I reported to Charles that I was trying to cover the waterfront: behave as if there were a tomorrow, call about film scores, plan dinner, and try to obtain pills so he could do himself in.

Mother's Day, May 14, "Cashing in on the original investment," Roberto calls it.

Dizzy Gillespie came to visit today, sly and boisterous, as is his way. He reported to Charles that his wife had lit a twenty-five-year candle for him and therefore Charles could not go anywhere until his time was up, which just about knocked Charles out. Dizzy put two fifty-dollar bills in the drawer of the bedside table. He brought two crushed Cuban cigars from his visit to Havana, which he had been saving in tinfoil in the refrigerator. He tried to put Charles's hand on the trapeze bar over the bed, but it wouldn't stay.

He was (it seemed to me) unduly rough. Charles cried out. Dizzy tried again.

There is a rapport between jazz musicians—at least male musicians—that is laconic and understood. It may be their way of remaining men in a rotten world. Or their aversion to the obvious. Or it may be their endlessly imaginative souls and spirits. Sometimes, to an outsider, it's as if they've blown their hearts away.

"I know you love me," Charles said.

"I love you," Dizzy said back.

Later that night while listening to an old Savoy reissue with Charles, I said: "Dizzy is crazy, isn't he?" I looked over, waiting for Charles to agree.

"He's beautiful," Charles declared.

Ornette Coleman came by the following day, another thoughtful visit of support from one of his peers. It was a bad afternoon and Charles dozed off while Ornette was still beside his bed. Somewhere inside me I couldn't help remembering Charles's "calypso player" dismissal of Ornette long ago at the Five Spot and wondered if a residue of that old competitive spirit remained under his eyelids.

There is only his illness. I sit at the phone seeking miracle medicines, uncovering pockets of ALS activity: a center here in New York at St. Vincent's Hospital; a physician outside San Francisco experimenting with a substance called Guarnadine; a cobra venom doctor in Florida. I investigate vitamin injections, biofeedback, hypnosis, acupuncture, new muscle relaxers from Switzerland, breakthroughs in Russia, medications in Italy from a Russian formula . . . When someone asks what I do, I no longer remember. I am enclosed in the apartment with matters as urgent as a head of state running a country that is under attack.

"He's going to die, Mom," Roberto says to me out in the hall. "You have to get used to it . . . He had a good life. We all come from somewhere. He'll go on . . ." He puts his arm around me. My efforts to be strong are wearing thin.

"We have to rehearse." Charles was speaking like a schoolteacher to Malcolm, the new nursing attendant, from his wheelchair parked in front of the bathroom.

"Now we'll rehearse going to the bathroom, making this turn in the hall. You have to leave space there for me to get up from the walker. Do you understand? And the shaving procedure. Do you understand?" Malcolm was giving it his all.

"Shave up. No, *up,* shave *up,* like the sky. You know where the sky is, man. Shave up. *Up!*" Malcolm finally got it.

"Not so long in one place, man. We'll be here all day . . ."

On the phone with Sonny Rollins later in the afternoon, the two of them were talking things out.

"I'm bad, Sonny. It's gotten worse. It's time."

"Maybe it's a reckoning . . ." Sonny said. "Maybe you gotta go on to something else . . . Right now I'm looking for a drummer. Gonna take some time off. Rethink things . . . What do the doctors say?"

"They ain't got no cure for this. The hospital would only hook me up."

"Have a lot of people come?"

"Not a lot. Some."

"You going out?"

"No, it's getting to be too big a strain. Cat bumped my head on the car door last night . . . Just don't let Sue put me in a fuckin' box. I want to be cremated. In India. I don't want to be anywhere near America. I don't want no musician's funeral. She knows that. Just remind her."

"Yeah, I've got my stuff made out. I'm going to be cremated and put in the Hudson River."

"Oh yeah? You'll be out there with Billy Strayhorn."

"He did that?"

"I want to be in strange territory if I can afford it. I don't want any undertakers messing with my insides. I want it all together." He laughed. "You goin' in the Hudson, man?" he asked Sonny. "Why not the East River? Why the Hudson? 'Cause it goes out to the ocean? You know, Swami Vivekananda and Ramakrishna were the only cats who got through to me. I thought they might come visit me when I split. I used to go to spiritual meetings at the Vedanta Society . . ."

He recounted Dizzy's visit. "Yeah, Dizzy was here. Still the same 'Get outta that bed, nigger!' shit. And then he said, 'See, you moved your hand.' He twisted it around and hurt it. Same old Dizzy! Looks good. Lost all that weight. All his stomach is gone! Didn't talk about himself too much. But he called back next day to say he heard I was doing something for the Ellington band. Told me to get up outta bed and do it . . .

"I'm getting up right now and get me some carrot juice. But I can't take too much 'cause I'm going to the Fats Waller show—yeah, *Ain't Misbehavin'*—and I can't be peein' too much at the show.

"Remember how we used to put fifteen cents in the jukebox movies and you could see him in person? Whoever's portrayin' him in a play shouldn't have too much trouble. You know he was a graduate of Juilliard? Yeah . . . Then, when he came out, he did what he decided to do . . .

"Miles? No, I haven't seen him. But I know he's feelin' good." Charles laughed deeply, his body shaking.

While he was talking to Sonny about Bird's death, Charles had tears in his eyes. Then he switched the subject to Sonny himself.

"Those rock musicians," he said, "they come and go by the thousands. You're a leader, Sonny. You're supposed to carry on the tradition. You're supposed to put them down. You're supposed to play

Sonny Rollins. The people out there, they'll listen to it. Not the masses, because this is a capitalist bullshit country.

"I heard your record over the radio the other day, but it didn't sound like you. The beat was off somewhere else. It sounded like somebody copying you. You gotta come over so we can talk the truth to each other. I used to try to find a name that was right, I tried jazzical, ex-slave music, black classical music, but the critics wanted to go on calling it jazz . . .

"You know, aside from baseball, it's the only creation America has, and the White House is about to admit that. I know you haven't deserted yourself, but you're not playing you. You know I can't swing like you. But I never stopped playing myself."

Later, when we were discussing how he and Sonny were having their ashes scattered in different parts of the world, I asked if he planned to come back to me afterward. He laughed and said, "I'm never going to leave."

Dexter Gordon stood in our living room swaying on his heels, recounting musician road stories for Charles with large gestures and a croaking voice. "You dig?" he said with pleasure. "I mean, there was my drummer backstage and these two cats slide in while me, I'm off in the corner unhooking my horn . . ." He paused so that his slow, long gestures could catch up with his words. "The set is over, you see, and I hear these two guys say: 'You *bad,* baby, you can *blow!* Where you from, bro?' and my drummer, he just shuffles from shoe to shoe and says: 'Nurk.' And me, I'm adjusting my horn and I'm cracking up because I *know,* you see, I've heard it before and so I've got my face all closed off and the two local dudes, they're saying: 'Huh? Wazzat?' And my drummer, he moves his shoulders up and down and says again: 'Nurk.' And I know these cats ain't never gonna figure that one out, 'cause all the cats from Newark, see, they say 'Nurk,' it's the way it is, and my drummer, he's so cool, baby, so slow and easy, he just stands there, not communicatin' . . ."

Dexter's voice was big and husky and amused, wrapped inside his recollections, canceling everything else in the room.

When Dexter left, Charles, who had other things on his mind during most of the visit, said to me, "Call the bass repairman."

"About what?" I asked.

"He will know the dates and makers of the basses."

"So?"

His voice rose clear and pragmatic from the bedroom. "That way, when you sell them, you can advertise what records they were played on. That way they can be *heard*."

The planning for death when it is near at hand is like a fever. Days come and go like surreal scraps of paper blowing in the wind: Tuesdays, Saturdays, they are all the same. Today I checked out the complicated procedures involved in having one's remains sent to India, where Charles wishes to be cremated ("I don't want no one touching me in this country") and his ashes scattered in the Ganges.

"I'd like to find out about burial in India," I said to a receptionist at the Indian Embassy.

"Beral?" she said.

"Burial."

"Borali?"

"Do you have anyone who speaks English?" I asked.

"We speak British English," she said stiffly.

I was connected to the consul general.

"I don't know. It's without precedent," he said.

"Everything he did was unprecedented," I said irritably. "What's so difficult about it?"

"You'd need to speak to someone at the Ministry of Home Affairs in Benares. The ceremony in the Ganges is in Benares. You know, it is a Hindu custom. One is cremated and then the ashes are immersed in the Ganges. But I don't know. If he were already in India, it would be different."

I called a jazz fan in Vancouver whose relatives are Sikhs. I spoke with Neshui Ertegun at Atlantic Records, who has business arrangements with India. He said he would see what he could do.

Late tonight we heard the entire recording of the new album, *Cumbia and Jazz Fusion,* over WRVR.

"You're super bad," Mr. Mackie said proudly in the hip jargon he was currently adopting. "You're gonna take over New York. That's my man!" He beamed.

Charles couldn't help smiling. "Still, I feel like a fool in a wheelchair," he said.

"Don't be ridiculous," Mackie replied immediately. "George Wallace goes everywhere, he does all his business from a wheelchair."

"He's an evil man."

"Yes, he is," Mackie agreed.

"Still, I feel castrated like this. I don't mind my legs, but I'm a musician, man, and they took my hands away from me. All I want back is my hands . . .

"Hey, Sue," he called over to me. "They want a film score! How can I compose a film score like this?"

Michael Chamberg, the coproducer of *Heartbeat,* had come by earlier to discuss a three-million-dollar Warner Brs. film on the beats, a story about Jack Kerouac and Neal Cassady. He needed a film score and a musical director.

"Well, you could sing the melodies and then talk the harmonies to someone," I said.

He was already composing on the tape recorder. "Yeah, I could do that," he said.

The subject moved on to the musical failings of other nurses: " 'Uh . . . uh . . . my God to thee'—that's how she sings. She's messin' my ears up, man . . . ." He was describing Hermaline's incessant

"Jesus singing." "I don't want no amateur shit around me." He looked over at Mackie. "At least Mackie's in key." He grinned as Mackie adjusted his pillow, pleased.

Under heavy rains and dark skies I met with Gerry Mulligan and his muscans at the Brazilian consulate to conclude the visa arrangements for his South American tour, which was replacing Charles's. The outside world, the other egos—how supremely unimportant they had become. I was uneasy every moment away from home.

And, still, we had no way of knowing that in a few weeks' time, Gerry's trip would alter the course of what was left of our life.

"Help me, Jesus! Get out of my body, Devil! I'm with you, God, Jesus, I'm in you, Christ!" Charles was standing up next to the bed, swaying and bending and holding on to Mackie, but standing nonetheless. He had had a dream: I was with him, we were trying to find our way to God. Earlier I'd read from Ramakrishna and we'd talked together in the dark holding hands. Now he managed to stand on his feet for a few moments, Mackie encouraging him: "Sway from side to side . . . you can do it! Move that way, stand up straight . . . put your head back!"

"Oh, yeah," Charles said, throwing back his head. "Oh, yeah!"

On the weekend we Medicabbed down to Cooper Union to attend a performance of *Revelations,* a piece Charles wrote in 1957. It was part of a Philharmonic series called "Prospective Encounters." Gunther Schuller conducted. I sat on the arm of Charles's wheelchair in the front row; behind us, in a roped-off area, were friends. Charles recognized a flute player onstage who had been at the original recording date twenty years before and they saluted each other with their eyes; Charles had tears in his. Trombonist Jimmy Knepper was there too. I wiped Charles's nose and my own throughout the performance, wondering if the pain of the concert was worth it. He received a standing ovation at the end.

Afterward we went backstage, where Atlantic Records had planned a belated birthday celebration, and remained until past midnight drinking champagne with friends and musicians. Despite the emotions of the evening, Charles still managed to point out to Gunther Schuller the errors he had made in the final jazz section ("It didn't swing"). Gunther swallowed graciously.

"When I did *Revelations,*" Charles said the following day, "it was going to be the way of the future. It was just the first movement. I wanted to show the traditional and then carve the way for the new music.

"Oh, it was hard," he recalled, "it was very hard to write that music."

That evening, he sang a composition into the tape recorder straight through from beginning to end as he lay in the darkness, his voice energy rising hoarse in his throat, his breath miraculously sustained. Each day he made note of the change—a swelling in his left hand, a loss of motion in his arm—reporting the failures like a purveyor of the evening news, a commentator on the decline of his state. Shouting out a musical line for arranger Paul Jeffrey, who was helping notate the new material, he said, in what was only an aside: "It's hard to get the time, I can't beat my hand anymore." He banged his left hand on the wheelchair arm a few times, trying to catch the right tempo.

"I used to worry about hurting my hands," he mused. "As a kid I always thought I was a coward. I lost most of the encounters. I mean, I didn't want to hurt nobody else either." He laughed.

"You'd be afraid as hell when you're supposed to fight. I was no braver later on. I know when two people weighing two hundred pounds are hitting each other both people get hurt. A guy hits you with his hand, he hurts his hand. That's why they use boxing gloves . . ."

He banged his hand one more time on the wheelchair.

"You know, I was traveling alone most of the time with my cello. I didn't make friends. That's the reason I got picked on. I still do. There was a white guy named Homer who always bothered me. One time when Britt Woodman saw me take the insults, he said, 'Man, you don't have to take that. Why don't you go outside and whip him?' I had been training, so I said, 'Okay, let's go.'

"So we went outside. I knew he couldn't fight. He didn't even know how to hold his guard up. I could tell the way he swung at me—roundhouse punches. So I caught a couple of his punches and one right cross and he was finished. A jab, a hook, and a cross. Miles Davis is a good boxer. He knows as much as the average pro for his weight. If he hadn't been a trumpet player, he might have been a champion. And Max Roach is good. And Walter Bishop." He looked out the window. "All those personalities . . ." He was staring at the Jersey skyline across the river. "You can tell they've traveled alone. They don't worry about nothin' too much."

One gray afternoon he said: "I'd slash my wrists but I can't move my hands."

For a brief period he wanted out. "I don't deserve this," he said. "It's not natural."

It was already too late.

"I can't even kill myself. I can't reach for the pills." He phoned Roberto and asked him to pick up fifty Doredons on Fourteenth Street. An hour later, after an invigorating massage from the nurse, he called back for some Dannon yogurt boysenberry ice-cream bars as well.

"Dannons and Doredon." Roberto shook his head as he entered the bedroom. "You're crazy, man." Charles peered up sheepishly. Roberto had scored only the ice cream.

The following day, however, we succeeded: fifty Doredons apiece from two different doctors. Late at night in the middle of a thunderstorm I sped across town to the offices of a legal expert for advice about mercy killings (no discussions on the phone).

"Murder," he pointed out solemnly, "is against the law. Mercy killings may be morally justifiable, but legally they are not. Murder without a motive is no excuse. Society makes moral distinctions, but the law does not. There is guilty or not guilty."

I consulted another attorney the next day. "Get a family doctor," he advised. "Someone you can call to sign the death certificate. Unless a relative questions it, there will be no autopsy." Still another attorney warned that if there were an autopsy and if Charles had too much medication and if someone could prove intention, a person could go to jail.

Roberto and Charles joked together about the impending overdose. "More Doredon," Charles croaked from his pillow as Roberto picked up bottles from the table and read the labels. "Uh-oh, fingerprints. Send me to jail, man . . . ruin my career . . ."

"You better be an attorney, mothafucka."

We have orchestrated the event. We have decided to harness George's severe and dependable drinking habit to our own ends. Roberto, myself, and George will administer individually a quantity of sleeping pills that, taken together, will constitute an overdose. Neither suicide nor murder, it will be an accident, a combination of circumstances. Charles was ready. He said George was so drunk tonight he wouldn't know the difference.

"My butt hurts. It's from sitting in this chair. Sitting with no more muscles to support me. My shoulders hurt. It's from being manhandled by drunk nurses who don't know how to lift me. It's from wear and tear on the bones. It's not arthritis. Don't cry. You're a big girl now. Everybody's got to die. But I don't deserve this. It's not a natural death. I'd go crazy like this. Like in the old days. You wouldn't want me to be crazy . . .

"George," he called out. "That's my broad, I'm hugging her." He was referring to the pillows under his arm. "You know what a hug is, don't you?"

"I hear you." George adjusted Charles's heavy arm over the two pillows nestled against his chest.

An hour later we began the rehearsal, the dry run, of the terrible event. "Hey, gimme eight of those yellow pills," Charles said when George entered the room. He indicated the bottle of Doredon with his eyes.

"No, not that one, the tall bottle next to the lamp."

George fumbled nervously among the twenty or so containers of pills stashed on the bed table. "Here they are," he said thickly. He poured out eight pills. Roberto and I raised straight-armed fists of triumph. Charles beamed. We had pulled it off.

"It's nice," he said later on, more or less to himself. "Another dimension. And then the pearly gates!" He smiled. "Only trouble is, the devil's out there waiting."

In the hall, en route to bed, Roberto said to me: "Charles is a good sport. It's a rough game. You mustn't worry. He knows what he's doing." Then he called to the bedroom, "I love you, man!"

"I love you, too, man!" Charles called back.

I approached his bed. "I can't do it," I said miserably. "Not tonight. Give me a week."

Perhaps the act of taking destiny into his own hands changed things. Perhaps he never meant it at all. Or perhaps he simply changed his mind.

"All right," he agreed.

We never discussed it again.

. . .

"You looked nice in your black tonight," he said. "We'll write all the songs tomorrow, do all the projects . . . the movie. Pilobolus, the string quartets." He was making plans, looking ahead.

"Find out about Les Paul and his wife. They recorded and then speeded up the sound an octave higher. I have to hear myself. I have to hear my voice the way it should be. I don't know if I can get up that high. *Eeeeee . . . Eeeeeeee* . . . I still can do it, I haven't lost my voice yet . . . How old am I, fifty-five?"

"Fifty-six."

"I still feel young . . . You know why I want to split? I don't want you to go through this. You shouldn't have to."

Mackie's routines resound through the apartment: the countdowns, the squeaking bed, the running monologue, the high-pitched laugh. "Come to me . . . No problem . . . Kick me down . . ." while Joni Mitchell's tape plays in the other room:

> *Manhattan holds me*
> *To a chair in the sky,*
> *With a Bird in my ear*
> *And boats in my eye.*

Charles called Joni on the phone. "It's not about Bird," he said. "It sounds as if it's about me." He thanked her for her hard work and told her she had imagination. He listened to the song one more time.

"Maybe if I take Doredon it'll be like hypnosis," he said cheerfully. "Maybe I'll break the chair and come out of this. I'll talk to you while I do it. I'll describe the feelings." After a while he said, "I'll take Scotch and milk with the pills so I won't be sick."

"I know someone who died like that," I said. "Alcohol and Doredon."

He frowned. Does he really imagine the pills would knock him out of a trance, out of his paralysis, and not into death at all?

"Nobody wants to die," he said quietly.

In the elevator, actors discuss their plays, musicians complain about their gigs, the sound of practicing echoes down the hall.

"I'm doing six weeks in Miami."

"Oh, yeah? Tomorrow we leave for Rome."

A tall skinny artist with an Afro and an enormous black Great Dane noticed Charles in his wheelchair.

"Hey, you look just like Charlie Mingus," he said. "He's a great bass player."

"The devil is in the room!" Charles shouted to Mackie, who was sitting outside his door in the middle of the night. "He put his hand over my mouth. I couldn't call out!"

Mackie ran to his side. "You were dreaming. It's all right."

The following morning Charles reported that the involuntary muscles in his lungs were going. "I have to think about breathing now," he said.

The specter of death is immense and awesome. It stands in the hallway. It waits in the corridor just outside our vision. In the bedroom the devil's hand is already blocking the air.

Outside, there are celebrations. A street fair is in the works: dance, theater, song. Jugglers on stilts recite poems. The street of porn films and massage parlors and burlesque is being rechristened Theater Row. Forty-Second Street between Ninth and Tenth Avenue. Home.

. . .

"Turn it off!" Charles said hopelessly as Mackie's pocket radio blared from the bedside table, a station replay of a concert Charles had performed in New Orleans the year before, with running commentary by a deejay who'd gotten it all wrong. "I wasn't inspired by Oscar Pettiford." Charles sighed. "I wrote that before Oscar Pettiford was even heard of. I was inspired by Duke Ellington, Debussy, Stravinsky, Bartók. It had nothing to do with Oscar Pettiford!"

Joni Mitchell called a moment later. He was still angry.

"I'm dying," he said into the phone as Mackie worked Dermassage cream into his legs. "At least I wish I were. I don't know how to anymore. I used to know."

I could hear her laughter at the end of the line, Joni trying to lighten the words. She asked how he liked the two new tunes she'd worked on. He was not in a mood for conversation.

"They're not as professional as the first one you did," he said. "One of them sounds like Lambert, Hendricks, and Ross."

They were an unlikely couple, Joni and Charles: Joni, a singer who didn't read music, who refused to risk her gifts or her intuition by submitting them to formal study. And Charles, who, as a teenager in Los Angeles, studied composition and music theory with the legendary Lloyd Reese, and mastered the classical bass with Herman Rheinshagen, the retired principal bassist of the New York Philharmonic. Joni's musical talents fell into place on their own, a natural outgrowth of her poetry.

"You're the hillbilly singer," Charles had said to her straight-faced from his wheelchair when she first walked into our living room. She stopped dead at the entrance and stared at him without speaking. He'd caught her off guard. She was standing beside Don Alias, tall, black, and handsome, the jazz percussionist who was living with her then. She was taller than I had imagined and looked surprisingly serious. Suddenly she relaxed. She looked at Charles slyly and burst out laughing. They liked each other from the start.

· · ·

It was midsummer, the beginning of July. We'd taken a train ride to Washington, D.C.—Charles in his wheelchair in a special coach jammed with press and performers—to picnic on the White House lawn with several hundred musicians. The world of jazz was about to celebrate the twenty-fifth Newport Jazz Festival with President Carter, a welcome, if belated, acknowledgment from the top that America's own music mattered. More important to us, in our failing world, by the end of the day Gerry Mulligan, the baritone saxophone player, had given us hope.

Under a blazing sun Roberto was standing beside Charles's wheelchair dressed in his new white suit and wing-tip shoes, surveying the inner sanctum of the American side of his heritage and taking snapshots to add to his mountains of Americana back home. At home, beside the reminders of his early years in Rome, a portrait of Theodore Roosevelt, dedicated to my maternal grandfather, was framed above his bed.

I thought of my mother on these very grounds at the turn of the century, sitting, aged four, on Teddy Roosevelt's lap, playing the piano. It was an overlapping family scenario as unimaginable as my return to the streets where my father first walked in immigrant shoes through Hell's Kitchen. Opposite Roberto's bed at home, a twenty-foot American flag covered two entire walls. Now, whenever Charles looked over at him, Roberto placed a patriotic hand over his heart. For the moment Roberto was the best thing going.

Jimmy Carter, in his shirtsleeves, was raising a paper cup to toast the assembled musicians. Dizzy Gillespie was preparing to involve his peanut-farming president in a rousing vocal duet of "Salt Peanuts." Gerry Mulligan was making his way through the crowd greeting friends when suddenly he spotted Charles's wheelchair and hurried over.

"Hey, man, I'm back." Gerry leaned over and gave Charles a hug. "It's over." Gerry had just returned from South America, where, along with Lionel Hampton, he had helped fill in for Charles's canceled tour. I'd last seen him storming through the corridors of the

Argentine embassy, protesting the inevitable visa hassles the day before his trip. Now, under a scorching sun, he was describing the windup of his tour in Mexico City. All at once he turned to Charles and began to speak so swiftly and in tones so low that I moved closer to listen.

His head was bobbing with excitement. "My friend . . . I have a friend in Mexico. You must see for yourself!" It didn't make sense at first, I didn't see the connection, but then he explained that his friend, Vincenzo, was suffering from the same incurable illness as Charles and that he was—as fantastic as it sounded—recovering! A remarkable and legendary healer known throughout Mexico, a seventy-two-year-old Indian witch doctor, according to Gerry, was accomplishing miracles.

"Her name is Pachita," he said. "I'll put you in touch. I have friends who can arrange a meeting!" He urged us to go.

While Gerry talked on, George Wein, the impresario of the festival, stepped up to the microphone on the stage and announced Charles's presence. The crowd rose to its feet. President Carter hurried over to Charles's wheelchair and embraced him. With the president's arm around his shoulders, Charles silently acknowledged the ovation with the slightest nod of his head.

And then an astonishing thing happened. George Wein stepped up to the microphone one more time.

"Charlie Mingus! Charlie Mingus! Stand up and take a bow!" he cried out for a miracle to the man frozen in his chair.

I couldn't look over. Without turning my head I imagined the expression on Charles's face, flanked by our nurse Mr. Mackie on one side and by the president of the United States on the other and now, for no reason at all, being asked to do the one thing he most desired: to rise to his feet.

He burst into tears. Behind his tears was a grimace of desperation I saw only in photographs. But that was a long time afterward.

He did not stand up.

Three days later we gathered our medical props and our favorite nurse, Hermaline, and boarded a plane to Mexico. Within a week we were among the jostling throngs of pilgrims outside Pachita's gate. We had simply packed up and left for the world of magic. Like the others who were gathered there, we had nothing more to lose.

Seven

Minutes after we landed at the Mexican airport, a crew of ambulance attendants in shimmering jumpsuits entered through a side door of the plane and quickly maneuvered Charles down a ramp toward a waiting van below. "Oh, they're looking so fine!" Hermaline kept saying to Charles as she tried to keep up with the mobile stretcher unit that was marching smartly ahead. "All clean in their suits! It's a regular army here for you!" When we reached our hotel in the fashionable Zona Rosa district of Mexico City, however, there was no welcoming army, not even a message at the desk. The hotel clerk called the three names I'd scratched down hastily at home, but not one of them, not Pedro nor Juan nor Jesus, answered his phone.

Our swift departure seemed suddenly absurd: landing in a foreign country without a plan, standing around a lobby like a canceled tour, failing to look beyond the next eight bars. Well, maybe it was a test of our endurance, I thought: the faith healers testing our faith, waiting to see how we'd behave.

We settled into a suite of rooms, ordered the medical equipment necessary for our survival, hired Arturo, a bilingual Mexican nurse, and began our wait. Day after day Charles sat grim and taciturn in his chair beside the window while we waited for word from our contact, a young French woman named Claudy whom Gerry Mulligan had promised would introduce us to the centers of witchcraft and healing he'd described so convincingly on the White House lawn.

"I guess she's vanished," I ventured to say on the third morning.

"She never existed at all," Charles replied from across the room.

On the fourth day, as the afternoon sun dropped behind the building opposite our hotel and I was calling the airport, at Charles's insistence, to book a flight back home, there was a sudden pounding at the door and Claudy glided effortlessly into our life. It was our first taste of the unpredictable events ahead. She laughed gaily, as if we hadn't been waiting for half a week, introduced herself, and began to tell us her story. As she paced our rooms, waving a glass of wine from the gift bottle she'd brought and already opened, she described the auto smashup she'd survived with her boyfriend two years before, her paralysis that had lasted for more than a year, the medical authorities who were unable to help, the miraculous reversal when Pachita cut her open with a knife, and, finally, the transcendent moment two weeks later when she danced through the nightspots of Mexico City.

"Oh, I dance!" She laughed, throwing back her head. "Of course, Pachita tell me no, too soon, not to do!" Her eyes sparkled. "But I dance!" She was wiry and small, her skinny thighs pressed tight inside leather pants beneath a jacket imprinted with blazing sequined flowers, a mix of current fashion and the timeless snubbing of taste. Her hair was streaked yellow, her skin cooked almost black by the Acapulco sun. She had a winning enthusiasm and a certain toughness that was softened by a throaty laugh. Hermaline eyed her with alarm. Born again into the Baptist faith shortly before leaving New

York, wary of the "demon healers" she remembered from her Jamaican village, Hermaline sensed the young woman before her was not among those she imagined to be the saved.

"I will help," Claudy cried gaily as she circled our hotel room. "Are many I help who need Pachita powers." In the same breath she spoke of leaving Mexico, extricating herself from this strange world before it was "too late." Then again she spoke of staying on, taking up someone's offer to run a disco in the chic village of Puerto Vallarte. "Something you do when you are old." She laughed. "Not yet, I think." She finished her story and her wine and hurried off as unexpectedly as she'd appeared. Her last words concerned Lola, her maid, who spoke Pachita's dialect and would serve as our interpreter the following day when, hopefully, we would meet the formidable healer herself.

The following afternoon we arrived at the gates to Pachita's courtyard in the northern slums of Mexico City, accompanied by Claudy, Lola, our own attendants, Hermaline, and the ambulance driver. It was a dark day with faint sounds of thunder in the distance, the sky as gray and tattered as the neighborhood we were entering. As we lowered Charles in his wheelchair to the sidewalk, the air clung heavy and forbidding with the smell of an imminent downpour.

We had followed Pachita's orders carefully and without question. Our van was parked exactly two blocks away from the crowded entrance to her quarters, as she had instructed. Through the gates we could see a large gathering of men and women, many of whom were whispering together as if they were in church, as if some fearful or holy event were about to take place. We entered the courtyard. Suddenly Hermaline turned back.

"It's like this in Jamaica!" she cried out, trying to break away, still carrying Charles's walker, heading toward the street. "I know it! It's the devil's work!" The air of mystery, the crush of humanity with its sour smell that filled the atmosphere with foreboding, had caught hold of her. Despite her protests, I ran down the street and pulled her back. "No!" she insisted. "I'm going out for mangoes."

"You'll do it later," I said, steering her back to the gates. There was no time to argue. "We'll go together," I promised. We were nervous, our imaginations already on edge. We had heard stories of patients rejected by Pachita who died soon after. Charles began coughing, his body wracked with cramps.

"Is that Charlie Mingus?" someone asked who was standing in line.

"No," I replied quickly, turning my back. We were not in the mood for fans, although he was popular in Mexico and they appeared unexpectedly—the ambulance attendant collected his records, our hotel clerk had attended last year's concert. Still, any recognition or reminder of his achievements rarely pleased him now, unless his special antennae approved the sensibility behind the remark. Then he might look up with a small smile and mumble, "Thanks, man."

Someone else asked if the man in the wheelchair was Mingus. He was an elderly man with a bright red scarf around his neck who looked as if he might have seen better days. He wished Charles a swift recovery so he could play music again. Then he recounted the story of a retarded child brought before Pachita by a physician who had stood by and watched as Pachita cut open the child's head and placed her hands inside the skull. "The physician—well, he thought he was dreaming," the man with the scarf went on. "The next thing you know, the doctor placed his own fingers next to hers, and then when Pachita closed the wound, she promised the child would recover." He paused and looked at us. "That's what happened."

We were listening attentively, ready to believe, when Claudy's friend Don joined us in line, the companion-nurse to Vincenzo, Gerry Mulligan's friend with Charles's disease. Gravely, Don continued the discussion. He described the operations Vincenzo himself had undergone, witnessed by prominent surgeons from Paris. "She cuts as a surgeon cuts," he said, "but she accomplishes in five minutes what it takes a surgeon two hours to perform."

A man behind us spoke up. "The wounds heal within three days and leave no scars," he said. "What she does inside the body . . ." He

looked off above the crowd and fell silent. "... is miraculous!" someone whispered.

"*Charles Mingus!*" a voice called out from the front of the line. Although we were far in back, three young attendants hurried over and
led Charles quickly through the crowd in his wheelchair toward a
low ramshackle dwelling in the distance. Our band of nurses and attendants followed swiftly behind. When I finally caught up with
them, they were crossing an unlit vestibule and were headed toward
some shabby yellow curtains that served as a room divider. Together
we passed through the curtains and entered a large waiting area.
There, in the center of a group of male attendants, a tall and impos-
ing figure stared at us intently from across the room. I had no doubt
that it was Pachita.

Furtively, I examined the big, broad-faced Indian woman, who
looked younger than her seventy-two years and seemed at first
glance—wrapped in layers of wrinkled aprons and skirts—more like
a common bag lady than a purveyor of miracles. Her powers, however, were soon apparent. As we assembled before her, an assistant
received the egg we had been ordered to bring along. Arturo, our
nurse, had dutifully purchased the egg in a market near our hotel.
Without questioning its purpose, we had carried it with us since
early morning.

Pachita stared at Charles for a long moment without speaking.
Then, without warning, she turned abruptly and moved off to a corner of the room. Here she conversed at length in a low voice with
Don and Claudy's Indian maid Lola, while her attendants stood to
one side. After a while she returned and drew close to Charles, addressing a few words to him in English. In the background where her
entourage was gathered, a strange ceremony was unfolding in front
of Lola. A member of the group was making stealthy anointments
over Lola's head and signs of the cross before her face—a sort of
cleansing ritual, Claudy explained later. Then another attendant approached us and removed an object I hadn't noticed, which looked

like a light brown purse or bag, from the spokes of Charles's wheel-chair. Pachita watched this activity from a distance. Then she turned and faced us.

"He has a living nerve virus," she said matter-of-factly in her Mexican Indian accent, clearly enough for me to understand. It was an astonishing declaration. All year long the medical authorities had referred to an unidentified virus that had attacked Charles's nervous system and departed, leaving it irrevocably damaged. Pachita's "living" virus—one still present in his body which could be located and removed, as she soon explained—was a word that sang with hope.

I watched her as she stood before us in a large bare chamber without candles or amulets or crosses or adornments, without the trappings of voodoo or of magic I had expected. She placed her hands on her hips and made her pronouncement: a large Mexican peasant woman claiming to be a reincarnation of Cuauhtémoc—the last Aztec emperor and nephew of Montezuma—a woman clad in old aprons and sweaters in a brightly lit room full of disciples who, without ritual or mystery or ceremony or celebration, was telling Charles not to worry, that he would be all right.

"You will get well," she said to him in English as she patted him between the belly and the chest. She was neither smiling nor severe.

Lola murmured under her breath: "She sees what she sees!"

Moments after we returned to the hotel a wild summer storm broke loose. Thunderclaps rattled the panes of the porch door off our suite. Hailstones bounced on the terrace. A horn sounded below. "Ever hear Bird play that?" Charles asked groggily from the bedroom. He had relaxed into a half-sleep after the reassuring events of the afternoon.

"There was a storm when Bird died," I remembered. "And one when Mingus lived," I added quickly. The hail slapped against our terrace windows as Don, Lola, and I wordlessly toasted the afternoon with hotel champagne and sampled the prickly pears, fresh figs, and chocolates provided by the hotel manager in Charles's honor.

The miracle, it began to seem, was not simply that we found Pachita but that we found her in time. Here in Mexico City, over seven thousand feet above sea level, Charles was breathing hard and irregularly, sometimes in gasps. Still, we did not acknowledge miracles. We remained quiet and secretive, afraid to consider a future at all. Too much certainty might result in a jinx on the cure. Charles's egg was back in its wrinkled brown paper bag on the marble dresser of our chic hotel on the elegant Reforma as, quietly, we waited for the magic to gel.

In the evening, Claudy arrived with the first batch of herbs. "I will come back later," she said, transferring the herbs from two large buckets to smaller containers and setting them on the table. "You must be patient now. In Mexico everything is slow . . . slow . . . slow." She stretched out her French triplets like a soothing bedtime story. "You must get used to this country. It is all tomorrow, you know. Even the dogs are lazy, they don't care. I've never seen anywhere in the world dogs that lie immovable in the streets while cars honk past them. You must get used to it!"

Charles, who was used to nothing in Mexico, remained in a panic, calling on a growing list of invented names for Hermaline that included Abigine, Aborigine, and Himalaya. He was in a state of emergency, whether asking for a pan to throw up in or dental floss to clean his teeth. Hermaline and I scuttled through our routines like Mexican water roaches under light. "You're a treat," she said encouragingly as she scurried past, referring to some small aid I had provided in the middle of Charles's gargantuan demands.

The following day, Claudy and Don arrived with more reinforcements from the occult: additional buckets of sticky herbal mixtures for massages prepared by Lola, six quarts of herbal elixir for oral consumption, bitter teas, exotic creams, and an enchanted wine that needed to ripen for three days and three nights on our hotel terrace under the sun and the stars. As for the boils that had plagued him for a week, Pachita prescribed a rotation of homeopathic remedies involving baked potato compresses on his buttocks to absorb the liquid, followed by hot tar applications to drain the pus.

After lunch we began our first massage. The herbs, which we heated on a small stove set up in the bathroom, were intensely and intoxicatingly fragrant. With our hands full of warm green oil, Arturo and I kneaded and massaged Charles all afternoon. A profound aura of well-being emanated from this heady mixture of healing herbs and began to settle over the room. For hours we rubbed his skin, pushing the oils through his pores, Arturo standing on one side of the bed, me on the other, Charles like a great whale between us, as we sought to bring life and regeneration to his body. I thought of the intimacy and exchange among men on the whaling ship *Pequod* as together they worked their fingers in the thick spermaceti of the whale, and I watched Arturo's serious face in the dim bedroom light with a sense of camaraderie as he grinned and winced with the movements of his hands.

However, by midevening Charles's spirits were no better and his health seemed worse. He was convinced his boil was threatening his life. "It's like a tiger biting into me!" he told Claudy over the phone. To me he added: "People have died from them. They're poisonous!" Although he was sharpening his protests with the old color and exaggeration, I remained for once unmoved.

"I've taken the serious things seriously," I announced coldly. "I've devoted myself to them for eight months. Your boil I do not take seriously." When we were dealing only with a serious illness, Charles was calm as a clam. No phony dramatics, no games. He conserved his energy in silence. Now, with a little confidence and some real hope, our quarters resembled a Sicilian wake. Hour after hour he moaned, "God save me. Save me, God," in an extended protest that ran into the night. From under the covers I reminded Hermaline that I had no sympathy for "bullshit theatrics." Nonetheless I considered hopefully that perhaps Pachita's herbal massage had caused mur-murings in his dying nervous system. Birth is painful: perhaps his dead motor circuits were coming to life, beginning to feel again.

When Claudy arrived with a special salve for the boil, she re-ported that Pachita had gone north to her hometown for a fortnight and would delay the operation until Charles lost weight. She implied it was necessary to allow time for the "evil" to dissipate—the ma-levolent spirits that had him in their spell. Before leaving, Claudy dropped the term "black magic." Charles, who was listening in the other room, promptly added her provocative remarks to a festering imagination that already reached into the most fearsome sockets of his mind. Now he had another reason to stay awake besides the boils, one more round of ammunition to help fight sleep, to call out, to travel his lonely road to the end of the night where the spirit world was waiting.

For the rest of the night the three of us—Charles, Hermaline, and me—sat fully awake in the darkness while, hour after hour, Charles protested his condition in a running fugue with Hermaline, who chanted "Oh Lord" or "Dear me, Jesus" from her position at the bedroom door. With increasing impatience, I attempted to point out the rational means of help to a man surrounded by terrible forces that, to me, remained nameless and unreal. Back in New York, if the devil was in the room, Mackie offered prayers or lit candles to exor-cise the demons that, together, they believed in. Now, in Mexico, Charles's imagination fermented in the dark, alone. When I said I didn't want to hear about it, he replied, "That's why I never discuss it with you." And when I said, "You don't have to suffer like this, you can get help," Hermaline's voice rose from the adjoining room: "Jesus will help you. Jesus will let you sleep . . ."

"Not if you're sitting here in the dark with a hot potato up your ass," Charles interrupted her angrily. He wanted the potato removed, although it had successfully opened his boil, the poison and puss spilling over into the mealy substance as Pachita had predicted. Hermaline removed the potato.

"Jesus was a human being," Charles continued. "He took out his penis from inside his robes and he peed when he had to. He was human. None of you knows what I'm going through with my boil. You, Hermaline, are presumptuous. You are blasphemous. Christ means humility and you are full of pride." Hermaline maintained an uneasy silence, waiting for his sermon to run its course.

"When I was thirteen," Charles went on, "I knew what I would achieve. I knew I would be a success in music, be famous, all that. You can't tell me now what I know or don't know . . . I know things. I know that my boil is open. I know that my boil is sore. I know that my boil is killing me. So you can all shut up!"

Shortly after dawn, when Charles had fallen asleep for perhaps five minutes, Don and Claudy appeared with a rented car outside our hotel. According to Pachita's instructions, we were to drive two hours south, under the shadow of Popocatépetl, to the temperate valley of Cuernavaca, where we were to find a home. Although Cuernavaca was once a vacation site favored by Aztec princes and later by the Spanish conquistadores, today it was a resort area attracting the merely rich. Pachita had chosen Cuernavaca for its climate and altitude, which were favorable to Charles's condition and to his weakened lungs. I remembered when his band appeared at the University of Mexico the year before, how musicians had eagerly accepted the hit of oxygen they were offered backstage—a customary provision for visiting performers. By midday, after Claudy, Don, and I had found a suitable place, walled in and private and only ten minutes outside of town, we called Mexico City. Charles was running a fever. Over the phone he said he was dying. When I suggested calling a doctor, he replied heatedly, "You don't change horses in midstream." We raced back through the mountains. Ninety minutes later I jumped out at the hotel.

"Six-ace-flash," he raved from his bed as I entered the room. "Two eyes are better than one." His fever had soared beyond the markings on the thermometer. "Don't spill the firecrackers," he said. "What'd I tell you? Another doctor's hat pretty soon . . . Soon they'll give me a plate to be chopped on . . ."

I put my arms around him and crawled into bed. His delirium raged on. There was little we could do. We were in the hands of the herbalists and the sorcerers now, the white witches and the healers. Standard medications for paranoia like Mellaril, or pain relievers like the electronic suppressor, sleeping pills, or Valium, or common analgesics like aspirin for fever were all part of the past. I got up and tried to call Claudy.

"You can see both ways in a love affair . . ." Charles went on. "The doctor said to close the pores . . . *close the pores!* . . . Oh, Lord, just let me keep on walking . . ."

"Charles has been voodooed," Claudy reported over the phone when I reached her. "Pachita must get it off him." Claudy instructed me to place a glass of water beside his bed in order to collect the evil spirits, to leave it there all night and empty it immediately in the morning. She said Pachita had warned her that she must get it off me, too.

"How will she do it?" I asked with curiosity. "Will I need to visit her in Chihuahua?"

"Pachita is not 'spectacular,' " Claudy replied with dignity, her French translations, as they were so often, tantalizingly obscure. "She doesn't need you there. She'll do it where she is." Claudy promised that she and Don would bring over the herbal medications. Don, who had taught water- and snow skiing at Club Meds around the world, been employed as a sound engineer on at least one film, and spent the past two years nursing Vincenzo, was at the moment with Claudy taking a vacation from obligation. Although the blond-tinted ends of his

hair were growing out (like Claudy's) and he looked the part of a resort stud on the make—well built, easygoing, available—he had a
passive warmth that was doubtless appealing to the ill. He and
Claudy were not well matched. She was high-powered and driven,
running on an energy level that could light the highway from here to
Acapulco.

By the end of the week, our hotel room had achieved new levels of
chaos. After we called the emergency hospital for the fifth time to
beg the two Mexican doctors who had already lanced Charles's boils
to return and check his lungs, they reported that his lungs were infected, with complications that might require surgery. They urged us
to go immediately to the hospital, where trained nurses, antibiotics,
and special treatments were at hand. In the middle of their diagnosis
Don burst through the bedroom door with the latest medications
from Pachita. As the doctors looked on with dismay, Don announced that we were to rub fresh excrement into the boils, cover
them with gauze, apply the *emplasto monopolis*—a tarlike stick that
required melting on our portable stove—and then follow with the
baked potato dressings, as usual.

Don had brought rock crystals called *alumbre* to clear the phlegm,
fresh orange leaves for congestion, and a special salve for Charles's
chest. Above all, Charles was not to go to the hospital, not to take
antibiotics, not to clean out his lungs. Dawn was approaching after
a long and exhausting night. The two young interns offered order, cleanliness, and the benefits of modern science. The alternatives
were all too familiar by now: a handful of age-old remedies laced
with a touch of pharmaceutical sophistication from a seventy-two-
year-old enchantress in a Mexican slum. They included the turmoil
of our hotel room (an electric stove on the bathroom floor next to a
pile of dirty sheets), the erratic changing of offbeat dressings that required frantic midnight calls to room service ("baked potatoes—no

butter"), and now, unbelievably, a blob of excrement on an infected wound.

I escaped to the terrace where Don joined me, alone. "You came all the way from New York to see Pachita," he said reasonably. "You must trust her. The medical doctors offer no hope." He shrugged. "What can you lose?"

I raced back inside. Charles had a fever of 105 degrees. I ran again to the terrace, accompanied by the doctors. They were sympathetic. They were not unfamiliar with witches. I returned to the bedroom and put the decision to Charles. Without hesitation he opted for Pachita. He declared he would remain at the hotel and the interns would remove the gauze dressing they had placed only twenty minutes before on his boils; they would do so at once.

"I need room for the shit," he said, referring to the excrement dressing. "Tell them to remove the gauze from my ass." He nodded to Hermaline.

"I'm not working at this time," she said agreeably. Her shift was long over.

"Go tell them to take the gauze out of my asshole," Charles thundered to Arturo, who understood perhaps one or two words of his commands. Arturo hurried into the bathroom looking for the bedpan. *"No!"* Charles bellowed again. *"Not the bedpan, muthafucka!"*

Arturo turned to Hermaline. "Is he insulting me?"

"No, dear, he likes you," Hermaline replied.

No one offered his services for the prescribed treatment. Charles himself had been constipated for a week. Suddenly he shouted: *"Bedpan!"*

Arturo ran to the bathroom one more time. Within minutes the magic prescription was delivered. I sometimes imagine that it was at this moment, in the marvel of this event, that our faith in Pachita began.

That night, while life hung in the balance, while it was essential to believe in the remedy, Charles continued to tamper with the cure.

With large doubtful eyes he observed every minuscule change in his condition. I thought he was dying—so closely did his symptoms and behavior resemble the terminal stages of ALS. His eyes were huge, as if absorbing life's final details. When he coughed they bulged like rubber balls in the pressurized cabin of a plane. His stare offered little hope. His voice was diminished to a whisper.

And then, at dawn, when his fever miraculously dropped and his boils began to drain normally, I almost imagined that Pachita had stepped in and saved his life during the night. But the most extraordinary moment was to come. After a week in bed the deadweight of his body should have made such an effort impossible, and yet he rose off the chair with ease, arched his back, lifted his head, and stood firmly on his feet! His hands did not slip on the walker. His weight did not strain our efforts to hold him up. He remained standing in front of his chair for several seconds, shifting from foot to foot the way Mackie once instructed. As the three of us watched, he actually sat down—instead of falling deadweight into the seat as he had done for the past few weeks. While we stood around him in silence, Charles's eyes filled with tears. Arturo wiped his face and Hermaline chirped on, "You should be laughing, not crying. Oh, Lord Jesus, it must be joy he feels, yes, Charles, you must smile."

We watched, and at last Charles smiled—the most magnificently warming and wondrous smile in all these months—the hope and astonishment shining in his face. I felt it shine in mine too, for I believed at last, without ambivalence or doubt, in his efforts to get well.

Against all odds we had leased a villa for six months while we waited with faith in Pachita, for the realization of her cures.

In Cuernavaca, the screen door slammed on its iron hinges and Hermaline appeared in the doorway, starched and efficient, reporting that Joni Mitchell was on the phone from L.A. with lyrics to "Goodbye Pork Pie Hat" ("We're all in it!" Joni said with excitement. "I've brought it up to date. I have a line about Charlie in Mexico with the faith healers. I hope he likes it. I couldn't keep myself out of it"). Hermaline came again to announce a call from the opposite coast— Jody reporting that Charles's drummer Dannie Richmond was fronting something called the Charles Mingus Quartet, which had just played the Village Vanguard in New York.

Instantly, Charles wanted our attorney to order them to "cease and desist." He didn't want his music played by "those kids."

"They've written me off," he said as he watched Arturo catch two flies in the palm of his hand with a single hook through the air and then dash them against the porch floor in one perfect arc. He was beginning to change his mind about Arturo. He stared at him now with pride, as he might have stared at one of his musicians after a particularly fine solo, and complimented him lavishly about the flies. Then he looked at me with unexpected sadness: "They don't think I'm going to live."

I'd grown accustomed to the failures of our life as the months had passed, the slowly descending scale of opportunity despite our dogged hopes. But at that moment if I could have sent the entire band to the bottom of the sea with a flick of my hand, I would have done it gladly.

Arturo, who resembled a Mexican version of the Italian comic actor Alberto Sordi, shared the events of our life with quiet irony. He had many talents besides his uncanny ability to catch the swarming flies that circled our heads. He selected the choicest mangoes, guava, oranges, or avocados from the trees in our garden as Charles's vast needs demanded. Despite his slim frame, he could change a tire, repair a broken oven, and lift the heavy jugs of fresh water onto the antique wooden table in our Spanish kitchen. He could clean out Charles's lungs while the technicians stood respectfully to one side.

He ran for groceries, prescribed medications for insect bites or diarrhea, lanced a carbuncle, killed a water bug, recommended one antibiotic over another, and, above all, shut his mouth tight when all formal medical knowledge was replaced by a spoon of shit. He had no message to force on a captive audience, no superior convictions for an ailing patient, unlike most nurses, who slashed and burned through the bedroom like jungle missionaries.

Watching Charles repose with his head on his chest beneath his pointy broad-brimmed hat from Spain, his body wrapped in a white jalaba from Tunisia, Arturo proudly noted Charles's resemblance to the Mexican revolutionary Pancho Villa.

Arturo was quickly becoming family.

Meanwhile, we lived in a splendid stately villa, full of history and art, surrounded by thick foliage that spilled over stone walls into well-tended gardens that overflowed with plant life and flowers. We were surrounded by elegance and order and taste, an appreciation of art and the yearnings of the spirit. If we were not hopelessly absorbed in matters of health, this would have been our Garden of Eden. As we listened to "Todo Modo" and *Revelations*—two of Charles's compositions most often on the turntable—a snake rattled ominously in the background.

If time was confused in New York, here it appeared to have stopped altogether. I calculated the days from the Fourth of July, which was a Tuesday—three days after Charles's extended band, directed by Paul Jeffrey, played selections from his music, recorded in the Atlantic studio last January, at an outdoor jazz festival in upstate New York. Arturo adjusted Charles's hands, unclasped his watch, and time moved on—his time continuum now in the hands of Pachita somewhere in Chihuahua in northern Mexico.

Late afternoons we set off on bucolic excursions through dazzling sun-drenched hills and farmlands accompanied by Arturo and by Eugene, Charles's son, who arrived this past week from California to serve as our English-speaking nurse when Hermaline leaves.

"I know where Hermaline will go first when she returns to New York," Charles said recently, staring at the ceiling as if the place in question were between the wooden beams. "A Chinese restaurant," he answered himself as she chattered on.

"Where would you go?" I asked.

"I'd go straight to a piano."

Arturo and Eugene together chained and padlocked the wheelchair into place in the backseat of our rented van as we prepared to set off through the countryside. The carpenter, whom we hired earlier in the afternoon to fashion a ramp for Charles's wheelchair—so that we could slide him into the garden or down the steps to the garage or up into the middle portion of the Volkswagen van (or *Combi,* as they call it here)—was a rangy six-footer. He, Arturo, and I took turns trying to push one another up the newly made ramp into the car, bending the wheelchair back on its rear wheels to test its clearance. At last, as the carpenter sat scrunched and nervous in the chair and Charles shouted orders from the porch, Arturo heaved and shoved the chair along the two rubber-matted wooden planks and tilted the carpenter triumphantly through the door.

"Give me the key," Charles ordered as we arranged him in the chair, eyes flashing, suddenly unnerved. "You're not going to tie up *my* ass! Not going to roll *me* down the damn cliff! Shit on *that!*" His eyes were challenging. *"Give me the key!"*

Nonetheless, Arturo patiently wrapped the chains around the wheels of the chair and Eugene affixed the padlock. Then we sped off along the back roads, Charles cradled in his chair, swooping through the winding curves that shook his flesh and helped release the pain.

That evening Eugene and I talked late into the night—our first exchange—seated at the long table in the dining room while he described his past and told me how he couldn't talk to his mother until he was twenty-five.

"Not until I was out of the marines." He laughed. "I could never just sit and talk." He poured himself a glass of local wine from the crystal decanter on the table. It sparkled warmly with reflected light from the chandelier that hung above our elegant place settings while he described life in the 'hood in Watts. "When I was a kid I spent most of my time in jail." He shrugged. "I got caught, that's all. Doing what everyone else was doing in the ghetto. I was thirteen years old when the trouble began." There was still an edge between us from the past—his mother had once sent him on a mission to New York to bring Charles back to her, twenty years after he'd left home—but we were making efforts to please.

When he showed me some silver charms from the village square he'd bought while out drinking with Arturo, I complimented him immediately: "They're beautiful," I said. Then I added: "They look just like some rings of mine." Instinctively, I looked at my fingers.

"Oh, they are nice," he agreed at once, looking at my fingers. Then we both noticed I wasn't wearing any rings.

During the day he massaged and exercised Charles, cared for his own small son, Kevin, who accompanied him from California, and concocted imaginative dishes in the kitchen. Despite brief moments when his eyes narrowed and his mouth set in a tight line, something like sweetness lay beneath his glib surface charm. Very California, I thought, with his exercises and natural foods and his long bloomer karate pants. Porkless and cigaretteless, he craved lots of "smoke" (he made his pot connection only a few hours after his arrival) and plenty of wine. His meditative tranquil side vied with the hustler and the Mingus energy. I couldn't help but like him.

Seated in the wheelchair, Charles relaxed for part of the day, but the nights were full of terror. I tried to reassure him, to insist on faith in Pachita, to overlook the "irritations" along the way. But then I did not have two large infected cysts between my testicles and my rectum, and it was no struggle for me to breathe. I was impatient with his fears, I did not want to recognize them. I wanted him to get well. I refused to accept that Pachita's way might fail, that the American doctors with their twentieth-century training were correct in their hopelessness.

"Would you like a good breakfast?" I asked, half-asleep. "Would you like some pancakes or a mango?" I remembered how I used to force myself to think of soft-boiled eggs on early mornings when the universe seemed to disappear into the void, when any reason at all to get up, even the slim reality of breakfast, was enough to dissipate the fear. I fell asleep again and when I awoke, Charles and Eugene were gone, the sun trying to break through this week of rain and overcast skies.

Sometimes I wondered whether I should have let go, should have spared Charles this return to life, if in fact it was a return. Perhaps he deserved an early death. In Italy Mamina, my mother-in-law, used to say, "Those whom the gods love die young."

Earlier today he reproached me with his life. He said it was my only error, to have brought him down here to continue the struggle. He'd been grouchy and demanding. Hermaline had been scrapping with him in her way until, finally, with a sanctimonious toss of her head, she said: "Well, if I was meant to die, I would accept it. I would just open my arms and let Jesus take me in. I wouldn't try to fight."

Charles's names for her now include: Himalaya, Hellamina, Himalady, Hermanilla, Godzilla, and Gargantua.

He began to complain about Arturo: "Arturo's a great day nurse," he said. "The best. He caught three flies in his hand at one time. But he's not a night nurse, he doesn't know how to turn me in bed."

Something happened to Arturo when Eugene came to town.

Charles went "over his head," allowing his son to give orders about technique to Arturo—to Arturo, a professional nurse! Next day Arturo missed lunch and could no longer understand my Spanish. Poison was in the air. Charles called him Artillo or Atilla the Hun. Charles remained loyal only to his most immediate needs, to whatever response he could muster from the crowd of attendants that surrounded him. Neither past nor future mattered. He had created in the shrewd center of his helplessness a powerful force at his command, directing the show sometimes with panic but always with that unfailing instinct for the weaknesses and strengths of those around him. I tagged along, feeling more and more like a minor accessory to his anxiety, which swelled like the open sea and carried us off on the crest of its hysteria, growing more powerful as the days move forward and Pachita's operation neared.

Despite his slight build and soft voice, Arturo ruled our staff with natural authority, the only one to successfully manipulate the maid and gardener, whom we finally fired last night. While the bedrooms went unattended, the meals uncooked, and the laundry unwashed, Arturo had his monumental daily Mexican breakfast served at the appointed hour, his uniforms starched and pressed, his bed made up, his rooms ordered and cleaned. During the long night hours, Eugene told me yesterday, he is using our car to smuggle Mexicans across the border.

Last night a young woman named Theresa, who ran an art gallery in Mexico City and was a friend of Claudy's, arrived at our villa— very Spanish-looking in her long black skirt and lace bolero, her dark hair tied behind dangling golden earrings, her elegant easy style, a mixture of reserve and warmth. Her mother was Mexican, which accounted for her authority and familiarity with the ways of this country. She moved in on our domestic problems immediately, firing a volley of orders to the community back in the kitchen.

Eugene took note of our new guest with interest.

Down at the pool, reading Octavio Paz's essay "The Day of the Dead," from *The Labyrinth of Solitude,* I recalled my helplessness last winter when I longed for someone, anyone—a friend, a minister, an adviser—whose faith was so genuine and stripped of nonsense that it might have produced a dialogue worthy of Charles's suffering. Now death was no longer a topic I lived with through my days and my dreams. How quickly one puts it aside when the least hope arises! Now again I imagined that life went on, that the day's sunlight was all that mattered as we warmed ourselves after breakfast on the long porch and tried to work the stiffness out of his limbs. August! I could hardly believe it. August! We had lived through the summer! Tomorrow we have another audience with Pachita, our last before the operation takes place.

Amid the squalor and apprehension of Pachita's courtyard, the crowd waited, serious and subdued, drawing little relief from the small tokens of art and life she had provided—the chattering canaries that swung in their cages overhead, the papier-mâché skylarks attached to her ceramic walls, the wooden statues of hens and ducks scattered in the mud below. (Her affinity with bird life was apparent. After all, legend had it that she was the reincarnation of Cuauhtémoc, whose symbol was the eagle.)

In the background even here rose the ubiquitous strains of "Saturday Night Fever," the latest disco hit. Yesterday, a Mexican torero was gored by a bull at the Plaza del Toros in Mexico City. The night before, somewhere in the world, Muhammad Ali, the world heavyweight champion, won a decision over his opponent Leon Spinks and regained his title. Glimpses of the real world still asserted themselves in radio snatches on the noisy streets.

The intermittent sound of knocking at the outside gate disturbed the air, although none of us moved to open it. The gate itself was a long window of yellow glass with black wrought-iron bars that splayed out magnificently like an Aztec sun. All afternoon we waited. When we finally were led into Pachita's chambers at dusk, we found her seated at a desk in a lighted room, her hair done up in pink curlers—the witch backstage. She stared up at us almost crossly for a moment and then touched Charles lightly on the shoulder.

"In six weeks," she said to him as unemotionally as if delivering a recipe for tamales, "in six weeks you will be cured!" She discussed the details with Arturo: no mud baths yet; a little chili is permissible; the operation would take place a week from Friday. On the way home Charles laughed from the backseat about the chili. "She's a comedian!" he said, chuckling into his chin.

Two weeks later, back in the slow festering heat of Pachita's courtyard, it was growing dark. We had arrived with our baggage at dawn, according to Pachita's instructions, and had watched the crowd slowly diminish all day long with no word from her attendants. Exhausted and disappointed, we were preparing to return home when her attendants suddenly appeared and announced that she would perform the operation this evening. They warned us that if Charles had no bottle of alcohol or stack of bandages like the others, she would not operate.

Arturo rushed into the night to search for a neighborhood pharmacy, while the rest of us—Eugene, Claudy, Charles, and I—waited uneasily inside the courtyard with the half-dozen men and women Pachita had selected, gathered in hushed groups outside her windows in the dark. The strong odor of alcohol seeped through the open shutters. Somewhere inside we could hear a baby cry.

When Arturo finally returned, triumphant, we had lost all sense of time. Still we waited. Sometime, long past midnight, Charles was called inside. We felt our way slowly through the darkness, stepping over bodies of patients recovering from their operations—

perhaps a dozen were stretched out on the floor of the vestibule—until we found the entrance to the operating room and Eugene wheeled Charles inside. Although we could barely make out the shadowy forms stationed at the far side of the room where Pachita sat beside a narrow bed, an assistant motioned us away from her corner. His concern was wasted; there was little we could see clearly in the dark.

Another helper moved past us, holding a long kitchen knife similar to the one Theresa's maid had used to cut up zucchini for dinner. He walked to Pachita's corner and handed her the knife. Then he approached Charles in his wheelchair and, in English, asked his name, if he was a musician, if he played music and composed.

"I used to," Charles replied.

"What happened?" the attendant asked.

"I can't move now. I can't move my hands or my legs." In the darkness, Eugene lifted Charles out of the wheelchair and managed to pivot his immense deadweight around by himself. Then he placed him on the bed, where two assistants turned him on his side. Pachita leaned over his back.

The operation had begun.

Eugene returned to our side of the room and stood directly behind Claudy and me as we waited nervously in the dark, placing his hands on our shoulders, pressing down hard. It was an unexpected and intimate gesture, an unspoken sharing of concern. For the first time in weeks I felt almost a bond.

"Does it hurt?" someone asked.

"I believe in God in Pachita," it sounded like Charles was saying. "Yes, it hurts," he added. The smell of alcohol was overpowering. When another attendant asked how he felt, Charles's voice was barely audible.

"Like Christ when they pierced him in the side," he said. The air was full of tension. Nonetheless, something in his voice made me wonder whether he had inserted the agony of Christ into the ambiguity of this night in order to sanctify the layers of voodoo and magic that surrounded us. Or whether, along with the pain and deadly seriousness, his natural flair for theater had surfaced.

Back in Cuernavaca the following morning, relaxing on the porch, he reviewed the operation: "I'd like to have her cut *my* steak," he said reflectively as we soaked up the noonday sun. "Won't *no* blood run out, baby . . . She *know* how to cut. She cut right through the *pores,* baby . . . there where the holes are already! . . ." He paused. "Or is it someone else who cut? Right from heaven? Someone up there cuttin' and directin' the show from up above with a laser beam . . . ? Shee-it, that's what it is," he said with sudden conviction. "A laser beam! From God through Pachita!"

And so the operation, that huge event we'd anticipated for so many days, had come and gone, its simplicity anticlimactic, almost as if it never happened. One wondered, really, if it had. Or whether Pachita had so thoroughly understood the perversities and failures of the human spirit that she cured sickness and pain with the patient's own subconscious. Was that her magic? Was disease curable by willing it so?

The bandage today seemed clean as a whistle, no blood stains seeping through. I resisted the strong temptation to inspect it before the required seventy-two hours were up, to peep under the elastic bandage covering the still-wet cotton reeking of alcohol, feeling like Orpheus, ready to blow everything in order to know with certainty.

Late in the afternoon, I accompanied Claudy to a lush villa in Cuernavaca belonging to Dante, the owner of two gay discotheques in Mexico City and Acapulco. Dante and three male friends in bikinis were lounging at the pool, spread out on straw mats in the sun, drinking rum and Coca-Cola. We joined them and discussed Pachita in French, Spanish, English, and Italian. The following gossip surfaced: one of the poolsiders, Manolo, the possessor of enormous blue eyes, had accompanied a friend with kidney trouble to Pachita's, where the healer removed the defective kidney and replaced it with "something else." The "something else" appeared to be working fine. Another of the young men, Michel, reported that his mother, a well-known dowager and social dragon of Acapulco, had herself operated on a friend during a trance in which Pachita handed her a knife and told her to carry on. Meanwhile, Claudy said she planned to question Pachita about the details of Charles's operation.

Now we had another twenty-four hours to endure, one more day before we were instructed to inspect the wound. Eugene, as it turned out, had already peeped under the bandage while Charles slept. We met for a conference in the kitchen, where he casually reported that he had seen nothing at all, no blood on the bandage, no wound, and suggested that we not mention it to Claudy "in case it might upset the spiritual wham wham." He proceeded to doctor a second bandage with iodine, water, ketchup, soy sauce, and alcohol, which he intended to substitute for the one now taped to Charles's back. He dried the prepared bandage in the oven, then stashed it on top of the refrigerator.

When I returned from the market Charles was in high spirits. He said Pachita had removed one of his kidneys.

"What do you mean?"

"Eugene said there was a lot of blood on the bandage."

"What does blood have to do with kidneys?" I remembered he'd heard about Manolo's kidney story yesterday.

"You have kidney trouble, don't you?" he asked. In fact, my kidneys had bothered me ever since we arrived in Mexico.

"Oh, you think she's going to give me yours?" I laughed.

"Yeah," Charles replied. "She probably has a going traffic in people's organs."

When I asked Eugene if he'd told Charles there was blood on the bandage, he denied saying anything until I repeated Charles's words.

"Oh, yeah, I mentioned it yesterday while I was massaging him."
Eugene sorts out the truth according to the whims of his imagination
or, more frequently, according to what is immediately advantageous
at the time. One night recently, when we were drinking beer and eating nachos in the village square, some small boys who were hustling
overpriced "silver" trinkets among the tables, gathered around us
with their hawkers' trays. Eugene bought some charms, bargained,
rapped with them at length, examined a silver bracelet—the most
expensive item—and finally sent them packing. Moments later he
uncovered his napkin and exclaimed with surprise, "Look here, see
what they left . . . ," and produced the silver bracelet.

"Eugene, that's terrible," Theresa said with a small gasp of
esteem.

"You outsmarted the street smarts," I said.

"Oh yeah," Eugene murmured as he fastened the clasp on his
wrist. "I been out there a long while."

Claudy called to say she was unable to speak with Pachita because
the wife and the mother of the president of Mexico were meeting in
her chambers. She said that scores of guardsmen and police were
overrunning the yard. "The wife of the president has problems
with her ovaries," she reported. In addition, the mother of the president was suffering with kidney trouble. As Charles still insists that
Pachita removed his kidney, we now have cause to wonder whether,
among all the other uncertainties, the mother of the president of
Mexico was walking around with the kidney of Charlie Mingus.

I told her Eugene had peeped under the bandage and seen
nothing.

"Pachita is not a charlatan," she replied firmly. "If do things is because necessary at the time. I will have lunch with her and see."

"You must promise not to say we lack faith," I said nervously.
"The important thing is that Charles believes in the cure."

"I talked to Vincenzo," Claudy continued. "Is coming to Mexico City tomorrow with two week's mud supply for Charles. Is much better. Spends nights alone now, gets up and does pee-pee, shaves himself, is beginning to walk. I hope Charles meet this week."

At midnight, although the lights had gone out in the house and a thunderstorm was brewing, Eugene left with the car, probably for more beer. In the middle of the storm, a crash echoed through the house.

"Ice," Arturo said.

"That was lightning, man," Charles said. "It struck the window."

"Ice," repeated Arturo.

"Go outside," Charles ordered me, "and see if you see ice. That's lightning, man." I went outside under the arcade and peered into the patio. The rain was pouring down in torrents, blown by the wind. I returned quickly inside.

"I'm not going to stand out there to check what's coming down," I said, rebelling. Charles ordered Arturo outside. He returned with a chunk of ice.

"Show it to me," Charles said, as I held it before his eyes. "Higher," he shouted. "I can't see."

Twenty minutes later, a bolt of lighting struck something outside and there was another loud crack against Charles's bedroom window, followed by a battery of hail. Just then Eugene returned, three sheets to the wind on his own weather chart. Whatever he had gone out for, added to the tequila from dinnertime, was not wearing well. He had changed to his Japanese lounging clothes and was stomping about the house, raunchy and mischievous, although the hour had arrived to remove the bandage. It was a hell of a time, I told him, to be out of control.

After another half an hour, around 1 a.m, when Eugene had calmed down a bit, we removed the bandage, Charles reminding him about the blood Eugene had said he'd seen earlier. Eugene flipped the "bloody" gauze bandage he'd prepared across the bed and onto the pillow in front of Charles's eyes.

"There, is that enough blood for you?" he asked.

"Throw it away," I said, scooping it up quickly. I ran to the bathroom and flushed the toilet. Meanwhile, Eugene was telling Charles there was no scar.

"That's a miracle," Charles said. "To cut into me, and all that, with no scar. Baby, that's a miracle!"

"I don't think it's a miracle," I said uncomfortably. "Pachita knows things other people don't. Some people think your music is a miracle. Some people think—"

"You can't run your intellectual shit on this one," he snapped. "This is spiritual. Ain't no one can do that, cut into the body and don't leave no scar."

"Claudy was opened from her neck to her spine and there was no scar," I said, trying to shift the conversation to something I thought I believed took place. "Or Vincenzo . . ."

"Three days," Charles mused, "before removing the bandage . . . forty days for the wine to prepare . . ."

Pachita worked with spiritual numbers. I could feel his faith in her settling. I drew some comfort from that. I held his hand in mine and he pressed his fingers into my palm. I could feel his nails. We talked about the operation. I asked whether there was pain.

"If she wanted me to feel pain I would have felt pain," he said.

"You said you did," I reproached him.

His eyes twinkled. "Well, when the knife went in four or five inches, there was pain, baby."

In the bathroom Eugene nudged me and held up his thumb and middle finger in a circular sign of triumph. We had pulled it off. I hurried out.

Still, it wasn't entirely clear just who in our household was running the show.

Charles and Eugene continued to discuss Pachita while Eugene prepared his bath.

"Well, I hope she's whatever you believe in, God or the devil."

"Oh, there's a God," Charles said.

"Well, I don't know," Eugene replied.

Charles said: "He walked the earth."

"If he did, I think he'd still be walking," Eugene said as he wrung out the washcloth.

"There's a God," Charles repeated.

"I hear you, man."

Was it a seventy-five-dollar fiasco? Some cheap theater in the dark? Flashing knives and scissors and the smell of alcohol? This morning, after a sleepless night, irritated or disappointed in Eugene, who must have been wearing thin under the strain of his demands, Charles woke me up so Eugene could "take a break" for fifteen minutes. The break stretched into three hours. Soon we were arguing and complaining, me about my kidneys, he about his sleeplessness; me that I need three or four hours of vacation. The nurses all get twelve hours a day and a whole day each week. Even Eugene gets twelve hours a day. Me, I'm always on call, or shopping or cooking or preparing herbs.

"I need someone to talk to," I complained. Even Charles won't hold a conversation with me; he cuts me off in the middle of any small enthusiasm.

"You're right," he said, "I can't talk anymore, I can't think. I'm going crazy. I can't sleep." And on we went. In his frustration he moved his legs so they hung over the side of the bed a little.

"Well, you're moving your body," I said.

"Yeah, I'd like to move it right off the bed and crack my head on the floor. I tried to do that in New York once. I tried to summon all my strength. I couldn't do it."

I watched him inch himself into different positions on the bed like a large fleshy crab, his naked body straining under the exertion. I thought about all that trapped power and remembered the days on Fifth Street in his studio when he was sometimes anguished or full of fury and I was fearful of his strength. For a moment, the slow movements of his body filled me with fear again until I was consumed with such sorrow and shame, I dropped my head.

Now his hands looked like the hands of a drowned man, puckered at the fingertips, with an odd translucence. Now they had the feeling of paper. Those hands that had created so much music were withering from lack of use.

Eight

You gonna miss me, baby
'cause I ain't comin' back no mo'
You gonna miss me, baby
my old raggedy soul . . .

Charles was on his back, singing in bed, imitating Jimmy Wither-spoon and his throaty vibrato. Eugene boogied into the bath-room to heat the herbal mixture prescribed by Pachita.

"You know, I like the blues better than bebop. Always did," Charles said in his big new voice. He continued to sing and exercise his voice as he had all morning—ever since he discovered that he could gargle again. Staring at the ceiling, his voice rose: "Urinal uri-nal urinal urinal urinal . . ."

Eugene was rattling pans and running water in the sink.

"*Piss, ba-by . . .*" he sang louder.

Eugene carried in the bedpan while Charles beamed, delighted with his newfound voice.

"Tamales!" he shouted suddenly. "Hey, Hometown," he called to his son. "Let's hit the country roads . . ."

Soon we were speeding through the countryside, Eugene at the wheel, over bumpy dirt roads and unpaved village streets, Charles bouncing like jelly in the wheelchair behind, grinning and gritting his teeth by turns as we careened around the circular *zócalos,* stopping to taste the local tamales—hot cornbread shaped inside corn husks—served up by old women out of giant metal pots steaming in front of poor huts and shanties that dotted the tiny village paths, mud paths that turned into mud roads and eventually snaked off to the mountains.

Eugene, who went scouting earlier in the week for wild cannabis—convinced it was growing in the area—was discussing his hopes with Arturo.

"You think is just there, like that, free for you?" Arturo laughed from the backseat, where he was attending to Charles. "Oh, no. If there, *amigo,* farmer shoot you, no question!"

Meanwhile, Eugene has been growing marijuana here at home. He has cultivated clandestine patches around the property. He makes forays each morning, carrying a plastic garbage bag full of water or cow manure or snail shit or anything else we have in stock that he thinks will increase its potency. He babies it with more attention than he lavished on his wife and child, who twice have come to visit. The day after his romantic interlude with Claudy in the guest room last week, he invited her to visit his crop. She declined, failing to perceive the rare expression of intimacy behind his offer.

He has planted it behind an abandoned mansion a half mile away. It grows on the rooftops of our villa. He has placed jars of it in shadowy clumps around the garden wall. A cellophane bag full of already-harvested green seeds dries in the sun on the kitchen sill while he researches ways to improve the local strain. One day he told us how he planned to transport his plants to California when he returned: hiding them in the paper hangers of his suits, or beneath the dogs' thick collars, or inside the handlebars of his son's tricycle that had been left behind. He wasn't troubled by the rules. "Someone else's justice," he called the white man's law, quoting Malcolm X as he'd done in school—"just us"—insider jokes he'd learned growing up in Watts.

As Claudy and I cooked the ingredients for Charles's herbal massage on the stove, Eugene leaned over from behind her shoulder, brushing his arm against her breast while he examined the sticky sap with a professional eye before we added it to the cauldron. Although she warned him against it—"No! Not good! Not to do"—he took a little, all the same. Soon the smell of "smoke" and the scent of candles and incense, along with the monotonous sound of chanting, issued from his quarters through the connecting bathrooms to the bedroom where Charles was still asleep.

After weeks of living together, as close and intense and involved as we have become, I realized that I knew almost nothing of Eugene's feelings, except that he seemed to be without a heart. And yet, if there was a redeeming side, it was the comic-strip hero who caught firecrackers in his hands at celebrations, the adventurer for whom there was no task, no risk, no undertaking too difficult to attempt. In a household already run on fantasy and excess, his willingness to try anything, his relaxed lunacy, fed the boundlessness of our hope. He pushed Charles tied in his wheelchair to the tops of pyramids or down the flowing staircase of Las Mananitas restaurant to the elegant gardens below, carrying the Mingus energy and imagination into the next generation—impetuous, moody, infuriating, reassuring. Whether he had soul was hard to tell: the street cynicism and survival buttons snapped on and off. Still, he had remarkable patience and was managing to help Charles in countless ways.

The prolonging of life, the stretching of this almost unspeakable ordeal over the long days, was it worth it, I sometimes wondered. Does the daily struggle match Charles's huge desire to go on living? That desire prevailed for at least part of each day as, determined in our independence, we headed off in the car by ourselves, rattling over country roads, Charles bobbing in the seat behind me, the chains holding him in place as I tried to think of places to go and consulted his wretched face in the rearview mirror while we made an effort to deny reality and pretend we were free and mobile. We were, for a while. At least we had the memory of how we were.

The two of us drove through the afternoon, exploring, buying live turkeys that flap imprisoned behind Charles who was imprisoned as we drove on through Mexico, where we never planned to live or know this other inscrutable culture: an American woman in blue jeans and a large black man in a wheelchair behind, stopping at stands where the woman opened the side door of the Volkswagen bus and delivered tacos to the man, while Mexicans stared without much curiosity and Charles ate and thought about the next place to go, anywhere, so long as it was not home.

Sometimes I thought of simply driving the car off the side of the road.

As I stood at the edge of the pool with indecision before returning to the house, Charles looked up from his wheelchair, which was parked at the end of the sloping lawn beneath the porch, with a slightly wicked stare.

"It will be just this sort of moment, knowing you," he said, "when you'll lift your arm and swat me into the pool." He was smiling. He summoned all his strength, pushed his hands forward slightly on the arms of the chair, and made ready for the move.

"Not yet. But it will happen," I said optimistically. We were speaking of renewed health. At least I thought we were. At a later date I would consider that idle suggestion as an invitation to murder, a last desperate exit out of his misery. Perhaps he already knew.

.   .   .

Tonight, September 15, in celebration of Mexican independence and Eugene's birthday, our family caravan, including Ron, our latest import from the San Francisco nursing agency, went out on the town under a sky of fireworks. Earlier, I constructed a towering birthday cake out of thirty-two bottles of Dos Equis, Eugene's favorite beer, with a big candle wedged on top and a bottle of tequila to grow on, along with a colorful blanket and dashing poncho I found in the market.

Charles and I sat on the porch while I exercised his fingers. I pressed back each knuckle, one by one, pressed the middle joints, folded and pressed the fingers, curled them into his palm in a fist, then opened them, according to his orders. Each joint on each finger was pressed back, and again back, and back farther still.

"More," Charles said, wincing.

"Does it hurt?"

"Man," he said, "of course it hurts. It's supposed to. Ain't nobody exercised these fingers in two days."

"Well, tell Arturo. He'll do it. So will Ron. Or Eugene. Or me. I did it yesterday, don't you remember?"

He eyed each finger critically as I handled it, expressing his displeasure when I fell short of his demands, describing each movement in detail. His fingers, his hands, were still under his careful discipline despite his inability to unlock their energies on his own.

After an extended argument with nurse Ron (whom Charles maintains is no nurse at all—he thinks a band of phonies in San Francisco is using names of real nurses to get jobs out of the country. He says Ron doesn't turn him correctly and makes mistakes a nurse

wouldn't make), we made up once again. I said I shoot my mouth off
a lot, but no hard feelings. I've traveled a distance from my re-
spectable roots, the genteel control essential to civilized behavior; a
distance from my father, who once set aside my gift to him of Saul
Bellow's *Henderson, the Rain King* because he found the language
vulgar and unacceptable, reminding me of the centuries it had taken
to separate man from beast, to fashion civilized man and gentlewoman. He was not about to throw it all away because of a word on
page five.

"But Shakespeare, your favorite author, is full of vulgarity," I
protested.

"Yes," he replied, "but only in the mouths of drunkards and
thieves."

I am countless scenes away from the gentlewoman I was.

Going to sleep at night resembles an audio obstacle course in the
middle of a 1960s light show. I lie in the jumbo-size bed sideways
across the middle, hugging the bedclothes and pillow in an effort to
block out sound and light and prepare to ignore the commotion and
state of emergency that continue around me throughout the night.

Charles shouts orders every few moments, the lights flick off and
on from one end of the room to the other and from bathroom to
bathroom, compounded by the enormously loud grating of the electric bed as it rises toward the ceiling or takes on various positions
(knees up, head down, bed up), the changing frequency of the water
bubbles in the oxygen tank as Eugene raises or lowers the pressure in
the tube that runs into Charles's nostrils, and then, worst of all, Eugene's fiercely unexpected bangings on the metal tank, which every
single time fill me with fear.

This morning, exhausted and full of infantile rage, I sang "O sole
mio" as loudly as I could under Eugene's window so that his rest
might be disturbed; so that he might experience a fraction of my

frustration and sleeplessness. Afterward I had a long, absurd argument with Charles in the garden.

Tonight, in an effort to make peace and to court me in style, he invited Eugene and me out to an after-hours discotheque—always in charge, always coming up with something unexpected. How I love that man! We sat in the aluminum-foiled dark of the discotheque like an Andy Warhol studio extension, Charles in his wheelchair, Eugene and me beside him at a table, while the strains of "Saturday Night Fever" pumped their way across Mexico, pumped their way across the entire world, if the daily marketplace here is any indication.

Today we drove to Theresa's elegant apartment in Mexico City to wait for Claudy's urgent call regarding an audience with Pachita later in the day. Eventually the phone rang—Claudy calling to say that Pachita was not available. "Pachita call me personally. Say Charles must bear some of pain. Is expected he have pain in legs and arms and shoulders as muscles start again to move. Say she already take out virus, is getting better. Will call him like with Vincenzo when is—"

"Don't call me, I'll call you," I interrupted angrily. Because now I had to tell Charles, had to watch the disappointment on his face, know the suffering that would continue. I went into the dining room, where everyone was assembled over chicken cutlets, fettucini and mushrooms, zucchini and tomato puree, where everyone was wiping their mouths with beige linen and lace napkins. The room grew silent. I repeated to Charles what Claudy had said.

"I am getting better, I am getting better, I am getting better," he said.

"Every day in every way, I am getting better and better." I repeated the mantra of Émile Coué, a popular healer of the 1920s. The room laughed uneasily.

"Who told us to come to Mexico, anyway?" Charles asked bitterly. "Claudy?"

The March 15, 1972, cover of *Changes*.

Sue, Charles, and Sonny Rollins at Norman Mailer's
fiftieth birthday party at The Four Seasons.

Charles composing at home.
Photo: Sue Mingus.

Partial score of "Sue's Changes." 1974.

Sue's surprise birthday party for Charles at home, on April 22, 1978. *Photo: Sy Johnson.*

Charles dictating musical instructions to Paul Jeffrey for new compositions that he sang into a tape recorder. Winter 1978. *Photo: Sue Mingus.*

At the White House in June 1978: Roberto (partially hidden by President Carter), President Carter, Mr. Mackie (the nurse), Charles, and Sue.

Sue and Charles confront New York, following the North African tour.

Joni Mitchell and Charles in Mexico.
Photo: Sue Mingus.

Eugene and Arturo prepare to kill
an iguana for Charles's iguana-
blood and wine potion.

Eugene pours the iguana-blood
potion into Charles's wineglass.

Sue makes a circle of life before scattering
Charles's ashes into the Ganges River.
January 1979.

Horses running along the beach of the Ganges River.
January 1979.

The Mingus Dynasty, at a recording session for its first album for Atlantic, in 1980. *Left to right:* Jimmy Knepper, Charlie Haden, Dannie Richmond, Jimmy Owens, John Handy, Don Pullen, and Joe Farrell.

Sue and the Mingus Dynasty in North Africa on a State Department-sponsored tour, in March 1980. *Left to right:* Hugh Lawson, Dannie Richmond, George Adams, Sue, the Commander of the Royal Moroccan Air Force, and John Handy.

The Mingus Dynasty in Argentina, outside a Buenos Aires television studio. *Left to right*: Clifford Jordan, Billy Hart, Roland Hanna, and Randy Brecker.

The Mingus Big Band at Fez in New York City, performing material from "Blues and Politics," in 2000.

The Mingus Big Band's Christmas card in 1995.

The Mingus Orchestra in 2000. *Photo: Jimmy Katz.*

"People must wait," I said feebly. "Pachita has her own sense of time. When Vincenzo first came to Mexico, he had an appointment on Monday. He stayed with friends for a week. When he wore out his welcome, he moved to a hotel. She didn't call. Three months later he got his appointment. It took Claudy over a year for hers." I was talking as fast as I could. "We've been lucky. You've already seen her twice . . ." Everyone was chiming in. Charles seemed to relax a little.

"Pachita is clever," he said. "She gets some lamb's blood, does her business in the dark, and then gets you to cure yourself with your own confidence." He was beginning to laugh. "Yeah, man," he said to Eugene, "a little lamb's blood—that blood had an odor on that bandage. Human blood don't smell."

No one can pull the wool—lamb's or otherwise—over Charles's eyes, I thought with pride.

"It didn't smell to me," Eugene said. "I mean, it wasn't no woman's blood."

"Yeah, man." Charles was beginning to enjoy himself. "It wasn't from no pussy." Everyone was looking relieved.

"I want some ice cream, man," Charles said suddenly. "Tell Arturo we're going out. I want pineapple and banana and strawberry and pistachio . . ."

"And vanilla and chocolate," I said.

"And rum raisin," Eugene added as our procession headed for the door.

Joni Mitchell arrived last night, followed by our friend Daniele Senatore and his pal Carlo Ponti, currently at Elektra Records, Joni's label. We met them all at the airport and swung home through the notorious Plaza de Garibaldi in downtown Mexico, where feasts of tamales and *pulche*—the murderously strong cactus wine essential to life here—were as available as the bands of mariachis poised to croon their tales of love and betrayal. I thought of Charles's tribute to them, "Los Mariachis," on his album *Tijuana Moods,* and wondered if he, too, was recalling the wild bordertown nights he once celebrated.

The following morning our household was spread across the garden after only a few hours' sleep: Joni, in a bright orange leotard, performing her yoga exercises. Later, she sat on the grass beside Charles and discussed their recording project. She said she needed another song or two so the album would have "more variation."

"I never wrote the same thing twice," Charles replied. "If there's a similarity, you are in control of that. It's the arrangements." He told her he no longer had any melodic range and could not sing another tune.

"Why don't you write lyrics for 'Reincarnation of a Love Bird' or 'Sue's Changes'?" he suggested. Later on, while he was playing a tape of "Orange Was the Color of Her Dress" for her, I realized his own drummer, Dannie Richmond, could be playing the same tune— one of the staples of the band—at that very moment at the Village Vanguard in New York.

"I know I tell long stories," Joni said later that night when we were emptying the crystal wine decanter and telling our tales. "I've inundated you. I've talked without stopping. It's because you're a new friend. It's as if I have to get all the information out so you'll be an old friend." It was an unexpected, swift, and easy friendship— something that bolstered me in my isolation, along with long talks with Daniele late into the night, glad for his mind and his heart and the plain good fun he was to have around.

Still, the projects and discussions that extend beyond Charles's illness were no more than the blur and noise of an outside world we no longer inhabited. Even the social occasions, the long drives, the rustic lunches, the bullfight we attended in Mexico City—Charles watching moist-eyed as his own sign, Taurus, charged into his moment of truth—the strolls in town, are giddy and indistinct.

.   .   .

"There's old Peanut himself," Joni observed when she first arrived and saw the color photograph of President Carter hugging Charles (signed with personal regards and mailed out by the White House) that sits on a wooden shelf near the dining room table. It was slowly losing its shape, bending at the middle from the heat and humidity and the constant rains.

A few days after Joni left, we found a silver frame for the photo in Taxco, the silver center for tourists in this area, one afternoon when Eugene, Arturo, Charles, and I were driving through the mountains on one of our small, always unpredictable excursions.

After only twenty minutes in Taxco, we were accused of stealing two rings from a silver shop; the police, who were instantly summoned, threatened to take Eugene, Arturo, and Charles in his wheelchair to the station. Arturo was incensed. Charles threatened to piss on the floor. Eugene made the usual casual small talk and jokey denials.

When we finally drove off, Arturo shouted through the window of our van at the Indian ladies, shopkeepers, and assorted carabinieri who had assembled on the street, that we lived in the governor's house in Cuernavaca, as though our lofty residence cleared us of suspicion. I, too, had shouted at the police, calling them idiots for accusing a man who was paralyzed in a wheelchair of theft.

Meanwhile, there was no doubt in my mind who had pocketed them.

"Where should we go now?" Arturo asked.

"To steal some more rings?" I said, looking sideways at Eugene.

To obtain the ingredients for our manure applications, I drove to the corner early in the morning, when several cows were freely grazing on a grassy area flanking the sidewall to our villa. I parked the car, took out a garden spade from the trunk, and ran after a large black-and-white heifer, scooping up the mounds of manure she was dropping along the way. Over my shoulder I could see the strolling

Mexicans as they peered out silent and expressionless from under their sombreros.

Back in the kitchen, I wrapped the "schitt," which was full of small seeds and healthy-looking blades of grass, inside plastic bags and placed it in the salad compartment of the refrigerator, hoping the maids would not find it. Their feelings about gringos were already ambivalent. Later I would add chopped parsley and yellow camomile flowers, according to Pachita's orders, perhaps prescribed for the humane purpose of offsetting the smell.

We initiated the manure applications down at the pool: a mix of one half-portion fresh grated parsley to two parts cow shit, heated over an outdoor burner sizzling on the porch. There was common agreement that the fumes would be less powerful outdoors. Charles submitted with silent dignity. He had protested for the past week—right up to the moment when he was confronted with Arturo's direct telephone call to Pachita (Arturo dialed her number and the enchantress herself picked up the phone) to discuss Charles's recalcitrance and any possible alternatives. Faced with her possible disapproval, he had rallied, leaning forward to assure Arturo, who was holding the receiver, that yes, he would do it, he would certainly do it.

The possibility of hope, of some new truth from this dumpy neighborhood witch (mistaking her for Pachita, I once followed another large, aproned woman down the street into a vegetable shop), was enough to make Arturo stammer and stutter, all smiles when addressing her, despite years of medical training repeating her name every few phrases in deference: "Pachita, how long should we leave the cow po-po on? Should it be heated, Pachita? Yes, Pachita. Thank you, thank you, Pachita."

Last week our usual caravan of Arturo, Eugene, Charles, and me ran into her unexpectedly on the street. She was sitting in the front seat of an automobile parked in front of her house and was in a surprisingly aggressive mood.

"People say I am a *bruca*—a witch. Fuck it!" she was saying to someone when we arrived. She was holding a small child and spoke to Arturo through the car window. Charles stared at her from his wheelchair on the street and told Arturo what to ask next. She eyed him from time to time, her left eye squinting. She asked why he wore a belt across his forehead and listened to Arturo's explanation about holding his head in place against the chair. Then she prescribed snails for his lungs, a "plaster" of cow manure with parsley for his chest, and hot comino oil to massage away the cramps in his legs.

Back home that evening, down at the pool, Charles sat in his chair, naked in the waning light, while Arturo applied cow dung to his stomach, wrapped loosely in thin gauze, and Muttley sniffed around the chair. As I passed through the small space between the arm of his wheelchair and the water, I thought: if his chair slipped and he plunged into the water we might not be able to get him out, he might drown.

He might drown. It was so simple. I could do it myself. The accident would be over in three minutes. No possibility of error or failure, as with the sleeping pills which might not work, or the overdose which might be difficult to explain—Charles not being able take them himself. Murder. But here was a way for an accident: Arturo out to lunch, Eugene sleeping on the far side of the house. It is an option if things get worse. He can still see, he can swallow, he has hope. But after Pachita's "fifty days" from the operation are up, if he is not better, a way out of his misery must be found.

"Completely alive or completely dead," he said yesterday. I ask Eugene occasionally what we should do. He sidesteps the question.

As his wheelchair becomes more uncomfortable, his innovations multiply. Recently we covered the backboard with sheepskin.

"It's gone from a Mercedes to a Rolls-Royce," Eugene observed this morning.

After spending all afternoon at the teeming La Viga marketplace in Mexico City searching for garden snails—*caracolas*—prescribed by Pachita for the latest cure, we returned to our villa. We dumped the twenty-five kilos of snails on the floor of the ornate patio bathroom off the kitchen. They would have suffocated in the burlap bag from the market or disappeared into the earth if we had poured them on the lawn.

Only a few hours later, they blackened the marble bathroom, clinging to the walls and ceilings, darkening the toilet, caking the door handle and the frame. They were as grotesque and ubiquitous as a plague, as horrifying as a scene in a Hitchcock film. They spread across the floor, covering the tiles. They climbed the pipes. They blanketed the gold-inlaid oval mirror and the porcelain sink below. Every inch of the room was alive with movement.

Sabino picked off two hundred for Charles's first meal. They require several rinsings to wash off their slime and eliminate their poisons, an hour to remove the tiny dark shells, after which they are boiled and, finally, fried in butter with garlic and parsley.

Although Mexicans don't eat snails, Sabino and Margarita carry on stoic and resolute. They have learned to live with a refrigerator full of cow manure and to circle the tall mounds of imported mud for Charles's bath that block the elegant courtyard. They have learned to sidestep the green bottles of Pachita's *aguardiente,* whose charmed contents ripen under the moon and stars; to ignore the chickens laying eggs indiscriminately off the pool; and to avoid the colliding geese and dogs and iguanas as they skid past our walls of flowering bougainvillea.

In the current order of things, programmed by a reincarnated Aztec prince and a loud-talking gringo in a souped-up chair, a million snails multiplying in the bathroom are just one more fact of life in the daily scenario.

Eugene did not show up from his short trip to California according to plan, although we waited at the airport all day long and Charles went crazy at home. Mary-the-substitute-nurse offered to help out on this third night in a row in which I have had no help and no sleep. It was a long, infernal night during which I succumbed to fits of helplessness and rage. A few times I wept.

"She is *unico*," Mary had said earlier to Charles as I bathed him and applied ointments. "She is so patient, your wife." Later, when I lost control—standing at the side of the bed, overcome with frustration and exhaustion, going into my fifty-sixth hour without sleep, my voice at a screaming pitch, staring wildly at the ceiling as if God might explain my crime or my punishment—Mary was tight-lipped and disappointed at the foot of the bed.

I regained control and continued the long vigil after noisily ripping off the granny gown I had donned only a moment before (ready to take Mary up on her whispered suggestion that I try to get some sleep) and angrily throwing on my khaki pants and shirt again—because Charles did not want to be left alone with a nurse whose English was so undependable—stomping back into the room to announce I was dressed once more and would not, oh no, attempt to snatch just an hour's sleep. Charles mumbled on, his momentous energy unceasing, full of reproach and a dozen indecipherable insults, born of the righteousness and madness of the ill, forged within its bestiality and suffering and all-consuming need, which reduces everything that is human and sensitive to the ravings of a lonely creature throbbing in bed in the final spasms of protest.

I remembered Rilke's description of his grandfather's dying, the hugeness of it filling the rooms of the mansion as he ordered his servants to carry him from bedroom to bedroom, roaring and bellowing through the halls as he lived the immensity of his death like the last terrible eruption of a volcano.

Charles calls out every twenty or thirty seconds. When finally I can bear it no longer, when finally I voice my fatigue and tell him that his need stretches beyond my capacity, when at last I have turned the light on and off for the fortieth time, turned the oxygen tank up or down, pulled the pillow in or out, felt for spasms that are not there, massaged comino oil into imaginary ripples, stretched his arms, re-adjusted the sheet, when it is after 6 a.m. and Brunhilda is barking out the night and the rooster is sounding the alarm again as it has done all night long with the confusion of Mexican roosters, when the sky is becoming light and we begin to make out objects inside the room, now, all at once, I hear Charles begin to snore. Mary is in the big chair suddenly asleep, and I sit smoking a cigarette in the bathroom and drinking instant Mexican coffee, my eyes burning, perceiving all at once my split image where the mirrors meet, a face that still fails to show the reflected agony of Charles's suffering. He snores on, it has been three or four minutes, a brief recharging of batteries, almost a whole cigarette.

Nine

It was November 1, the Day of the Dead, a day of celebrations in cemeteries, dances, and pageantry. Special cakes in the shape of skulls filled the bakery windows. "Is not macabre," Claudy said over the phone. "Is full of life and mystery and art . . ."

Here at home, however, there was no art or pageantry, only Charles's failing voice and the steady changes in his condition. When he couldn't count the usual one-two-three-four as we lifted him to his feet this morning, he modulated to four grunts instead: "Uh-uh-uh-uh."

I sit here smoking two cigarettes, drinking coffee, and eating a piece of death cake—*pan de la muerte,* according to the sign—a round, high, white sugar cake that looked like a squashed tam-o'-shanter. I'd just called Claudy to remind her it had been four months and he was getting worse, to ask whether Pachita had ever promised and failed to deliver. I'd called out of a need to be told something, anything, I suppose the truth. After seven decades of firsthand experience with bodies and minds that were not working properly,

227

doesn't Pachita know a hopeless disease from one that could be treated? Was she a legend, a reality, or merely a dupe? Was she a witch gone senile? Even witches deteriorate, they don't just go out in a puff of smoke.

"Is not a charlatan," Claudy responded with some annoyance. "If say something, is for reason." She paused. Before hanging up, she repeated, "Is not a fake."

"Don't go right home," Charles said after dining on oxtails and fettucini at Las Mananitas. Driving shakes him up and calms his pains. I suggested we drive all night long. And so we drove, bumping over dirt roads, hoping he might sleep, stopping frequently along the way to adjust his chair. Once Arturo and I spent half an hour on the side of the road, redoing everything one more time: removing the backboard, the blue-and-white tube, the chains, the long bandage-scarf, the wooden wheel support below, the pillows under his feet, and then starting over again from scratch.

The windows were steamed. We were on the old road to Mexico, the "Libera"—not the new toll highway—and there was not another car in sight. The police seldom patrolled here and it was unsafe to stop, as Arturo noted more than once. He was muttering in the blackness—while we did and undid Charles's covers—"Your money or your life," as if the Mexican highwaymen had already arrived. I was beginning to get nervous. I remembered a Flannery O'Connor story called "A Good Man Is Hard to Find" about a calamitous roadside encounter. We heard a rustling sound from the woods. "They'd just as soon take your life as not for a few pesos in these parts," Arturo said under his breath. We worked faster. Charles, undaunted, continued his demands.

And so we drove through the Mexican night over winding roads and across mountains, a slip of moon visible in the direction of Popocatépetl, the dark slopes and shadows and silhouettes of the swiftly passing landscape forming a blurred and spectacular reality of their own as Charles, lumped and jostled in his chair, found a tenuous peace in the night.

For a moment he spoke in his sleep.

"What?" Arturo asked.

"I'm in a trance sometimes, man, I don't know who I am."

And then after the pain set in again, after hours of discomfort, we stopped for ice cream. Afterward, in the rearview mirror, I saw his face lit with pleasure, human, recognizable, a little tune rising from the backseat in the dark.

While we were in Mexico City, Sabino and Margarita threw out the cow shit I had stashed away, without telling them, in the salad compartment of the refrigerator. Not as shocking as a dead cat, perhaps; still, one would like to have overheard that conversation.

I started to read aloud the liner notes for the new album that Atlantic Records had just mailed us. Charles stopped me almost immediately. The title had been misunderstood. It read "Me Myself and I" and he was not interested in hearing it.

"Me, Myself—*an Eye,*" he said impatiently, "the *Eye of God,* of the *loved and beloved,* the *eternal.* They don't understand a thing."

An English fan had sent a taped interview with Charles that also arrived today. It was made in London in 1972. In it he says: "Music is my life. Without it I'd be dead. All I need is score paper and a piano."

Later in the bedroom, he said: "I think Pachita has gotten together all the people in the spiritual world, all the people in the land of hell and the land of heaven, all the king's horses and all the king's men, and I think she can't put Humpty Dumpty together again. . . . But then, maybe he never fell at all. Maybe he was just a poor fool in love."

.   .   .

At home from the hospital, Mary pinch-hit during the day, a slow, sunny, tenuous Sunday waiting for Eugene, who was still in Mexico City. Charles was nervous and high-strung, on the edge of panic. To speak clearly now he must make the superhuman effort of lifting his head.

"I have no voice box," he said at breakfast. Still, he refuses to simplify or modify his commands by limiting himself to one or two words. Stubbornly he maintains the complex convolutions of thought, feeling, and metaphor that are the materials of his spirit. As we strain to hear, his demands unfold in long narrative form, reproaches full of historical detail, the past failures of a reckless nurse who missed a beat or botched a cue or his conviction that his well-being, and perhaps his life, depend upon the precision with which we fold a sheet.

Several days ago I suggested a shorthand arrangement—questions that could be answered yes or no. Today he had a slight remission and his normal voice briefly returned. When I walked into the living room he glared at me with an indignation that must have been simmering for several days. With all the strength and fury he could muster, he exclaimed: *"Fuck yes or no!"*

On Monday, he was feeling better. We set off on a journey for Ixtapan de la Sal, driving through a stupendous mountain range that resembled a bed of sleeping women, sensuous dark curves that lay along the horizon as softly seductive and inviting as goddesses in repose. Everywhere the land and sky seemed peopled with divinities, erotic and awesome. I could barely keep my eyes on the road.

As we swung around a bend, we passed a family of Indians gathered under an enormous tree who held up iguanas for us to see. Charles's unmistakable sounds of interest from the backseat caused us to back up and purchase two jumbo iguanas for three dollars apiece.

"The blood of the iguana has no smell," the old woman said as she held the scaly reptile by its tail high in the air. "When you kill him, you cut the back of his neck with a knife and catch the blood."

"It's good to drink," added the old man. "It's good for health. You can mix it with wine or with beer."

"Or with Coca-Cola," said the young boy, holding a smaller iguana by the tail. Rattlesnakes and pythons were on sale back at the house, but we reluctantly sped on.

At home we arrived in a commotion of iguanas: Margarita screamed; Sabino observed from far off; Eugene, after careful examination, announced he would have a pair of new shoes made from their skin.

"Better than alligator," he said.

Early morning. Our household was assembled on the back patio of our villa. We set a bottle of Mexican blanc de blanc Hidalgo with three wine goblets on the glass table. Then we placed a pan to catch the iguana blood at the edge of the courtyard where Arturo and Eugene were waiting, armed with ropes and knives. Margarita and Sabino sat close together on the wooden bench. Charles watched critically from his corner.

Eugene held the iguana tight under his palm as it hissed and opened its bright pink mouth in the direction of Muttley, whose nose was quivering flat on the ground. His body was ready to spring. Slowly Arturo delivered the death blow, clean and professional, catching the spurting blood just as the first rays of sun blinked through the thick branches of our orange tree.

As we were pouring the blood into goblets, a local physician, Dr. Calva, appeared at the entrance to our garden and then backed hurriedly off the terrace. "I don't want to interfere with your ritual," he murmured.

"It's not voodoo," I said irritably. "We're preparing to eat the iguana and are sampling its blood."

"I suppose if turtles carry typhoid, iguanas do, too," he observed from the far edge of the patio.

"We eat turtles in soup," I replied.

"Nicely boiled," he countered softly. Charles refrained suddenly from sampling his drink. I sipped mine with determination. It tasted powerful, possibly the zap of early morning wine. Eugene downed the rest, liberally laced with chilled Mexican blanc de blanc.

"Oh well. Oh well. Oh well. Oh well. Oh well. Oh well." Charles sat at the breakfast table, exercising his voice. "Oh. Well."

Somewhere in the dry rolling fields of the Mexican night, fifty kilometers from home, is a place called El Huerto, or the Orchard. The name suggests an irrigated land and is a metaphor for the bordello village tucked inside its folds. Through the center of this village runs the Callano de la Speranza, the Street of Hope. On either side of its narrow lane are rooming houses interspersed with bright taco bars, 1,400 rooms in all.

Driving through the countryside in our van during one of our midnight excursions, hoping to stumble on a late-night snack, we found ourselves part of the crowd on the Street of Hope. Charles, dressed like a visiting sheik in his white Arab robes, might have been lining up a harem.

Our van moved slowly down the narrow street.

We parked the car, lowered Charles out of the van, and entered one of the bars. Eugene winked at the bartender: "It's not often that Mom, Pop, and son frequent the bordellos together." Soon we were back in the van full of tacos, beer, and too much loud music, moving slowly down the road. We passed baggy-trousered Mexicans shuffling by archways that revealed door after door like public dressing rooms at the beach. We continued down the dirt street until mud holes and rocks rendered the way impassable.

In one of our final trips to the big market to buy herbs, Charles informed me bitterly that I did not know "how to follow orders." Under other circumstances I might have considered that a plus. Now I felt only the sting of his dissatisfaction. At the market Eugene disappeared, leaving Arturo and me the backbreaking job of lifting Charles's wheelchair out of the car by ourselves. While we negotiated terms with the herb lady, Charles, sitting slightly apart from us, alone in his chair, called me over and unexpectedly burst into tears.

"I get offended too, sometimes," I said. I put my arms around him. I assumed he was concerned about our squabbles. Then I noticed a peso sitting on his shirtsleeve. "What's that?" I asked.

He looked up at me. "Someone put it there," he sobbed. I held his head in my arms.

Arturo came over. "What's this? What's this?" he asked Charles. "What happened?"

"Someone gave him a peso," I said.

Arturo frowned. "It's like that here in Mexico," he said quickly. "It's what people do. That's life," he said, appealing to Charles's worldliness. "You and I, we are men. We are sophisticated, we don't care about it.

"It's good luck," he suddenly added. "Yes, put that coin in your pocket, right there. It's good luck." He smiled encouragingly. I wanted to hug him. He laughed. "Come on, come on," he said to Charles. "Let's go buy some fruit, yes? There is a fruit you have never had. I want you to taste."

We made our way to the best fruit stand in the market. Four little girls and a little boy stood near the stand and gaped curiously at Charles. They crowded close to observe him. They stared with the cold, cruel directness of children. I tried to put myself between their watchfulness and his misery. I said angrily to the boy in Spanish, "What are you looking at?" He drifted away. I stepped hard on the toe of a small foot behind me. Unfortunately, the remaining children belonged to the fruit stand lady.

From the family stand we moved to the voodoo section of the market, where I bought a "devilfish," a dried skeleton of a strange creature that resembled a monster. It was hanging above the herb stand beside the strings of religious beads and magical artifacts and good-luck garlic wreathes.

"Why do you want that?" Arturo asked disapprovingly as I forked over 150 pesos.

"To pray to," I said bitterly.

When we were all in the van, Charles said from the backseat, "Drive!"

"What?"

"Arturo, drive!" he said and grinned as if he had a trick up his sleeve. We drove along the highway for half an hour. When we reached home—a whole hour before Arturo's day was up—Charles said: "Arturo, you stay here. Sue and I will drive by ourselves." He grinned again.

"Okay, okay," Arturo agreed. Before returning into the house, he spooned out one of the exotic "granada" fruits he had purchased at the market for Charles, standing beside the wheelchair in the back-seat of the van.

"Where do you want to go?" I asked Charles when Arturo had gone inside.

"Get Aneho rum," he said mysteriously in his shorthand speech.

"Then what?"

"Curves," he said.

I wondered if he was contemplating our drunkenly careening off the highway to the sweet release of death.

"You want to jiggle around the curves?" I asked. He was silent. "Why did you want to leave Arturo?"

"To give him a break," he replied.

I hadn't realized he was repaying Arturo's kindness with some precious time off.

On the Plaza d'Ayala we found our rum, swigged down a third of a bottle, and then "Drive!" he said again. We set off for the old Aztec village of Tepotzlan, following a long, narrow road that wound through solitary hills where groups of horses wandered free in the night and where crosses and chalk-white stones shone bright as streetlamps under the reflecting moon.

As the moon vanished, giant mysterious shapes began to cover the horizon, dark phantom silhouettes that seemed to haunt the overcast night. We drove on and on through this magical time alone, the air unexpectedly warm and soft and sweet as spring. Hours later in a burst of light, the magnificent cathedral loomed incandescent over the sleeping town, hanging above Tepotzlan's cobblestone streets and colonial roofs like a giant lantern. Charles had orchestrated another moment out of time. Chair-ridden and paralyzed, he still dredged up more life, miles more, than most men on their feet.

"A slow rehabilitation," Pachita said, as we lined up before her the following day. "But is getting better." She stood in a dimly lit room with her attendants before an array of flowers, a receiving line in this shabby country club of the ill, as the sick and the invalid were ushered in through the gingham curtains, one by one. She came over before we left and patted Charles's stomach: "You must have faith. You must believe in God and you will be cured." She touched his forehead and asked for a blessing. After giving Jesus a list of medications, she said, "Tell the boy (*muchacho*) he is going to get well."

. . .

As we sat parked on the street near a bus stop where several dozen Indians were waiting, a small boy stood and stared curiously at Charles strapped into the wheelchair in the back of the van. Charles looked back at him for a moment and then launched into a series of weird faces and grimaces that sent the boy packing. It's the first thing he's done in three days with any enthusiasm.

"You've got to pull out of it," I said.

"You believe in her?" he asked.

"Of course."

"Fifty days are up," he said.

In the middle of the night Charles responded to a question I had asked that afternoon concerning some records he might like from New York.

". . . And tell them to send Monk," he said suddenly at 2 a.m., as if there had not been a lapse of eight hours since my question.

"What's that?" I said, awakening.

"Monk and Duke Ellington."

"What?"

"The tapes!"

"Oh, you want Monk, too? You haven't mentioned him for a long time," I said, yawning myself into consciousness.

Eugene cut in: "He wants the record with Duke, Dad, and Monk."

"Your father never made a record with Monk," I said, now fully awake.

"Yes, he did," Eugene insisted. "My mom has it. It's with Duke, Dad, Monk, and Max Roach."

"No, there's a tune Charles wrote called 'MDM,' for Monk, Duke, and Mingus."

From the dark recesses of the bedroom the maestro himself cut in. "Ask me," he said indignantly. "They haven't done me in yet."

We turned to inquire. "Was there or wasn't there?" I asked.

Charles's diction was now muddied and incomprehensible. As usual he refused, on principle, to answer any questions with a straightforward yes or no. I went back to sleep, waiting for clarification in the morning.

In the sun, on the patio, as Jesus was straining the wine from the gourd—Pachita's treatment for his saliva problems—Charles confirmed that he and Monk had never recorded together.

Later that day, I regressed to those first weeks over a year ago when I was emotionally out of control. It is difficult on the heart to spend much time alone with him without the nurses, who are a buffer to the disease, their good spirits professional, helping to keep reality at a distance. He noticed my eyes were wet and continued to give orders as he does throughout the day.

"Put my hand on your neck."

"On your neck?" I asked.

"On yours," he said in his gruff voice.

I put his hand on the back of my neck and leaned my head on the arm of the wheelchair. Then I realized he was no longer organizing his comfort but was shaping an embrace, his dead limbs arranged in a hug of reassurance. He stroked my head, moving his hand a little back and forth and exerting the slightest pressure. I started to cry. He continued to stroke my head. We said nothing.

The air was thick, electric. Above his wheelchair we could almost feel the August stars crackling in the night. We sat together listening to the din of tree frogs and crickets, their sultry buzz mingling with the incessant screams of cicadas in the open fields. We could almost taste the air. It was heavy and overripe with fragrance. There was too much beauty, I thought. I was afraid of slipping into its seductive spell, at least here in the wake of his suffering.

Not that sensuality and romance had ceased because of illness.

They remained center stage, he saw to that. When the nurses disappeared for lunch, we'd go off to the bedroom. Or, at the end of the day (if it had been a bad one), he'd invite me to unwind over cocktails in the elegant gardens at Las Mananitas, where we'd arrive with our raggedy carnival of nurses, bandages, and props, proud and noisy at the top of the flowing staircase.

But tonight he was in the wings, removed. His voice was barely audible, his mind fixed on his pain.

"Chapter Eleven," he said unexpectedly. I looked at him, slumped in his wheelchair near the pool, and wondered what adversary was on his mind. Some former critic, or death itself? To whom had he been pleading bankruptcy? All bets were off, that much was certain. Or perhaps he'd been talking money with his son.

I laughed. "Are you calling Chapter Eleven on Eugene?"

"Don't have to," he replied. "Daniele will take care of him." Matters with his son were often oblique, burdened with expectation, two sides pulling away at each other, balancing old debts. I was never certain what they meant.

I was certain only that dying, slow dying, required enormous attentiveness. Everything was new and surrounded by urgency, the focus as sharp and personal and terrifying as when one was a child. Nature and her monsters were in the corners again, whispering.

"If I get out of this," Charles said, "I'll have a lot to tell."

The lights and noise and maneuverings in the bedroom—compounded, as always, by Eugene's bumping into my bed as he turned Charles all night long like a goose on a spit—left me sleepless and crazed. When I shrieked at dawn after a particularly whopping jolt, Eugene accused me of "having an attitude."

"If anyone has an attitude around here," I snapped, "it's not me." I left for the marketplace two hours later—my only legitimate refuge, like an escape into church—as the whoops and cries of Eric (who had arrived for Christmas), Eugene, and Roberto down at the pool already pierced into the day ahead.

When I returned, Charles sent word that he wanted to talk to me in the bedroom.

"Well, what do you want?" I asked, wheeling him inside.

"You," he said. "I want to say four sentences while you listen." I sat down in front of him.

"I was thinking about things this morning," he said. His voice was tender. He waited a moment before going on. He was letting an interval of time, a certain number of beats, soften the rough edges between us. "I love you," he said. "I was watching the kids. They are all right. Your son is beautiful. I don't know what will happen in the future. I don't talk as fast as I used to. But I want to say what I want to say from the heart. You are a good person, a good person . . .

"Person . . . person." He was practicing his pronunciation. "Person."

I jumped up laughing, and put my arms around him. "I love you madly," I said in my best Duke Ellington rendition.

"I'm better today." He smiled. "My lungs are better. There was smoke outdoors and it didn't bother me for a long time."

I wheeled him back outside. Roberto and Eugene were playing chess on the porch while Eric romped with the dogs below. For lunch the five of us shared some hot roasted goat from a trattoria in town. Life was ready-roll again, off on its circular racetrack.

2 a.m. After the nightly drive, Eugene set up the Christmas tree, which we decorated with Mexican paper ornaments and garlic wreaths from the voodoo section of the market. We had so much trouble sawing the stump that Charles suggested we decorate it horizontally.

3 a.m. He was coughing mercilessly and the gargle was not clear-

ing his congestion. I sped into town to look for an all-night pharmacy that sold a rubber tube for our hand pump, running the lights and ignoring traffic signs, the dogs skidding across the back section of the Volkswagen bus as we careened through the dark streets. At the emergency hospital a group of bland-faced Mexican interns said they could send an ambulance but could not come themselves to clean out his lungs at home. I called Eugene to see how serious it was.

"Do the doctors speak English?" Charles wanted to know.

"This is Mexico," I said. "If it's an emergency and they speak Sanskrit, what the fuck does it matter?"

Charles decided if they did not speak English it was not an emergency.

4 a.m. Eugene asked me to go across town again for another oxygen tank.

5 a.m. Charles requested that I prepare one of the prune-apple-honey-egg-milk-nutmeg-banana supremes in the blender.

5:15 a.m. As he drank it with difficulty through a straw—he can barely swallow and I believe he is close to death—he whispered: "It's as hard to suck as a virgin titty" (which phrasing required about ten minutes for us to decode).

5:30 a.m. Eugene dropped Charles.

"He was paid to do it," Charles later said angrily when Eugene went to wake up Jesus for his opinion of the cuts—a large gash on his right temple and a cut on his forehead between his eyes. Eugene was apparently trying to remove the brown box from under the front wheels and the chair tipped over. When I came out of the bathroom he was washing the wound and cutting tape strips to hold it together, cool and matter-of-fact.

10:30 a.m. The doctors arrived, sewed four stitches in the cut on Charles's temple, administered several shots of novocaine, and departed. While Jesus was preparing the herbal mixture in the other room, Charles said darkly, "Get two pairs of boxing gloves."

I laughed. "For you and Eugene?"

"For Daniele," he muttered. "For Daniele and Eugene. He'll take care of him."

On New Year's Eve, Eugene went to his girlfriend's, Hilda the dentist, for a boisterous family celebration. It was odd, I supposed, that we never called her just Hilda, at least among ourselves. She was Hilda the dentist. Like the song about Rosie the Riveter during the war. Charles probably started it. He was in the habit of calling people by their jobs. Or musicians by their instruments. "Hey, Bone!" he'd say to the lead trombone player. Or "What's up, Sticks!" to the drummer. Like my father calling everyone Mimi. I suppose he didn't have to learn their names.

Back at home Charles and Arturo sat in the bedroom with the oxygen machine in the semidarkness, misting by candlelight. Daniele, Gabriela, Eric, and I dined at the long table, also by candlelight, listening to the distant firecrackers and guns go off at midnight. Charles did not join us. I made a pot of lentils for the sake of tradition (Italian) and went to bed.

Eugene: "What sort of funeral do you want?"

Mingus: "Do what you like, I won't be there."

January 5, 1979. The sun flickered across the ceramic tiles toward the far corner of the patio where Charles sat in a dazzling patch of light beside Eugene. I was preparing to leave for Mexico City to pick up the visas for our retreat back to the States. Our six months' lease was up and we were heading home. I knelt beside Charles's wheelchair to ask whether he wanted some sashimi from the capital. His appetites, undiluted by fourteen months of illness, were as driven and passionate as they were the night he ordered twenty-five Ramos gin fizzes. Only two days ago I raced through the neighborhood looking for pineapple ice-cream pops with as much urgency as our nightly oxygen runs.

"Dad and I have made a truce," Eugene called over his shoulder on his way to the kitchen.

"I'm glad about the truce," I said softly to Charles.

"That's right," Eugene continued, returning with a tray full of teas. "He's going to get into bed later on."

"Good," I replied. Bed was something Charles had avoided for a week. As I prepared to leave, I asked again about the fish. Sashimi was his favorite treat. He lowered his eyes without speaking.

In the evening, when I honked outside the garage, Sabino opened the gates with uncharacteristic speed. In the living room, Jesus was seated by himself at the long table. Eugene entered through the glass doors.

"Your bracelet wasn't ready at the silver shop," I warned him.

Eugene shrugged. He didn't seem to care.

"Is Charles by himself?" I asked.

Eugene looked at Jesus. "Dad died at three o'clock this afternoon of a heart attack," he said. I stared at him blankly. After all these months of wrestling with hope, it had happened anyway. I ran to the back room and lifted the blue sheet that covered Charles's head. A stretch bandage binding his face and holding his jaw in place gave him almost a smile. Eugene and Jesus had performed their job professionally. Eugene was watching from the door.

"Even his eyes looked relaxed when they stared at me after it happened," he said. "I kept going back to the room after he died. Even two hours later. I thought he might still be alive, holding his breath. You know he could stop his heart if he wanted to . . ." I remembered how Charles was afraid of that power, how he'd expressed his fear in a composition called "Half-mast Inhibition," explaining the title to me once—impatiently, as though it were perfectly obvious—that "half-mast" was death itself, a lowered flag, and "inhibition" his own reluctance to transcend his life on earth through meditation.

"I couldn't believe it," Eugene continued. "I said, 'Why me?' I'd always told him, 'You'll never die in my hands, I know what to do.' And I do. And still, he died."

What happened when Eugene transferred him to the bed? Was it fear that stopped his heart? It was as if he knew it would happen in bed and refused to go. His instinct was like that: he foresaw danger and sometimes mistook the cause. I thought of the crutches he'd found that moonlit night, shouting his fears up and down the block like Cassandra. His mistrust of Eugene may have been only his vision, his knowledge, of how his death would come to pass.

I wondered if he knew that day; if it was why he refused the fish.

I lowered the sheet. Something in my stomach or heart or wherever pain settles in most easily forced me to remember that barely an hour before, I was racing through the mountains on a bus from Mexico City, learning the lyrics to a drinking song from a band of rowdy teenagers who were sitting across the aisle, laughing and encouraging me to sing. Despite the other passengers, our voices rose, chorus after chorus, until finally we were shouting our song. The old bus rumbled through the rough countryside, lurching from side to side, and I watched the familiar Mexican landscape fly dizzily past my window with no burden on my heart—no intuition at all that, as we headed merrily to Cuernavaca, Charles was dead at home.

Ten

"Sue and the holy river
Will send you to the saints of jazz—
To Duke and Bird and Fats—
And any other saint you have."

—*Joni Mitchell*
"Mitchell/Mingus" album cover, 1979

At the airport Eugene and I raced through the corridors, late as usual, weaving in and out of the noisy crowd, Eugene pulling behind him the large rectangular metal urn filled with Charles's ashes. Instead of the sleek, custom-designed, black leather carrying case of which Charles would have approved—and which predictably Eugene failed to retrieve on time from the leather shop—the urn was wrapped in a brightly colored Mexican blanket and strapped to a small luggage carrier on wheels. It veered dangerously down the terminal aisle in a blur of yellow, red, and green, skidding to the left and right while Eugene plunged on ahead, as reckless and precarious as he was last summer when he used to race Charles's wheelchair downhill at the market, Charles smiling grim and proud behind, tied to his chair as it shot free and utterly out of control toward the street.

Laughing, Eugene glanced back, his face obscured behind spectacles, cigar, and mustache like Groucho Marx as he darted from gate to gate, his long serape cape flying in the air, and suddenly we heard the merry-go-round music blaring from the airport speakers overhead and, laughing still, Eugene danced up the aisle, disappearing in the distance with Charles's ashes like the end of some Fellini film, a madcap clown in our last parade.

On board, with the ashes beside me, I thought how Charles would have ordered dinner and champagne for the urn as he regularly did for his bass violin, ticketed and paid for on the adjoining seat, explaining the logic of an extra meal to any greenhorn stewardess he encountered. Eventually, the appetite of his bass became known to airlines around the world so that twin trays were sent without argument to the bulkhead where the two of them waited.

In New Delhi, a tall, elegantly groomed Indian official at the American Embassy stared down at me from his desk: "You don't offer a Sikh a cigarette," he said as I quickly snapped shut the case inside my purse. He was a relative of a young Mingus fan in Vancouver and was my only contact. When I explained that my husband had wanted his ashes scattered in the Ganges, he suggested I take a driver with me, someone who could help arrange the ceremony. He realized, as the consulate general at the Indian Embassy in Mexico City had realized when I had gone to pick up my visa the week before, that I had no idea what I was doing, and he was trying to help.

"Be careful," the consulate general in Mexico City had warned me. "Drugs are smuggled into the country in coffins and you might be stopped." His warning barely registered. He suggested I take Charles's ashes to the village of Hardwar on the Ganges River in the foothills of the Himalayas—the closest holy city to New Delhi. Better by far, he had said, than Benares, where I told him I was planning to go. I was headed to Hardwar now, for no more reason than a kindly government employee in Mexico had named a town.

"You will need to bathe in the river," the Sikh official before me continued. "There is a separate place for women. You will wear a sheet or throw a towel over yourself, but no swimming suit, please! It is cold, colder than here in New Delhi. They will tell you what to do." He was wearing a turban and his beard was wound tight under his chin; it looked as if an elastic were holding it in place. What lay ahead was abstract and unimaginable and I could think of nothing to ask. I stared at his beard. It looked complicated and time-consuming and I wondered if he braided it from scratch each morning. When I saw he had risen to his feet and was waiting to accompany me to the door, I rose as well.

"The goddess Ganga represents joy in this life and hope in the life to come," he continued. "When you pay the Brahmin for the service, it will be eleven rupees or twenty-one or any number divisible by ten, plus one. A round number signifies completion. By adding one, you suggest continuity, something that goes on . . ." He bowed stiffly and disappeared into his office.

An hour later I was clinging to the backseat cushion of a rented car speeding precariously across the flatlands, headed toward the mountains. Our destination was the holy city of Hardwar in northern India. My driver-guide, Mohinder Singh, stared in the rearview mirror, no doubt wondering why an unveiled American woman was traveling with a large metal box in her lap on a mission he had not fully understood. He threw the skin of an orange out the window, wiped his hands on a scarf around his neck (he'd blown his nose into the same scarf a few moments before), and rolled up his window against the clamor of oxen, scooters, human rickshaws, wildly speeding buses, camels, and the endless stream of barefoot men in ragged white cotton leggings and turbans that crowded the highways across India, tens of thousands of men—not a woman in sight.

The metal box I was carrying with Charles's ashes now served as an armrest and steadier as we hurtled down the road. Mohinder Singh responded easily to my questions about the customs and traditions of his country, pointing out that Hardwar was "a vegetarian city," that cows were holy, that I would need to remove my leather shoes. At dawn we reached the sacred city of Hardwar.

Mohinder parked the car near a high wall plastered with garish commercial ads that ran along the grand stone stairway to the holy pier below. The movie star faces and their bright earthly goods stared down from a world as distant as heaven itself. Beneath the posters scattered vagrants lay sprawled asleep on the cold ancient steps, their thin rags and gunnysacks offering little protection from this freezing January morning. When Mohinder and I reached the pier, its world of the dead was teeming with life. Here, where the great god Vishnu once left his footprint, early mourners and mendicants already jostled among the crowd, elbowing away the threadbare cows that lumbered past. We squeezed through the rows of lepers who were seated on mats, waving their thin arms like broken flower stems in the wind, holding aloft begging cups that jangled with nearly worthless coins. Mohinder explained that alms to the poor would ease the soul's journey to its next incarnation, although the incessant clattering of their cups to draw attention was soon lost in the greater din and dreamlike disjunction of the pier.

I too walked in a dream, wandering along the shore with Mohinder past barbers who sat cross-legged on the cold ground, shearing the heads and faces of men so they might enter the immortal river.

We ducked the clumps of loose hair sailing in the brisk wind and headed toward a tall flimsy structure near the shore that looked more like a lifeguard's perch or a referee's seat at a tennis match than the holy man's roost it turned out to be. I thought back to the private club where I'd first played tennis long ago, behind a brick wall that concealed our white clothes and wooden racquets, high above the streetcar tracks where trolleys no longer ran. Now only the tar-embedded steel lines, which the city hadn't bothered to remove, recalled another time. That, too, was a dream.

On his rickety seat an old Brahmin whom Mohinder said could officiate at the ritual I required—though I would need to bargain—was hunched above, his long yellow hair and thin garments streaming in the wind. He seemed wary and nervous, more like a three-card-monte player in Times Square than a spiritual guide, as we agreed on a sum of eleven rupees, or ninety cents, and set a time for the scattering of Charles's ashes the following day. Behind the Brahmin's chair a ragged creature veered along the bank, releasing the ashes of a relative into the water from a soiled paper bag. Downstream, an old man fished the same riverbed for valuables, for rings or gold teeth. Everywhere vendors called out their wares to the bereaved.

I stumbled along beside Mohinder Singh through this Coney Island of the dead, its gaudy pasteboard temples dotting the pier like movie props, as we made our way among bands of peach-garbed Krishnas who floated through the masses with scant hairlocks sticking off their bald heads like pubic hair. We walked past an old woman whose dried nipples hung loose and visible when the wind raised her wet sari as she washed herself in the frigid waters. We saw men who themselves watched everything from the shore until, finally, I stood still in the center of all this bustle and strangeness and tried to find some common feeling, some claim or connection to the activity around me that belonged to something so entirely removed, so exotic and intimidating, that my heart sank and I knew I needed time.

I was an outsider here, as I was in Mexico—as I had been so long ago with Charles—unfamiliar with Hindu traditions, ignorant of the sacred texts, a woman marching in a land where women were invisible or encased in veils. I wondered if this was what Charles had in mind or whether I should grab my clothes and run past my guide to the shabby little hotel in the center of town where I could be alone and mourn in my own fashion.

Mohinder Singh, eager to return to New Delhi, encouraged me to perform the customary ablutions, here and now—the preliminary purifying ceremony required before I could release Charles's ashes in the river next day. And so, at his instruction, I approached the private sector for women and descended the steps to the covered area below. Here I undressed and covered myself with a white length of material that I wrapped hastily around my shivering body. Then I walked straight over to the stone bank and plunged into the river, heading down the watery steps without pausing, down farther until my body was submerged, and then, when the freezing waters reached my neck, I cried out loud "Charles" and held that word with all my strength.

The bitter cold, my own feelings of misery and loss, my nakedness, the alien world I had entered, the sordidness and lunacy of the pier merged together now like a deadweight and pulled me under. As the waters closed over my head I called out Charles's name one more time, and then something happened. The weight carrying me below was gone, replaced by the shock of cold, the shock of exhilaration, a sudden lightness that coursed through my body and must have been the baptism necessary for me to touch something, if only for a moment, of this other world I had entered. I rose out of the water and stood dazed and shivering on the pier while a holy woman, who sat cross-legged on a high table, placed a red mark on my forehead, and the other women pointed to where my clothes were piled on the platform and indicated that I should get dressed. I looked up the steps to where my guide was staring at me, bold and curious as I trembled, the sari around my waist, my breasts freezing, the sari falling below my thighs, and I no longer cared about the differences or my nakedness or the bitter cold. I dressed without hurry, feeling light and free, as weightless and removed as the chill wind that blew along the shore. Perhaps the Ganges had worked its miracle, had cleansed and changed me as it does the faithful.

I crossed the bridge to a small square lined with temples where I ordered *poohri* bread from a food stand and watched an old woman with her two sons at a table nearby whose hands shook so badly that one son held them still while the other pulled some faded yellow cotton gloves over her fingers. She leaned her head on his shoulder with a weary, almost defiant gesture that reminded me of Charles, and I knew that her sorrow belonged to me as well and allowed myself one moment of raw memory beside this old woman, closed my eyes in the warm afternoon sun and missed Charles deeply for the first time.

Mohinder Singh was waiting on the far side of the bridge. I asked him to drive me farther north into the Himalayas to a sacred, simpler village he'd described called Rishikesh, where I could release Charles's ashes away from the frenzy of the pier. I'd learned enough about holy places, I decided, to choose my own.

Hours later, I stood on a suspension bridge in Rishikesh forty kilometers upstream, where the Ganges was closer to its source and had regained its strength, tumbling swift and luminous hundreds of feet below. Here, at the end of the world where mountains rose straight into the sky and where all the beggars and bustling crowds had vanished, we could see in the distance an ashram that overlooked the river. Mohinder nodded when I asked if he thought I might be allowed to stay. We parked the car and continued on foot.

For a few pennies from a market nearby, I'd purchased a colorful wicker basket for Charles's ashes, as well as the fruits and flowers I would need for the ceremony, and, with Mohinder's approval, had heaved the ugly gray container from Mexico over the bridge. Below, in a small courtyard near the main temple of the ashram, the Brahmin in charge examined me through half-closed eyelids while he meditated in the sun and, after a time, led me to a small house that was one empty room with a small balcony above the Ganges. He carried in the clean white bedding himself and laid it on a cot. As the sky darkened and fresh night air drifted in from the river, I could hear chanting from another ashram across the water where a candle-lit procession was moving along its banks. Soon chanting from our own temples began, accompanied by slow erotic drumbeats and the tolling of bells. I stood on the balcony and listened. Above, the heavens were alive with stars.

Something sensual and palpable was mingling here with the life of the spirit, some call to life. In the distance a man sounded the mournful notes of a conch shell, the transcendental call of Krishna. At the foot of the stairs to the temple were three pairs of men's shoes. A young boy crossed the courtyard, humming. I remembered Allen Ginsberg's long Hindu chant the night he married Charles and me, accompanying himself with small flat cymbals between his fingers and chanting: "Hare Krishna, Hare Krishna, Hare Hare, Krishna Krishna, Hare Rama, Hare Rama, Hare Hare, Rama Rama."

The air was thickening with something I'd felt before, charged and undefined, a vitality that accompanies the end of things. I'd been frightened by its intensity in my father's library a few hours after his death when I awakened in the middle of the night, yanked from sleep in the room where he had spent so many hours over his books, shaken by a multitude of sparkling lights that played along his bookshelves in the dark. The lights were vivid and unexplainable, but more terrifying was the quality of the air. It was thick and unfamiliar, as if I'd been locked out of my own world and thrust into another; it was alive like an animal. I could feel it move. I had grabbed the floor lamp beside my father's armchair bed and snapped on the light.

In India, the air was different, it seemed urgent and wanton and full of possibility. In the library I'd felt only its terror. Here on the other side of the world, I stood on my balcony and felt at home, as if I belonged to the vastness of the night.

I remembered my father as he lay dying, paralyzed and soundless in a hospital, only a dozen years before Charles would be paralyzed and soundless, too. Across the small space between my chair and his bed we had stared at each other, wordless, from early morning through the final hours of light, with more intimacy than in an entire lifetime together. I sat shy beside this dignified man who was my father and did not throw my arms around him as I would today, fearing his displeasure and his pride. ("It's the way I am," he once told my brother, refusing a hug. "If you can take me like this, we will be friends.") Charles, incapable of distance, closed his gaps at every turn. At seventeen, he was challenging death, the greatest gap, as freely as he challenged life, tempted by its power, meditating in his room, certain he could will himself into another world. That same year he wrote "The Chill of Death," and then—later, when he was no longer tempted—his out-of-body experiences led to his insomnia, to the man who never slept, afraid now that he might leave his body for good and not return.

I remembered one late night long ago when he burst into my apartment on Eighty-seventh Street and headed straight to my piano. It was an old upright piano with missing keys that stood in the entrance hall to the living room. He sat down at the piano bench and began to improvise a tune:

"Death: I wish you was a wo-o-m-an-n-n . . ." he sang. He stopped and took a long swig from a bottle of Chianti he'd brought along in a paper bag. Then he continued: "Death: I wish you was a gi-r-r-r-r-l-l . . ." He laughed, pleased with himself and with our being together, pleased with his idea of death, making up the words as he went along, singing into a recording machine that was sitting on top of the piano. His voice grew lusty as the night wore on, and Fritzie, my German shepherd, who was lying with his nose over the pedals at Charles's feet, began to croon a high canine wail, aware that something was happening. Somewhere in an old box I have a tape of Charles and Fritzie together, singing.

Eleven

"The duality of the material world is felt in terms of heat and cold, misery and happiness. . . . One is in full transcendental knowledge who is free from this duality."

—*The Bhagavadgita*

Early morning before the sun rose over the Himalayas and the air was still frozen from the night, when old men and young boys were crossing the sands to the river beneath my window to bathe naked in its glacial green waters, I decided it was time to release Charles's ashes. Below, the men were removing the thin faded cloth wrapped around their bodies and unwinding their turbans. Wearing only loincloths, beyond climate and cold, they splashed the holy water over their skin or immersed themselves in its depths. It was a sacred time, and here in this small settlement up the river from the bustle of Hardwar, the Sadhus and Brahmins, the saints and the swamis, prepared for the day.

I left my balcony and walked across the courtyard to the main temple. At its entrance I removed my wooden sandals and waited for the swami to motion me inside. He was sitting on the floor with his helpers, overseeing the packaging of grain in small triangles of paper to be distributed among the poor. The swami had a shawl around his shoulders and was wearing socks. He made a sign of greeting, palms together, and I sat down opposite him. With the help of a translator, I told him I was prepared for the ceremony.

I was aware, as was the swami, that I would not leave my other life behind or stay on until I had merged with this land in which I was a visitor. I would not grow any closer to the sky and sacred air around me than I had grown in these few days. And although I dreaded the mindless demands of a secular life in the center of Manhattan and the unwelcome return to a new life without Charles that I could scarcely imagine, I indicated to the swami that I was ready for the ceremony, ready to move on. The swami called in a young Brahmin to accompany me to the river.

It was not yet dawn when we descended the long steps and stood together on its freezing shore. I had placed on the sand the bright wicker basket with Charles's ashes beside the garlands of marigolds and roses and the coconut that would serve as my offering of milk to the Mother Ganges. The Brahmin handed me a piece of burning incense and motioned me to draw a circle of life in the air while he chanted a prayer of passage from this life to the next. Then he put his lips to the mouth of a conch shell, blew a long plangent note, and waved me to the shore. I entered the Ganges and released my gifts of life and death: flower and fruit, ash and bone, and immersed myself in the water in a last embrace as Charles's ashes swirled around me.

As the ashes drifted off on their journey, I stood under the cold sky and remembered the long months in Mexico, the endless rites of passage, the mysteries, the stubbornness of our belief, and knew that whether it was all a dupe—whether Pachita wore pink haircurlers before the gig or the blood of the iguana had no smell or whether, here in India, the swami in the cold winter mornings wore his cotton socks—what mattered was only the roar of the wind past our windows as we careened, nurses, sons, and wives, beside a speeding wheelchair through the mountains of Mexico, driven by Charles's urgency in search of peace or, when peace was impossible, at least one more dinner. He had died as voluptuously as he lived, reinventing his days as they ran out, being fed in the most sumptuous restaurants of the land.

I climbed the bank and stood on the shore shaking with cold, the wet ceremonial cloth clinging to my skin. In the distance I could see a group of untended horses running along the beach. As the sun rose behind the dark stretch of Himalayas that covered half the sky, orange carp were visible glistening beneath the surface of the water. With a fragile sound of bells, the young priest waved his fingers in the air. The ceremony and the long months were over.

I continued along the beach. He died for a year, I thought; perhaps I had no fears left. I'd awakened in peace that morning as I had not awakened since they told me Charles would die. I was cut loose now, freed from attachments, permitted one moment of Hindu eternity in time. I walked along the sparkling riverbank and my step was light, as bright and insubstantial as the sunlight at my feet.

Epilogue: The Ongoing Discussion

"And so that's what he said. He said: 'Let's finish
the discussion on the bandstand.' "
> —*Mingus remembering a conversation*
> *with Charlie Parker*

A few months after Charles's death, I was asked to assemble a
small band to perform as part of a two-day Mingus tribute at
Carnegie Hall. I had never done such a thing and had no idea
where to begin. I searched through a stack of Mingus record albums
and decided on an ensemble of four horns and a rhythm section,
based on a lineup Charles had used on a Columbia recording in the
late fifties. All the musicians I called, except of course the bass
player, had played with Mingus.

To everyone's surprise, this impromptu seven-piece band sounded
more authentic than anything on the show. The reason was simple
and completely unforeseen: no one else at the two-day event played

Mingus music! Except for one Alvin Ailey member who danced to a Mingus recording, his music did not figure at all. Mingus composition was so identified with Mingus himself, it seemed, that other musicians were unwilling to trespass the turf. This revelation became the inspiration for continuing that early septet which became known as the "Mingus Dynasty." It was the first forum for Mingus composition that did not have at its helm the driving force and vivid personality of Mingus himself.

People said it would never work.

It's been a long road from the inception of the Mingus Dynasty to the present. I will not forget at the outset of my first domestic tour, in the spring of 1979, only five months after Charles's death, overhearing the musicians gossip about me when I called downstairs for room service and the hotel waitress rested the phone beside a large bowl of grapefruit and oranges on the counter where several musicians in the band were seated over morning coffee. When she went off to place my order, I could hear them discussing my incompetence at the bar.

"Hey, man," one of them said. "She doesn't know the first thing about what she's doing." I couldn't believe what I was hearing. The speaker was the same musician who had helped and advised me from the start, the one I thought was in my corner the most. Lesson Number One. Not long afterward, on the same tour, I was crying in the front seat of a rented car in a motel parking lot by myself, following some wounding words about my choice of hotels (oh, how important they are!), when the piano player came over to the driver's window and spoke to me through the open crack at the top. He told me I would become a trouper. He said it was hard knocks at first but I would learn and survive. No apology. Just a tough, accurate message from someone on the inside.

After two decades on the road as "one of the guys," I have many stories and many more lessons. Like the musician who regularly got his own room in another hotel, as a matter of principle, no matter how hard I tried. There were only two classes, he'd announce as he left us all behind: "First class and no class." Or the time I walked two miles under a burning sun in my high heels to argue with some union truck drivers on strike in Belgium who were manning the tollbooth at the border and refusing to let any large vehicle pass. At least two hundred trucks and buses were stalled on the side of the road. I implored the strikers in bad French but good logic to let our Italian bus full of Americans, which was headed for Holland, through the Belgian strike line. I returned triumphant, two hours later. In my absence, several musicians on the bus had been chanting a Buddhist mantra ("nam-myoho-rengey-kyo") under the direction of our bass-playing spiritual master. As I reported the good news, the chanters loudly celebrated their own success. Mine, it turned out, was peripheral.

I remember one musician who never stopped being angry about the injustices around him and who normally gave me a wide berth. Eventually, he bonded with my young son when they went fishing together in Woodstock. It was a day when Roberto caught a big old fish lolling near the shore by dropping a rock on him. It was their secret and it cemented their brotherhood. It helped me, too. And then one day when someone entered the dressing room after a gig and asked for a musician who happened to be black and I directed him toward someone else who happened to be white, my son's new friend said: "You really don't see color, do you?" From then on we were friends.

In fact, we were a family, most of us, able to discuss our particular throw of the dice when we needed to. You get to know people pretty well when you travel on the road month after month, sometimes year after year. You develop a language. Each tour has its own vocabulary, its own expressions that arise from the days and events of the tour. Its own code. The trombone player on his way to the elevator after a gig, knowing it will be only three hours before we will all congregate again in the lobby for the next departure, says over his shoulder: "Sleep as fast as you can." The drummer sees a burnt-out, leftover character from the sixties in long raggedy skirts and scarves, tie-dyes and beads, in the airport and says, disapprovingly: "Funk de dunk and mugley!" Then he slaps five with whatever musician is standing by and repeats: "Mugley! That's *worse* than ugly." The flute player says, "The pressure is all mine." The trombone player turns around as he leaves the dining car on the German railroad and, referring in his own mind to the upcoming evening gig, says to us: "I'll see you when you're better dressed." These impromptu observations become riffs of the road, phrases that are repeated, sardonically, familiarly, for the rest of the tour and then, later on, years later, perhaps repeated across a street in Dayton, Ohio, at a serendipitous encounter, when they have turned into family history.

"Hey," a voice calls out to you from the past, as you're about to enter your latest hotel: "Funk de dunk and *mugley,* bro . . ."

Charles and I did not discuss the nuts and bolts of what would become of his music, but he knew, as any composer knows, that it would live on. He may have known, with his gift for prescience—and some mischief, too—that I would be involved. After all, he left me in charge of his publishing company, though I had no notion what that entailed. In Mexico we lived life as an emergency moored in the present, soaking up the sun, following Pachita's orders, and trying to beat the rap. We did not consider the future at all.

I am not a professional musician and do not perform onstage, but I have come to feel a part of Mingus music and a kinship with the extraordinary musicians who keep it alive. One of my favorite expressions of support came long ago from the piano player Sir Roland

Hanna when we were traveling through Argentina with the first Mingus Dynasty. On our way to a television studio where I was to make some preliminary comments about the band, Roland, who had already seen me fumbling with interviewers, gave me some tips. After the show, which I'd gotten through safely, he wished to show his approval.

"That was fine," Sir Roland said. "You were okay. You're a . . ." He searched for the right word. We were walking along a sidewalk outside the studios, headed to our hotel, when he turned and paid the highest compliment of all.

"You're . . . a *musician*!" he said proudly.

Today, when I walk into a concert hall and listen to the first few notes of a Mingus performance, I can probably tell you whether the musicians have a tub or a shower in their hotel bathroom, whether they have a comfortable bed in the adjoining room, and whether there is a color TV. I have spent over two decades with Mingus bands frequently on the road and have learned that whatever treatment musicians receive in the afternoon will translate directly into the music at night. I have discussed this with concert promoters and booking agents, some of whom believe that music exists apart from life, from musicians who perform it and from the creature comforts that are so essential to well-being on the road. Someone should write a simple manual—the demands are hardly complex—because those needs will affect what you hear in the concert hall as surely as the sound system or a vaulted ceiling.

Mystical reminders of Charles's presence sometimes occur. A bass string snaps at the beginning of a concert, or a trombonist's acute senses pick up vibrations within the music that he knows are coming from somewhere else. One late night while I was preparing a "fake book" of Mingus compositions for publication, seated at the living room table in the Manhattan apartment where I still live, surrounded by pages from a composition entitled "Reincarnation of a Love Bird," a feather fell on the music I was examining. I brushed it away and looked at my watch: 3 a.m. I went on working, but I thought about the feather. It was an odd thing to be falling at that hour. It was an odd thing at any hour. I remembered a poem Charles had written called "A Feather Falls," about a feather he'd seen floating through the air at Carnegie Hall at a rehearsal just before he played a tribute concert to Charlie "Bird" Parker. It had led him to write a piece of music called "Reincarnation of a Love Bird," the music I was now preparing.

I decided to search for the feather on the floor. Perhaps I had imagined it. Just then a sharp slam-bang resounded above as something struck the empty wrought-iron birdcage near the window. A tiny black bird was swooping about the room. It landed on the table and stared boldly from a few inches away. Its feet were planted squarely on the sheet of music called "Reincarnation of a Lovebird."

When I went into the kitchen to pour some water into a bowl, the bird followed. When it alighted on the counter beside me, I knew I would change my life for that bird, put up screens, bird-proof the exits. For now, I closed the door to the porch through which it had evidently flown, and went to bed. While I was reading, the bird slowly squeezed through a crack at the bottom of my bedroom door, examined the room, flew onto my bookshelves near the slightly open window, and went to sleep. In the morning my little friend was dead, perhaps of a chill. I buried him in a plant between Charles's bass violin and the piano.

In the decades since Charles died in 1979, a number of repertory bands have been established to carry on his music, including the Charles Mingus Orchestra and, most notably, the Mingus Big Band.

For more than ten years, the Big Band has performed Thursday nights in Manhattan at a place called Fez. The familiar role of Charles Mingus as virtuoso bassist, bandleader, and personality on stage has begun to make way for his much larger role as a composer—perhaps the greatest change in perception since his death. His legacy includes one of the most personal and varied bodies of composition in American music and is the second largest in jazz. The Library of Congress has acquired the entire collection of his works. His music scores reside in its archives along with those of Haydn, Mozart, Stravinsky, and especially Beethoven, whose ink-blotted, coffee-splattered, undulating lines charge across the pages like a storm at sea and most resemble Mingus's own.

His jazz symphony and two-hour masterwork, "Epitaph," with its ironic title and five-hundred-page score, was never performed in his lifetime. "I wrote it for my tombstone," he said prophetically, three decades before its premiere. Ten years after his death, with the help of the Ford Foundation, the National Endowment for the Arts, British Channel Four, musicologist Andrew Homzy, editor and conductor Gunther Schuller, and many others, and after a nerve-racking year of planning and preparation, "Epitaph" finally premiered at Lincoln Center, on June 3, 1989. I produced it myself. It was one of the most harrowing events of my life. Until the last moment—including the final dress rehearsal when new music was still arriving by messenger from a team of copyists working around the clock—we had no idea whether the concert would be a triumph or a bust. In what seemed like a miracle, everything worked. The music was magnificent, the hall was sold out, and the *New York Times* called it one of the most important musical events of the decade—the first extended work since Ellington's "Black, Brown, & Beige" in 1943, and three times as long. Gunther Schuller called it the "Gotterdammerung of Jazz."

Since then, three missing sections of "Epitaph" have come to light, discovered by Andrew Homzy, who pieced together the original version measure by measure like a detective from hundreds of yellowing manuscripts in a wooden trunk in my living room. In a chance discovery, he solved the last mystery while doing research in the Lincoln Center music archives where he found the missing scores and paved the way for a final and complete premiere of Charles's masterpiece, in the future.

While touring with musicians, I have learned much about music and more about those who perform it. I have watched the dedication, complexity, mischief, and intransigence that go into performances. Any musician will tell you that Mingus music requires multiple skills. A drummer once described it as a three-ring circus; he should have said four. You need to read like a classical player, improvise like a jazz musician, play well in the ensemble, and, on top of everything else, have a personality. I have seen how behavior that causes trouble in one context may, in another, provoke the explosive magic and exultation that bring a concert to magnificent life and the audience to its feet. The music grows and expands with such contradictions.

I am reminded of a recent concert in Aarhus, Denmark, in which two musicians were screaming at each other backstage only moments before one of their finest concerts. A reviewer in the audience heard the rumpus through the curtains and thought it was a Charles Mingus tape from the past, used intentionally to incite the musicians into a preconcert creative frenzy. He wrote this, admiringly, in his review the following day.

In 1995 I founded a record company called Revenge Records. Its purpose was to steal back Mingus material released illegally by record pirates around the world and to rerelease it on our own label; to pay the sidemen who were never reimbursed; and, above all, to outsmart the pirates by underselling them in the commercial marketplace. For many years, long before I started Revenge Records—as a more effective way of confronting the pirates and the stores that, often unwittingly, support them—I entered stores and stole back Mingus music, walking off with a dozen illegal Mingus records under my arm, without being stopped. Until one day in Paris I was caught red-handed. The store guards waited until I passed through the doors to the Champs Elysées and then surrounded me on the street. Waving their walkie-talkies in the air, they forced me upstairs to the office of the store manager, who was standing tall and irate beside his desk, phone in hand, threatening to call the police.

I encouraged him to do so. I suggested he also call the television news stations and radio programs, as well as the offices of the principal jazz magazine in France, which happened to be across the street, so that I could explain to all of them at once why I was removing illegal products from his store. The manager replaced the phone. We had a lengthy discussion about record piracy, from two points of view. After a time, I was allowed to leave the store with my stolen CDs, which I had refused to surrender. I knew my success was limited: I knew those depleted bins would be restocked the following day. As I walked back to my hotel, the notion of Revenge Records was born.

I remember when interviewers used to ask him despite the breadth of his legacy how he fit into traditional categories that included European classical forms, bebop, Dixieland, gospel, Latin rhythms, and the blues—all genres of music he drew upon in his compositions, and then transcended. He would look up and sigh: "Can't you just call it Mingus music?" More than two decades later I think he'd be pleased—if not at all surprised—to know that we can.

As for me, I've been enveloped in his sound and sometimes his fury: hiring and firing musicians, publishing and producing music, occasionally storming the stage. It is a role that, in the old days, I could scarcely have imagined. The demands seem to germinate inside his music, as musicians discover when they respond to its lashings and incitements, the demands for personal expression that live on inside his notes. "Play yourself!" he used to holler to musicians and to the world.

The discussion goes on.